MATH ADVENTURES

A Key to Academic Math Advancement

GRADE 6

_____

_____

_____

Author: Ace Academic Publishing

Ace Academic Publishing is a leading supplemental educational workbook publisher for grades K-12. At Ace Academic Publishing, we realize the importance of imparting analytical and critical thinking skills during the early ages of childhood and hence our books include materials that require multiple levels of analysis and encourage the students to think outside the box.

The materials for our books are written by award winning teachers with several years of teaching experience. All our books are aligned with the state standards and are widely used by many schools throughout the country.

Prepaze is a sister company of Ace Academic Publishing. Intrigued by the unending possibilities of the internet and its role in education, Prepaze was created to spread the knowledge and learning across all corners of the world through an online platform. We equip ourselves with state-of-the-art technologies so that knowledge reaches the students through the quickest and the most effective channels.

For inquiries and bulk orders, contact Ace Academic Publishing at the following address:
Ace Academic Publishing
3031 Village Market Place,
Morrisville, NC 27560, USA
www.aceacademicpublishing.com

ISBN: 978-1-962517-13-3
© Ace Academic Publishing, 2023

Introduction

About the Book

Welcome to "**Math Adventures - A Key to Academic Math Advancement**"! This workbook is specifically designed to align with the school curriculum and help students improve their analytical and logical thinking skills. With over **750 questions and several word problems**, this book aims to cover all the required syllabus for students in Grade 6.

Our workbook is an excellent resource for end-of-the-year state tests given by schools, as well as a great review book during the summer. Whether you are looking to improve your math skills or simply keep them sharp, "**Math Adventures**" provides a comprehensive and challenging set of problems to help you achieve your goals.

Our authors have extensive experience in teaching and developing math curricula for students at all levels. **They have carefully crafted each problem to challenge students and help them develop key problem-solving and critical thinking skills.** The book covers a wide range of topics, including arithmetic, algebra, geometry, and data analysis, providing students with a well-rounded education in math.

We believe that with practice, anyone can master math. "**Math Adventures**" is designed to help students build confidence in their abilities and develop a love for the subject. With clear explanations, helpful hints, and detailed solutions, this book is an excellent tool for anyone looking to improve their math skills.

Thank you for choosing "**Math Adventures - A Key to Academic Math Advancement**". We hope that you find it useful and enjoyable!

Common Core Math Workbooks

Common Core English Workbooks

The One Big Book Workbooks

Math Adventures Workbooks

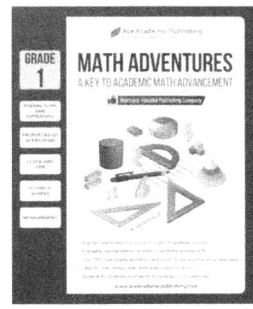
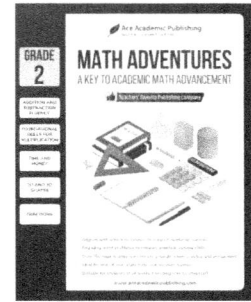
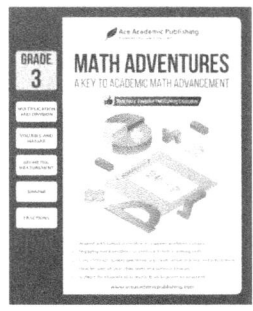
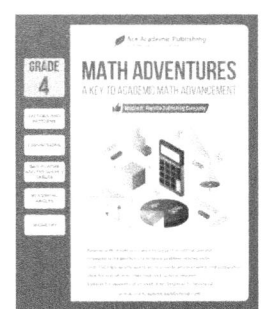
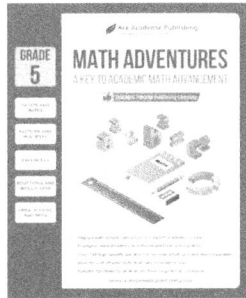
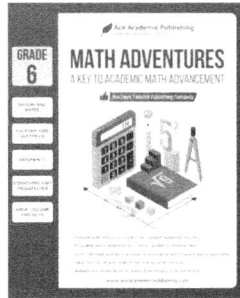
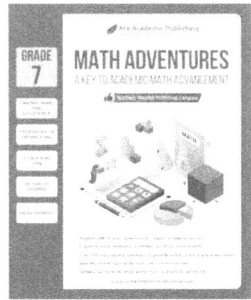

Early Learning Workbooks

TABLE OF CONTENTS

TABLE OF CONTENTS

CHAPTER 1

RATIOS AND RATES

SHADOW MATCHING GAME

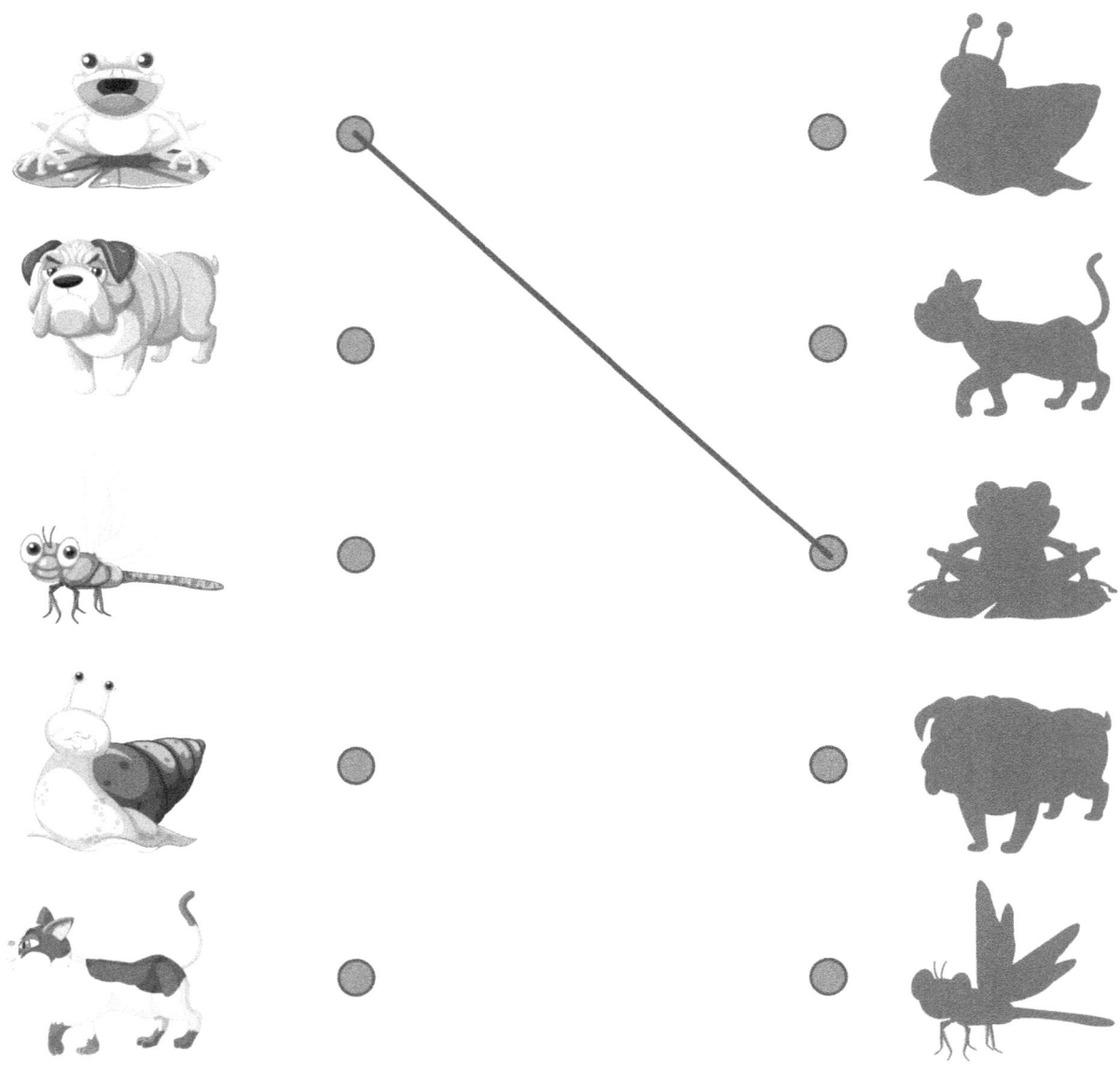

WRITE A RATIO

A ratio represents the comparison between two values or quantities and is often used to simplify or compare different situations. We use the word "to" when expressing ratios in word form. There are multiple ways to write ratios:

- as a fraction,
- using the word "to",
- with a colon.

As a fraction:

Write the ratio of two numbers as a fraction, where the top (numerator) is one number, and the bottom (denominator) is the other number. For example,"If the shop has 1 cat for every 3 birds, you can write it as the fraction $\frac{1}{3}$" is already correct. It accurately describes how to represent the ratio of cats to birds in the shop as a fraction, where the numerator is 1 and the denominator is 3. The resulting fraction is $\frac{1}{3}$.

Using the word "to":

The ratio between two numbers can be written using the word "to". For example, two numbers 3 and 5 are in ratio "3 to 5".

Using a colon:

Ratios between two numbers are usually written as two numbers separated by a colon. For example, two numbers 5 and 6 are in ratio "5 :6".

Example: There are 14 hens and 8 geese on a farm. Express the ratio of hens to geese as a ratios with a colon, as a fraction, and in words.

- As a colon, the ratio can be written as 14:8,
- As a fraction, the ratio can be written as $\frac{14}{8}$,
- In words, the ratio can be written as "14 hens to 8 geese" or "14 to 8".

RATIOS AND RATES

1.1   Write a Ratio

1 The ratio of boys to girls in sixth grade is 3:5. If there are 32 students, how many girls are there?

(A) 12   (B) 16   (C) 18   (D) 20

2 A grocery store sells 16 bottles of apple juice and 24 bottles of orange juice. What is the ratios of orange juice to apple juice sold?

(A) 14:1   (B) 3:2   (C) 2:3   (D) 21:1

3 Points A, B, C, and D lie on the same line. The distance between points A and B is 1.4 cm, the distance between points B and C is 1.9 cm, and the distance between points C and D is 2.1 cm.

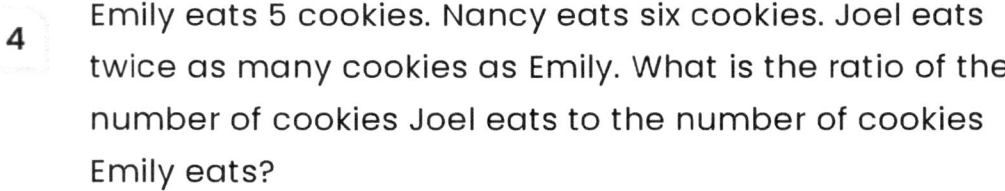

The ratio of BC:AD _____.

4 Emily eats 5 cookies. Nancy eats six cookies. Joel eats twice as many cookies as Emily. What is the ratio of the number of cookies Joel eats to the number of cookies Emily eats?

(A) 5:2   (B) 1:5   (C) 25:5   (D) 2:1

5 The cookies recipe calls for $\frac{4}{6}$ cup of flour, $\frac{3}{5}$ cup of sugar, $\frac{1}{2}$ cup of butter and 13 cup of milk. What is the ratio of sugar to milk? The ratio of sugar to milk

_____.

6 Parker is making breakfast for her family. Four of her family members are allergic to eggs. Parker and six other family members are not allergic to eggs. Which ratio represents the number of family members who are not allergic to eggs to the number of family members who are allergic to eggs?

(A) $\frac{7}{4}$ (B) $\frac{4}{7}$ (C) $\frac{6}{4}$ (D) $\frac{4}{6}$

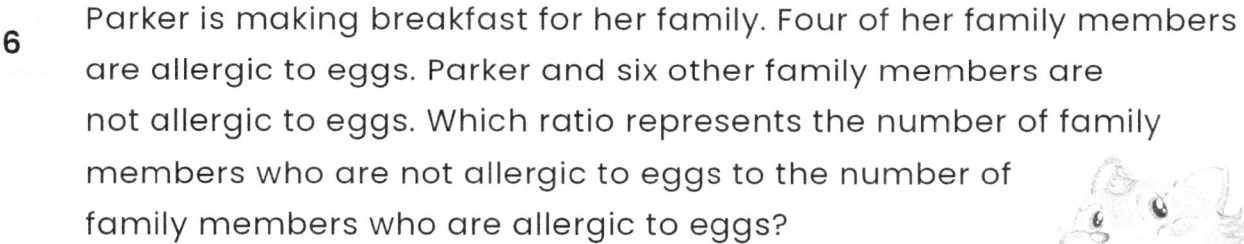

7 It takes one XXL pizza to feed four people. How many pizzas are needed to feed 36 people?

(A) 7   (B) 8   (C) 9   (D) 10

8 A water container with a capacity of 100 gallons contains 25 gallons of water. Find the ratio of empty spaces in the container to the capacity of the container.

(A) 25:100   (B) 75:100   (C) 75:25   (D) 30:70

RATIOS AND RATES

1.1   Write a Ratio

9   Mr. Helen has 35 students in his class. More than half of the students are boys. Which ratio could represents the ratio of girls to boys in Mr. Helen's class?

(A) 2:3   (B) 3:2   (C) 4:1   (D) 5:1

10   A fishing pond is maintaining a ratio of four sunfish to two perch. If there are a total of 180 fish in the pond, how many of them are sunfish?

(A) 150   (B) 120   (C) 100   (D) 80

11   A Basketball team won $\frac{2}{3}$ of all games. What is the ratio of games lost to games won?

The ratio of games lost to games won _____.

12   Mercy answers 14 questions correctly and 6 questions incorrectly on his math test. What is the ratio of correct answers to the total number of questions on the math test?

(A) 14 to 6   (B) 6 to 20   (C) 14 to 20   (D) 20 to 3

13 In a dance club, $\dfrac{5}{6}$ of the dancers are girls and 25 are boys. What is the ratio of girls to boys?

(A) 4:6   (B) 30:5   (C) 5:20   (D) 25:30

14 If the perimeter of the rectangular picture frame is 60 cm, and two times the length of the picture frame is three times its width. What is the length of the picture frame?

(A) 12   (B) 15   (C) 18   (D) 20

15 Rosie answered x out of 40 questions correctly on her test. What could be the value of x, if the ratio of incorrect answers to the total number of answers is 9:40?

(A) $\dfrac{1}{2}$ (B) 49   (C) 20   (D) 31

16 In their last game, the Warriors scored 222 points and the Cavaliers scored 88 points. Which ratio compares the number of points scored by the Cavaliers, to the number of points scored by the Warriors?

(A) 11 to 1   (B) 44 to 111   (C) 8 to 11   (D) 111 to 88

RATIOS AND RATES

1.1   Write a Ratio

17 There are three numbers in the ratio 4:8:2. What is the ratio of the sum of the first two numbers to the sum of the second two numbers?

(A) 6:5   (B) 5:5   (C) 6:6   (D) 1:1

18 Oliver answered x out of 45 questions correctly on his test. What could be the value of x, if the ratio of incorrect answers to correct answers is 11:34?

(A) 10   (B) 11   (C) 34   (D) 30

19 The perimeter of the rectangle is 20x cm. The width of the rectangle is 3x cm. What is the ratio of the length to the width?

_____

20 The following table shows the number of pets owned by children. What is the ratio of children who have owned 3 or more pets to those who have owned 2 or fewer pets?

Number of pets	0	1	2	3	>3
Number of children	10	6	15	8	2

_____.

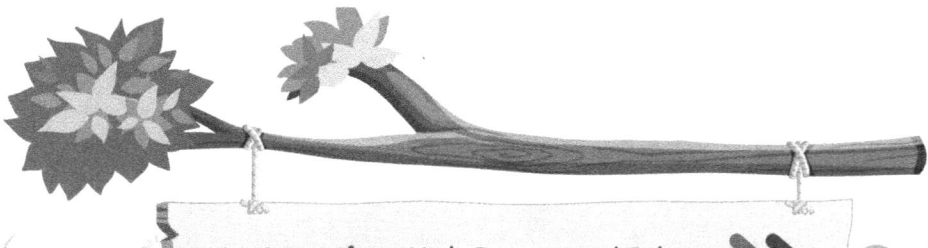

Next Section: Unit Rates and Prices »

UNIT RATES AND PRICES

A **rate** is a special ratio in which the two terms are in different units. For example, if a 7-ounce can of tomatoes costs $9, the rate is $9 for 7 ounces.

A **unit rate** describes how many units of the first type of quantity correspond to one unit of the second type of quantity.

A **unit price** is a cost per item (per one liter, one kilogram, one pound, etc.)

Some common unit rates are miles (or kilometers) per hour, cost per item, earnings per week, etc. In each case, the first quantity is related to the unit of the second quantity.

Rates and unit rates are used to solve many real-world problems.

1 bag of oranges cost $1.25

Example:

If Alex buys 5 bags of oranges for $8.40, what is the unit price of bag of oranges?

Solution:

5 bags of oranges cost $8.40
1 bag of oranges cost $8.40 ÷ 5 = $1.68.

1.2 Unit Rates and Prices

1 **Find the unit rate:** 15 pens in 5 boxes = _____ pens per box

(A) 2   (B) 4   (C) 3   (D) 5

2 **Find the unit rate:** 45 minutes for 9 cupcakes = _____ minutes per cupcake.

(A) 11   (B) 7   (C) 9   (D) 5

3 A rate of 984 watermelons for $ 164 = $ 7.5 per watermelon.

(A) True   (B) False

4 A rate of 600 liters in 15 minutes = 40 liters per minute.

(A) True   (B) False

5 Prince walked 6 miles in 2 hours. If Prince walked 27 miles, how many hours did he walk?

_____

6 There are 8,656 students standing in 1,082 rows around the school. How many students are in each row?

_____

7 If a 7 oz cake costs $280, then the unit price is $ _____ per oz.

(A) 90   (B) 60   (C) 40   (D) 70

8 If John drives 38 miles in three hours, the unit rate is _____ miles per hour.

(A) 11   (B) 7   (C) 9   (D) 5

9 If 2,400m is traveled in 25 minutes, then the unit rate is _____ m per minutes.

(A) 78   (B) 92   (C) 84   (D) 96

10 If 5,500m are driven in 50 minutes, then the unit rate is _____ m per minutes.

(A) 5.1   (B) 5.5   (C) 6.6   (D) 6.9

RATIOS AND RATES

1.2   Unit Rates and Prices

11   Roy runs $4\frac{5}{4}$ miles in $\frac{3}{4}$ hour. What is Roy's rate per hour?

_____

12   Twenty pumpkins cost $3.40. What is the pumpkin's unit price per pumpkin?

_____

13   April works for 4 hours and gets paid $20.80. How much is April paid per hour?

   Ⓐ $ 5.20   Ⓑ $ 4.80   Ⓒ $ 5.80   Ⓓ $ 4.20

14   Doug walked 1,200m from point A to point B and then 2,400m from point B to point C in 2 hours. What is Doug's average speed?

_____

15 Grayson rode his bike from 4:40 to 5:10 and went 6 miles. How fast did Grayson travel per minute?

- (A) 0.1 km per minute
- (B) 0.2 km per minute
- (C) 1.2 km per minute
- (D) 2.1 km per minute

16 A butterfly flew 35 miles in 30 minutes. How many miles can the butterfly travel in per hour?

- (A) 30 miles per hour
- (B) 35 miles per hour
- (C) 55 miles per hour
- (D) 70 miles per hour

17 Kevin and Larry are riding on the highway. It takes Kevin 35 minutes to go 140 miles. If Larry rides at the same rate, how long will it take for him to reach 240 miles?

_____

18 Manuel makes $48 by selling eight sofas. Tristan makes $91 by selling 13 sofas. What is their average gain rate?

- (A) $ 8
- (B) $ 13
- (C) $ 17
- (D) $ 7

RATIOS AND RATES

1.2   Unit Rates and Prices

19   Diana is shopping for chili sauce. Her favorite brand is available in two sizes, 500 oz for $15.00 and 900 oz for $18.00. Which size is the best value?

(A)   500 oz bottle is the better value

(B)   900 oz bottle is the better value

20   The juice shop charges $ 6.50 for a case of 9 bottles of juice and $1.13 for 4 packs of sugar. What is the unit price for one bottle of juice and one pack of sugar?

(A) $ 0.92   (B) $ 0.78   (C) $ 1   (D) $ 1.20

Next Section: Equivalent Ratios

EQUIVALENT RATIOS

Two ratios that have the same value are called equivalent ratios. To get a ratio equivalent to a given ratio we multiply or divide both the terms of the given ratio by the same non-zero number.

Example:

Consider the ratio $\dfrac{10}{6}$. Write three equivalent ratios to the given one.

Solution:

1st ratio: Multiply the numerator and the denominator by 2:

$$\dfrac{10}{6} = \dfrac{10 \times 2}{6 \times 2} = \dfrac{20}{12}$$

Solution:

2nd ratio: Divide the numerator and the denominator by 2:

$$\dfrac{10}{6} = \dfrac{10 \div 2}{6 \div 2} = \dfrac{5}{3}$$

RATIOS AND RATES

1.3 Equivalent Ratios

1 The ratios below are equivalent. True or false? $\frac{7}{9}$ and $\frac{21}{28}$.

(A) True   (B) False

2 The ratios below are equivalent. True or false? $\frac{103+5}{91-7}$ and $\frac{18}{14}$.

(A) True   (B) False

3 The ratios below are equivalent. True or false?

14 of $\frac{7}{5}$ and 18 of $1\frac{4}{5}$.

(A) True   (B) False

4 Mia cuts 324 apples in 12 minutes. Jamie cuts 184 apples in 8 minutes. Are their unit rates equivalent ?

(A) Yes, they are equivalent   (B) No, they are not equivalent

5 Two families participate in a cooking competition. The Charles family cooks 220 dishes in 11 hours. The Dylan family cooks 390 dishes in $19\frac{1}{2}$ hours. Are their dishes per hour equivalent?

(A) Yes, they are equivalent

(B) No, they are not equivalent

Equivalent Ratios   1.3

6 The sides of the first rectangle are in a ratio of 5:7. The sides of the second rectangle measure 14 cm and 10 cm. Are the ratios of the sides equivalent in both rectangles?

Ⓐ Yes, they are equivalent   Ⓑ No, they are not equivalent

7 The vegetable shop has 465 carrots in 15 boxes. Which choices below represent an equivalent ratios?

Ⓐ 185 carrots in 4 boxes   Ⓑ 315 carrots in 13 boxes

Ⓒ 279 carrots in 9 boxes   Ⓓ 232 carrots in 7 boxes

8 Which of the following ratios is equivalent to the ratio of the shaded area to the whole area?

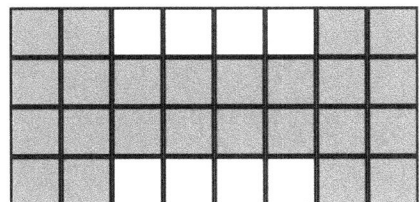

Ⓐ 5 :7   Ⓑ 3 :9

Ⓒ 1 :3   Ⓓ 3 :4

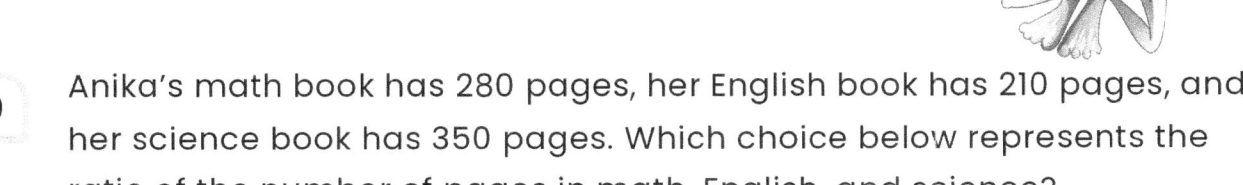

9 Anika's math book has 280 pages, her English book has 210 pages, and her science book has 350 pages. Which choice below represents the ratio of the number of pages in math, English, and science?

Ⓐ 4 :5 :7   Ⓑ 4 :3 :5   Ⓒ 1 :7 :3   Ⓓ 3 :4 :1

RATIOS AND RATES

1.3 Equivalent Ratios

10 Are the ratios AC : DC and AB : DB equivalent?

(A) Yes, they are equivalent   (B) No, they are not equivalent

11 Write the ratio in its most basic form $\frac{324}{72}$.

_____

12 What is the value of r, if the ratio $\frac{r}{18}$ is equivalent to the ratio $\frac{r+6}{9}$?

_____

13 It takes Annie 2 hours to finish 17 math problems. If Annie needs to finish 51 math problems, how many hours will she need?

(A) 8   (B) 12   (C) 6   (D) 9

14 Angela made $ 36.54 by selling eight boxes of dried blueberries. At this rate, how much will she make if she sells 16 boxes?

(A) $ 56.12   (B) $ 64.28   (C) $ 52.24   (D) $ 73.08

15 Write the following ratio in its simplest form.

51:595

(A) 3:35   (B) 1:25   (C) 13:12   (D) 4:18

16 Nile bought six sofas for $ 551. How many sofas can buy for $ 1,010.13?

(A) 12   (B) 11   (C) 15   (D) 17

17 The ratio of black pens to blue pens is 4:7. What is the total number of pens, if there are 80 black pens?

(A) 140 pens   (B) 180 pens   (C) 220 pens   (D) 250 pens

18 Write the following ratio in its simplest form. 38 : 513.

_____

1.3   Equivalent Ratios

19 If the ratios $\frac{x+8}{50}$ and $\frac{3}{5}$ are equivalent, Then what is the value of 'x' ?

(A) 18   (B) 22   (C) 26   (D) 34

20 What is the value of p, if the ratio $\frac{p}{12}$ is equivalent to the ratio $\frac{p+3}{6}$?

Next Section: Solving Proportions

SOLVING PROPORTIONS

A **proportion** is a statement that two ratios are equal.

It can be written in two ways:
- as two equal fractions ab=cd;
- using a colon, a :b=c :d.

$$\frac{a}{b} = \frac{c}{d}$$

Cross product rule.

In proportion, the product of the means equals the product of the extremes

$$a \times d = b \times c$$

Example:

Solve the proportion $\frac{x}{3} = \frac{4}{2}$

Solution:

Cross multiply $2 \times x = 4 \times 3$

$2x = 12$

$x = \frac{12}{2}$

$x = 6$

RATIOS AND RATES

1.4 Solving Proportions

1 The 6th-grade class has 33 girls and 45 boys. What is the ratio of girls to boys as a fraction in its simplest form?

(A) $\frac{11}{15}$ (B) $\frac{11}{12}$ (C) $\frac{3}{5}$ (D) $\frac{3}{9}$

2 Solve for q. $\frac{13}{3} = \frac{4}{q}$.

(A) $\frac{12}{11}$ (B) $\frac{12}{13}$ (C) $\frac{13}{12}$ (D) $\frac{4}{3}$

3 Determine whether the following proportion is correct: $a=3$

$\frac{4}{12} = \frac{1}{3a-6}$ (A) Correct (B) Incorrect

4 Agree or disagree. Are the ratios proportional?

15:18 and 25:30

(A) Agree (B) Disagree

5 Jackson ran 2 miles in 15.2 minutes. At this rate, how far can Jackson run in 30.4 minutes?

(A) 5 miles (B) 2 miles
(C) 4 miles (D) 7 miles

6 A motorcycle covers 240 miles in 4 hours. How many miles can the motorcycle cover in nine hours if it maintains the same speed?

(A) 410 miles   (B) 280 miles   (C) 360 miles   (D) 540 miles

7 Red and white balls are inside of a bag with a ratio of 6:11
Based on the ratio, complete the table below.

Red	White
6	11
18	X
a	77

_____

8 The numerator of a fraction is 6 less than the fraction's denominator. The ratio of the numerator to the denominator is 3:2. What is the fraction?

(A) $\dfrac{3}{4}$ (B) $\dfrac{3}{2}$ (C) $\dfrac{4}{3}$ (D) $\dfrac{8}{3}$

9 The table below represents the relationship between the distance from home, in miles, and time spent driving in hours.

Distance	Time(hours)
630	7
270	3
810	9
450	5

What is the unit rate of miles per hour?

_____

1.4   **Solving Proportions**

10   Ari collects 240 coins each year. Using equivalent ratios, fill in the table.

Month	1	5	7	11
Coins				

11   Use the table to find the constant of proportionality.

A	28	42	63	91	119
B	4	6	9	13	17

If we switched the rows, what would be the new constant of proportionality?

_____

12   The constant of proportionality for a proportional relationship is $\frac{5}{7}$. Which of the following points fall on the graph of the relationship?

(A) (21, 31)   (B) (15, 14)

(C) (25, 35)   (D) (21, 25)

Solving Proportions   1.4

13 On the map, 1 inch represents 15 miles.
What is the actual distance between two schools,
if the distance on the map is 8.2 inches?

    A) 123 miles   B) 157 miles

    C) 162 miles   D) 193 miles

14 What is the scale factor if the scale is 8 cm = 320 m ?

    A) 5:2,000   B) 3:1,000   C) 1:7,000   D) 1:4,000

15 The actual size is 30 m, and the scale size is 3 cm. What is the scale
factor?

    A) 3:2,000   B) 1:1,000   C) 2:5,000   D) 3:4,000

16 The scale size is 25 cm. The scale factor is 5:16.
Determine the actual size in m

    A) 0.8 m   B) 1. 2 m   C) 0.4 m   D) 1.5 m

1.4   Solving Proportions

17 A scale drawing of a house has a scale factor of 1 :5. What is the scale size of the length in cm, if its actual size is 150 m?

150m

(A) 1500 cm   (B) 2000 cm

(C) 3000 cm   (D) 5000 cm

18 A map has a scale of 1:12,000. A school is shown on the map as a square with a perimeter of 72 cm. What is the actual area of the school?

(A) Actual area of the school = 5.24 sq. km

(B) Actual area of the school = 4.19 sq. km

(C) Actual area of the school = 6.91 sq. km

(D) Actual area of the school = 4.67 sq. km

19 Sarah sketched the route she takes each day. What is the distance from Sarah's home to the beach?

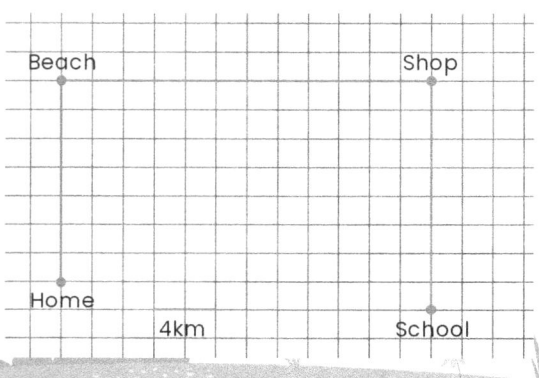

(A) 7 km   (B) 14 km

(C) 16 km   (D) 10 km

20 Diagrams A and B are scale drawings of the same field. What is the scale of the Figure B?

_____

RATIOS AND RATES

1.5 Chapter Review

1 Avery eats 172 grapes in 4 minutes. Dixie eats 217 in 7 minutes. Are their unit rates equivalent?

(A) Yes, they are equivalent (B) No, they are not equivalent

2 Which of the following ratios is equivalent to the ratio of the shaded area to the whole area?

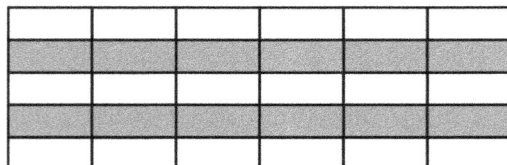

(A) 7 : 2 (B) 2 : 5

(C) 5 : 3 (D) 1 : 2

3 Write the ratio in its simplest form. $\frac{437}{69}$

_____

4 Solve for b $\frac{29}{11} = \frac{2}{b}$

(A) $\frac{29}{11}$ (B) $\frac{22}{29}$ (C) $\frac{29}{22}$ (D) $\frac{11}{29}$

5 A shop sells 20 laptops and 28 smartphones. What is the ratio of smartphones to laptops?

(A) 12 : 7 (B) 1 : 9 (C) 7 : 5 (D) 3 : 11

6   What is the scale factor if the scale is 11 cm = 550 m ?

(A) 1 : 5,000   (B) 2 : 1,000   (C) 3 : 4,000   (D) 4 : 1,000

7   What is the missing value in the table?

P	13	?	21	26
Q	104	136	168	208

(A) 19   (B) 18   (C) 16   (D) 17

8   Find the unit rate: 492 slices of pizza from 41 pizzas = _____ slices per pizza.

(A) 10   (B) 12   (C) 15   (D) 19

9   **True or False:** The ratios below are equivalent.
80 pens for 10 students
32 pens for 4 students

(A) True   (B) False

RATIOS AND RATES

10 A bakery makes 10 deliveries every six days. At this rate, how many days will it take to make 5 deliveries?

_____

11 The vegetable medley has a ratio of 3 to 5 for carrots to beets. Which of the following choices will keep the medley at the same ratio?

(A) Add 1 carrots and 2 beetroots

(B) Add 4 carrots and 7 beetroots

(C) Add 3 carrots and 5 beetroots

(D) Add 7 carrots and 9 beetroots

12 Which ratio below forms a proportion with the ratio $\frac{2}{7}$?

(A) 6 : 21   (B) 6 : 28   (C) 6 : 35   (D) 6 : 42

13 Jennifer drove 140 miles in 7 hours. At this rate, how long will it take her to drive the remaining 40 miles?

(A) 5 hours   (B) 2 hours   (C) 7 hours   (D) 6 hours

14 Which ratio is equivalent to the ratio $\frac{7}{9} : \frac{14}{3}$?

- (A) 1:5
- (B) 1:2
- (C) 6:5
- (D) 1:6

15 What is the solution of the proportion $\frac{56}{a+2} = \frac{8}{3}$?

- (A) 11
- (B) 13
- (C) 19
- (D) 23

16 The table shows some values of a and b, where a is proportional to b. What is the value of Z−W?

a	W	36	27
b	48	96	Z

- (A) 50
- (B) 56
- (C) 52
- (D) 54

17 The ratio of boys to girls in the piano class is 7 to 3. How many girls are in the piano class, if there are 56 boys?

- (A) 18
- (B) 24
- (C) 36
- (D) 40

18 A model of a gate uses a scale of 3 inch to 1 ft. The height of the gate is 45 feet. What is the height of the model?

- (A) 135 ft
- (B) 112 ft
- (C) 152 ft
- (D) 104 ft

RATIOS AND RATES

19   If it takes 10 people 12 days to design 7 books, how many days will it take 5 people to design 14 books?

_____

20   There are pens, paper, and erasers all in one bag. There are 150 items in all. The ratio of pens to pencils is 3:5. There are 37 more pens than erasers. How many erasers are in the bag?

_____

Next Chapter: Fractions ≫

CHAPTER 2

FRACTIONS

SHADOW MATCHING GAME

LCM AND GCD

A number that can only be divided by 1 and itself is called a prime number.

Examples of prime numbers are 2, 3, 5, 7, 11, 13, 17, 19, 23 and 29. The number 1 is not considered a prime number because 1 goes into everything.

The list of all the prime-number factors of a given number is called prime factorization of the given number.

Greatest Common Factor:

The greatest common factor (GCF) of a set of whole numbers is the largest positive integer that divides evenly into all numbers with zero remainder.

To find the GCF of two numbers:
- list the prime factors of each number.
- multiply those factors both numbers have in common. If there are no common prime factors, the GCF is equal to 1.

Example: Find GCF (24,36)

Solution:

$$24=2.2.2.3$$
$$36=2.2.3.3$$

Bold prime factors have the product that is the greatest common factor of numbers 24 and 36. Hence, GCF (24,36) = 2.2.3=12

LCM AND GCD

Least Common Multiple:

A **multiple** of a number is that number multiplied by a whole number.

The **least common multiple (LCM)** of a set of whole numbers is the smallest number (not counting 0) which is a multiple of all of the numbers.

To find the LCM of two numbers:

- List the prime factors of each number.
- Multiply each factor by the greatest number of times it occurs in either number. If the same factor occurs more than once in both numbers, you multiply the factor by the greatest number of times it occurs

Example: Find LCM (24,36).

Solution:

$$24 = 2.2.2.3$$
$$36 = 2.2.3.3$$

LCM (24,36) = 2.2.2.3.3 = 72.

1 Find the greatest common factor for the numbers 36 and 54.

(A) 9   (B) 12   (C) 18   (D) 27

2 Find the least common multiple for the numbers 63, 81, and 108.

(A) 2,268   (B) 2,374   (C) 2,716   (D) 2,912

3 Amy wants to give some stickers to her friends. There are 64 animal stickers and 96 bird stickers. She wants each friend to receive the same number of animal and bird stickers, without any stickers left over. What is the largest number of friends Amy can give the stickers to?

(A) 24   (B) 32   (C) 48   (D) 52

4 Mercy has 152 red balls and 104 white balls to put into boxes. What is the largest number of boxes she can have with an equal number of red balls and an equal number of white balls in each box (assuming she uses them all)?

(A) 34   (B) 26   (C) 14   (D) 8

2.1 LCM And GCD

5 Ann wants to make fruit salad bowls. She has 30 apples, 70 bananas, and 90 raspberries. Each bowl must have the same amount of fruit. What is the largest amount of fruit she can use if she uses them all?

(A) 10   (B) 15   (C) 20   (D) 25

6 Max has math class every 2nd day and science class every 5th day. If he had a math class and a science class on July 1, when is the next day he has both math and science?

(A) July 8   (B) July 15   (C) July 11   (D) July 21

7 Justin is thinking of a number that is divisible by both 42 and 49. What is the smallest possible number that Justin could think of?

(A) 186   (B) 294   (C) 328   (D) 432

8 The product of two numbers is 78,450, and the LCM is 2615. What is the GFC of these numbers?

(A) 25   (B) 20   (C) 30   (D) 39

9 Energy drinks come in cases of eight and water comes in cases of ten. There are 16 players on the baseball team, what is the least number of packs needed so that each player has an energy drink and water with none left over?

_____

10 Mercy bought 20 sets of black hair clips, 36 sets of yellow hair clips, and 60 sets of pink hair clips to make gift boxes. She wants to have the same number of sets in each box. What is the greatest number of boxes she can make without having any of the hair clips left over?

(A) 2   (B) 6   (C) 8   (D) 4

11 Jack has 75 apples, 50 oranges, 40 bananas and 35 strawberries. He wants to divide the fruits into groups so that each group has the same number of each fruit. What is the greatest number of groups he can make? How many of each fruit will be in the group?

_____

FRACTIONS

2.1   LCM And GCD

12 The vegetable shop is making identical vegetable baskets. There are 56 mushrooms, 70 onions, and n radishes. They want each basket to have the same number of vegetables. If the largest number of baskets they can make is 14, what is the smallest possible value n? How many of each type of vegetable will be in each basket?

_____

13 Callie uses GCF to rewrite the sum 1568 + 1248 using the distributive property. What is her answer?

(A) 24(29+35)   (B) 46(23+28)

(C) 32(49+39)   (D) 52(31+43)

14 William uses GCF to rewrite the difference 1320 - 825 using the distributive property. What is his answer?

(A) 105(9-2)   (B) 165(8-5)   (C) 210(2-1)   (D) 225(4-1)

15 Can you find one pair of numbers x and y satisfying condition, if GCF(x,y) = 18 and LCM(x,y) = 540 ?

_____

16 Tom is playing with toy cars. He wants to arrange them in rows 8, 16, and 32. These rows must forms a perfect square.
What is the smallest number of toy cars Tom can use?

(A) 4096   (B) 4128   (C) 4232   (D) 4312

17 The product of two numbers is 56448 and their GCF is 32.
What is the LCM of these numbers?

(A) 1384   (B) 1542   (C) 1764   (D) 1894

18 The product of two numbers is 51420, and their LCM is 3428.
What is the GFC of these numbers?

(A) 11   (B) 15   (C) 17   (D) 19

19 What is the least number which when divided by 20, 22, 24 and 26 leaves remainders 19, 21, 23, and 25 respectively?

(A) 15348   (B) 16518   (C) 17159   (D) 18215

FRACTIONS

2.1 LCM And GCD

20 Angela and her brother arrive at the zoo at 11:00 a.m. They agree to meet near the lion's cage to check in with each other throughout the day. Angela checks the lion's cage every 32 minute. Her brother checks it every 28 minute. At what time will they meet at the lion's cage again?

Next Section: Divide Fractions ≫

DIVIDE FRACTIONS

The **reciprocal** of a fraction is just switching the numerator (top number) and the denominator (bottom number).

Divide decimals by whole numbers

To divide decimals by whole numbers:

- Use long division to find the quotient.
- Divide as usual. Keep dividing until the answer terminates or repeats.
- Put decimal point directly above decimal point in the dividend.
- Check your answer multiplying quotient by divisor.

When checking the answer, use rounding and estimating.

Example: The reciprocal of $\dfrac{3}{4}$ or $\dfrac{4}{3}$

To divide fractions

- Take the reciprocal (invert the fraction) of the divisor;
- Multiply the numerators and the denominators;
- Simplify the fraction if necessary.

FRACTIONS

2.2   Divide Fractions

1 What is the value of $\frac{5}{9} \div \frac{15}{18}$ = ?

   (A) $\frac{4}{7}$ (B) $\frac{3}{5}$ (C) $\frac{2}{3}$ (D) $\frac{1}{2}$

2 Harry has $\frac{7}{12}$ of a pie. He divides his portion of the pie equally among nine friends. What fractions of the whole pie will each friend receive?

   (A) $\frac{7}{108}$ (B) $\frac{7}{9}$ (C) $\frac{108}{7}$ (D) $\frac{9}{7}$

3 Jack and her friend are dividing 26 pears. Jack shares his portion equally with his two brothers. Which fraction represents the number of pears each person receives?

   (A) $\frac{3}{26}$ (B) $\frac{3}{13}$ (C) $\frac{26}{3}$ (D) $\frac{13}{3}$

4 Casey has $\frac{7}{10}$ of a pizza. Casey wishes to give one-tenth of a pizza to each member of her families. How many members are in Casey's family?

   (A) 1   (B) 7   (C) 9   (D) 8

5 Janet is making pizza. She uses $1\frac{5}{4}$ cups of cheese for each pizza. How many pizzas can she make if she has $6\frac{3}{4}$ cups of cheese?

(A) 3   (B) 6   (C) 12   (D) 24

6 Tom has $4\frac{4}{5}$ pounds of apples and $1\frac{3}{5}$ pounds of oranges. The apple weighs how many more times as much as the garlic?

(A) 7   (B) 4   (C) 3   (D) 9

7 Erin wants to walk $4\frac{1}{2}$ miles. If the length of one lap around the track is $\frac{3}{4}$ a miles, how many laps does Erin need to walk?

(A) 13   (B) 10   (C) 8   (D) 6

8 Sam has $14\frac{2}{2}$ cups of apple juice and $15\frac{4}{3}$ cups of orange juice. He drinks $\frac{5}{4}$ the cup of apple juice and $\frac{7}{3}$ a cup of orange juice each time. What drink will end earlier : apple juice or orange juice?

(A) Apple juice   (B) Orange juice

2.2   **Divide Fractions**

9

Hector has $7\frac{3}{5}$ pounds of onion and $3\frac{4}{5}$ pounds of garlic. How many times as much as the garlic does the onion weigh?

(A) 2   (B) 5   (C) 6   (D) 9

10

The product of two fractions is $44\frac{1}{3}$. If one of the fractions is $\frac{19}{30}$, what is the other fraction?

(A) 35   (B) 70   (C) 95   (D) 140

11

The length of a rectangular park with an area of $85\frac{4}{4}$ m² is $7\frac{1}{6}$ m. What is the width of the park?

_____

12

Adam was raised \$ 130,176 by selling televisions. Each television was priced at \$ $90\frac{2}{5}$. How many televisions sold?

(A) 1,120   (B) 1,230   (C) 1,360   (D) 1,440

13   Fill in the gaps

$$\frac{8}{13} \div 2 = \frac{8}{13} \div \frac{2}{1} = \frac{8}{13} \times \frac{1}{2} = \frac{2 \times 2 \times 2}{13 \times 2} = \underline{\hspace{2cm}}.$$

14 Divide fraction $3\frac{3}{5}$ by given whole number 3.

(A) $\frac{9}{5}$ (B) $\frac{3}{5}$ (C) $\frac{6}{5}$ (D) $\frac{7}{5}$

15 Max collected $\frac{2}{9}$ of a pound of potatoes. He has to divide them equally among eight baskets. How many pounds of potatoes did Max put in each basket?

(A) $\frac{1}{24}$ (B) $\frac{1}{36}$ (C) $\frac{1}{48}$ (D) $\frac{1}{56}$

16 How much pie will 5 people get if they share $\frac{2}{5}$ a pound of pies equally?

(A) $\frac{2}{25}$ (B) $\frac{25}{2}$ (C) $\frac{5}{2}$ (D) $\frac{2}{5}$

17 There is $\frac{1}{7}$ of a box of chocolates left. Six friends want to share them equally. If the whole box initially has 84 chocolates, how many chocolates will each friend have?

2.2   **Divide Fractions**

18   Divide the fraction $7\frac{3}{6}$ by the whole number 9.

Ⓐ $\frac{9}{5}$ Ⓑ $\frac{3}{6}$ Ⓒ $\frac{5}{6}$ Ⓓ $\frac{7}{5}$

19   Which expression best describes the bar model below?

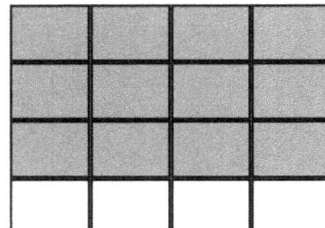

Ⓐ $\frac{3}{4}$ −4   Ⓑ $\frac{3}{4}$ x4

Ⓒ $\frac{3}{4}$ +4   Ⓓ $\frac{3}{4}$ ÷4

20   Zara had left $\frac{1}{8}$ of a pack of stamps. She divided them equally between 4 her children. What fraction of the package of stamps did each child get?

_____

Next Section:
Expressions with fractions »

EXPRESSIONS WITH FRACTIONS

Expressions with fractions typically involve mathematical expressions that contain one or more fractions. An expression can be a combination of numbers, variables, and mathematical operations like addition, subtraction, multiplication, and division. When fractions are included in an expression, it means that the quantities involved are not whole numbers.

Operations with fractions

1. Addition:

$$\frac{a}{b} + \frac{c}{d} = \frac{ab+bc}{bd}$$

2. Subtraction:

$$\frac{a}{b} - \frac{c}{d} = \frac{ab-bc}{bd}$$

3. Multiplication:

$$\frac{a}{b} \times \frac{c}{d} = \frac{ac}{bd}$$

4. Division:

$$\frac{a}{b} \div \frac{c}{d} = \frac{a}{b} \times \frac{c}{d} = \frac{ad}{bc}$$

EXPRESSIONS WITH FRACTIONS

PEMDAS! (Order of operations):

P – Parentheses first

E – Exponents (powers)

MD – Multiplication and Division (left-to-right)

AS – Addition and Subtraction (left-to-right)

Example: Evaluate the expression $\frac{4}{8} \times \left(\frac{1}{2} - \frac{1}{4} \right) + \frac{5}{8} \div 5$

Solution: Follow the order of operations:

1. $\frac{1}{2} - \frac{1}{4} = \frac{4-2}{8} = \frac{2}{8} = \frac{1}{4}$

2. $\frac{4}{8} \times \frac{1}{4} = \frac{1}{8}$

3. $\frac{5}{8} \div 5 = \frac{5}{8} \times \frac{1}{5} = \frac{1}{8}$

4. $\frac{1}{8} + \frac{1}{8} = \frac{2}{8} = \frac{1}{4}$

1 Evaluate the expression: $\dfrac{1+\dfrac{1}{1+\frac{1}{5}}}{1+\dfrac{1}{1-\frac{1}{5}}}$

(A) $\dfrac{24}{29}$ (B) $\dfrac{27}{20}$ (C) $\dfrac{23}{25}$ (D) $\dfrac{22}{27}$

2 What is the value of $\dfrac{7x}{y}-\dfrac{x}{7y}$, if $x=1\frac{1}{7}$, $y=\frac{7}{8}$?

(A) $8\dfrac{328}{343}$ (B) $7\dfrac{213}{243}$ (C) $8\dfrac{317}{312}$ (D) $7\dfrac{368}{234}$

3 Prince, Peter, and Philip have a coffee shop. They decide to split the $240 profit as follows: Prince will get $\frac{3}{8}$ of the total profit and Peter will get half of Prince's profit. How much money will Philip get?

(A) $ 95   (B) $ 100   (C) $ 105   (D) $ 115

4 Solve for y: $\dfrac{5}{8}+\dfrac{3}{4}\,y=\dfrac{13}{16}$.

(A) $\dfrac{1}{2}$ (B) $\dfrac{1}{4}$ (C) $\dfrac{1}{8}$ (D) $\dfrac{1}{16}$

2.3   **Expressions With Fractions**

5 Ben cuts $\frac{6}{7}$ m from a piece of ribbon $3\frac{2}{4}$ m long. Is there enough ribbon left for two pieces $\frac{5}{28}$ m long each?

(A) Yes, there is enough ribbon

(B) No, there is not enough ribbon

6 The line plot below depicts the growth of seven tomato plants in their third week after sprouting.

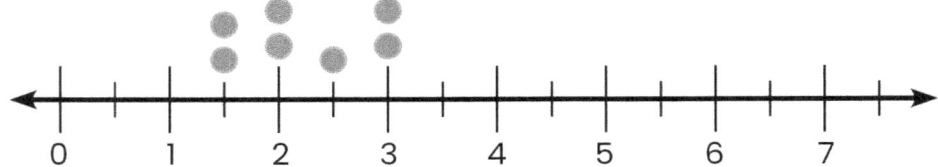

What is the total length of all plants, in inches? What is the difference between the tallest and shortest plants?

_____

7 Use <, >, or = to make true number sentence without calculating.

$(\frac{5}{6} + \frac{10}{11} \div \frac{5}{11}) \times \frac{1}{15}$ _____ $(\frac{5}{6} + \frac{10}{11}) \div \frac{5}{11} \times \frac{1}{15}$

8 Simplify $(\frac{5}{6} - \frac{1}{12}) \times \frac{7}{9}$.

(A) $\frac{12}{7}$ (B) $\frac{5}{9}$ (C) $\frac{7}{12}$ (D) $\frac{9}{5}$

9 Evaluate expressions $\left(\dfrac{2}{9} + \dfrac{5}{18}\right) \div \dfrac{14}{27}$

(A) $\dfrac{26}{21}$ (B) $\dfrac{28}{27}$ (C) $\dfrac{21}{26}$ (D) $\dfrac{27}{28}$

10 Ben needs to order muffins for 18 friends. Each friend should get $\dfrac{1}{12}$ a muffin. How many muffins should Ben order?

_____

11 There are 24 hours in a day. Adults work for $\dfrac{2}{8}$ of the day and rest for $\dfrac{1}{4}$ of the day. How many hours should adults spend working? How many hours should adults spend resting? Which expression below represents the total time spent working and resting?

(A) 8 hours   (B) 12 hours   (C) 16 hours   (D) 20 hours

12 Simon is making 10 chocolates. He mixed $3\dfrac{1}{2}$ cups of cocoa powder, $\dfrac{1}{4}$ cups of sugar and $1\dfrac{3}{4}$ cups of cocoa butter together in a bowl. How many cups of the mixture will go into each chocolate bar?

(A) $\dfrac{15}{4}$ (B) $\dfrac{20}{11}$ (C) $\dfrac{11}{20}$ (D) $\dfrac{4}{15}$

FRACTIONS

2.3 Expressions With Fractions

13 Martin has 11 pears. He leaves $\frac{1}{6}$ for herself and the rest he shares with his seven friends. How much does each friend get?

(A) $1\frac{13}{42}$　　(B) $2\frac{11}{34}$　　(C) $1\frac{6}{52}$　　(D) $2\frac{17}{41}$

14 Demi had $4\frac{1}{2}$ kilograms of flour. She kept $1\frac{3}{4}$ kilograms for herself and the rest she divided between her sister and her brother. How much flour does Demi's brother get?

(A) $1\frac{2}{7}$　　(B) $1\frac{7}{9}$　　(C) $1\frac{3}{8}$　　(D) $1\frac{5}{2}$

15 Yesterday, Roy walked $5\frac{1}{5}$ miles and Ari walked $2\frac{1}{10}$ miles more than Roy. They walked the same distance today. What distance did they cover altogether in three days?

(A) $35\frac{2}{5}$　　(B) $53\frac{1}{10}$　　(C) $39\frac{3}{7}$　　(D) $41\frac{1}{8}$

16 Mark has 50 balls. $\frac{1}{5}$ of her balls are red. The rest of the balls are white or blue. The number of white balls is equal to the number of blue balls. How many of his balls are blue?

(A) 15　　(B) 20　　(C) 35　　(D) 40

17   Tara finished $\frac{1}{7}$ of the project on Wednesday. On Thursday, she completed $\frac{1}{14}$ of the project. How much of the project does Tara have left to finish?

_____

18   Lara, Maya, Kelly combines their savings. Lara's part was $\frac{1}{8}$ of the sum, and Maya's part was $\frac{3}{8}$ of the sum. Kelly had how many times more savings than Lara?

_____

19   Jack ran $\frac{5}{9}$ of a mile each day for 8 days. On the 9th day, he ran $1\frac{1}{9}$ miles. How many total miles did Jack run?

   (A) $1\frac{4}{9}$ (B) $3\frac{2}{7}$ (C) $5\frac{5}{9}$ (D) $7\frac{4}{7}$

20   Five friends each ate $\frac{2}{15}$ of a pizza. What fraction of a pizza left?

Next Section: Chapter Review ≫

2.4   **Chapter Review**

1 Find GCF (256, 728).

(A) 6   (B) 8   (C) 10   (D) 12

2 Find LCM (198, 352).

(A) 3,004   (B) 3,046   (C) 3,168   (D) 3,246

3 If GCF $(a,b)=24$ and LCM$(a,b)=720$,
can you find one pair of numbers a and b satisfying condition?

_____

4 The product of two numbers is 68,356 and their GCF is 46.
What is the LCM of these numbers?

(A) 1486   (B) 1498   (C) 1524   (D) 1568

5 Calculate $15\frac{3}{4} \div 9$.

(A) $\frac{9}{2}$ (B) $\frac{4}{9}$ (C) $\frac{7}{4}$ (D) $\frac{2}{9}$

6   Divide the fraction $5\frac{2}{6}$ by the given whole number 8.

(A) $\frac{5}{6}$ (B) $\frac{3}{2}$ (C) $\frac{4}{7}$ (D) $\frac{2}{3}$

7   On the number line below, which point represents $5\frac{1}{2} \div 11$?

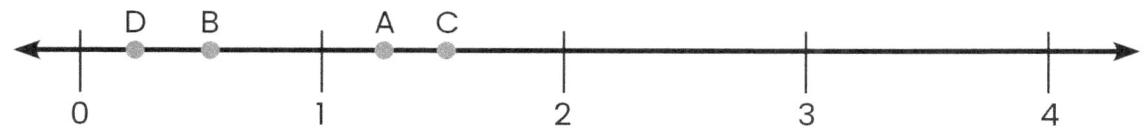

(A) Point A   (B) Point B   (C) Point C   (D) Point D

8   Sarah spends $\frac{6}{11}$ hour, three times a day, with her parrot. She also spends $\frac{2}{11}$ hour, twice a day, feeding her parrot. Select an expression, which shows the amount of time Sarah spends with her parrot per day.

(A) $\left(\frac{6}{11} \times 3\right) + \left(\frac{2}{11} \times 2\right)$ (B) $\left(\frac{6}{11} \times 3 + \frac{2}{11}\right) \times 2$

(C) $\left(\frac{6}{11} \times 3 + \frac{2}{11}\right) \div 2$ (D) $\left(\frac{6}{11} \times 3\right) - \left(\frac{2}{11} \times 2\right)$

9   Solve for m: $\frac{7}{12} + \frac{1}{3}m = \frac{11}{18}$.

(A) $\frac{7}{2}$ (B) $\frac{11}{4}$ (C) $\frac{1}{12}$ (D) $\frac{1}{3}$

2.4   **Chapter Review**

10 The following line plot shows the growth of 10 chili plants in their third week after sprouting.

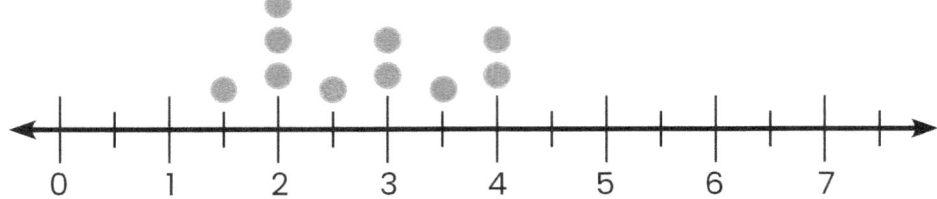

What is the total length of all plants, in inches? What is the difference between the tallest and shortest plants?

_____

11 Taylor is writing about a number that is divisible by both 84 and 112. What is the smallest possible number that Taylor could be writing about?

A) 336   B) 384   C) 462   D) 496

12 Randy earned $94,604 selling smartphones. The price of each smartphone was \$87$\frac{5}{4}$. How many smartphones were sold?

A) 1,012   B) 1,072   C) 1,125   D) 1,289

13 Nolan wants to pour a 2 L bottle of water into $\frac{1}{6}$ L glasses. How many glasses does Nolan need?

A) 6   B) 8   C) 10   D) 12

14 Each day Walter walks $3\frac{1}{2}$ miles to shop, $1\frac{2}{4}$ miles to work, and $1\frac{7}{4}$ miles home from work. How many miles did Walter walk altogether in 8 days?

(A) 54   (B) 62   (C) 76   (D) 80

15 Rosie baked a cheesecake for her sister's birthday. $\frac{19}{31}$ of the cheesecake was eaten during the celebration. The next day, Rosie ate one-third of what was left. How much of the cheesecake did Rosie still have left?

(A) $\frac{31}{17}$ (B) $\frac{11}{31}$ (C) $\frac{8}{31}$ (D) $\frac{31}{9}$

16 Aaron practiced his violin for $2\frac{1}{2}$ hours. He should practice for $20\frac{5}{2}$ hours this month. How many times should he practice this month?

(A) 5   (B) 7   (C) 11   (D) 13

17 Harry wants to plant 64 mangoes, 84 cherries, and 104 oranges in his garden. He is going to plant the same number of trees in each row, and each row should be planted with only one type of tree. What is greatest number of rows Harry could plant in such a way?

2.4   **Chapter Review**

18 Grayson has three watermelons weighing $2\frac{4}{4}$ kg, two watermelons weighing $2\frac{1}{2}$ kg, and one $1\frac{7}{3}$ kg watermelon. What is the total weight of all Grayson's watermelons?

_____

19 Calculate $21\frac{2}{3} \div 13 = ?$

(A) $\frac{6}{5}$ (B) $\frac{5}{3}$ (C) $\frac{5}{4}$ (D) $\frac{7}{2}$

20 How much chocolate cake will 8 people get if they share $\frac{5}{8}$ a pound of chocolate cake equally?

(A) $\frac{64}{5}$ (B) $\frac{25}{7}$ (C) $\frac{5}{64}$ (D) $\frac{7}{25}$

Next Chapter:
Factors and Multiples

CHAPTER 3

FACTORS AND MULTIPLES

SHADOW MATCHING GAME

IDENTIFY FACTORS

<u>Factors</u> are the numbers you multiply together to get another number. For example,

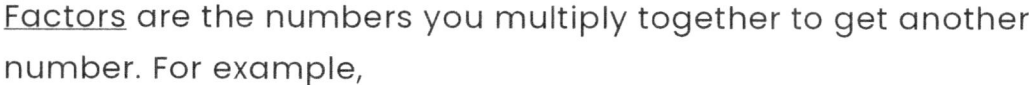

$$a \times b = c$$

!!! Factors must be whole numbers. If you divide and get a decimal or a remainder, then this number is not a factor. !!!

1. Any natural number is divisible by 1
2. The last digit is even 0,2,4,6,8
3. The sum of the digits is divisible by 3
4. The last digits are divisible by 4
5. The last digit is 0 or 5
6. It passes both the 2 rule and 3 the rule above
7. Double the last digit and subtract it from a number made by the other digits. The result must be divisible by 7.
8. The last three digits are divisible by 8
9. The sum of the digits is divisible by 9
10. The number ends in 0

An easy process to find the factors of any number:

*   All whole numbers have 1 themselves as factors, so your first two factors are 1 and the original number.
*   Work your way up from 1 and use long division to see if each number divides into the original number. For example, start with 2 and see it divides into the original number.
*   At some point, your factor list will close and there won't be any more whole numbers left that divide into the original number.

IDENTIFY FACTORS

Example: Find all factors of 12.

Solution:
1. 1 and 12   1 × 12 = 12
2. 2 and 6   2 × 6 = 12
3. 3 and 4   3 × 4 = 12

If you continue to check numbers for being factors, you'll get numbers 4, 6 and 12. Hence, the list of factors is 1, 2, 3, 4, 6, 12 .

1   List all factors of 33. Write the list of factors in ascending order.

(A) 1, 3, 11, 33   (B) 1, 2, 3, 4, 11 (C) 1, 4, 11, 33   (D) 1, 5, 11, 33

2   Mercy forgot the first number of her password: *23456, but remembered that it is divisible by 3 and 7. What was Mercy's password?

(A) 523456   (B) 123456   (C) 323456   (D) 423456

3   List all factors of number 15. Write the list of factors in ascending order.

(A) 1, 5, 11, 15   (B) 1, 2, 3, 5, 11   (C) 1, 3, 5, 15   (D) 1, 3, 5, 11

4   Michale thinks of a 3 digit number that begins with 31. It is divisible by 5 and by 7, but is not divisible by 2. What number does Michale think of?

(A) 305   (B) 323   (C) 325   (D) 315

FACTORS AND MULTIPLES

3.1   Identify Factors

5 List all factors of number 36. Write the list of factors in ascending order.

(A) 2, 3 , 4, 8, 12, 17   (B) 2, 3 , 4, 6, 9, 12, 18

(C) 2, 3 ,5, 6, 7, 12, 18   (D) 1, 3, 5, 11

6 Bessie has several pens. If she arranges them in groups of six, she will have one extra pen. There are no extra pens if she arranges them in groups of five. Which of the following could be the number of Bessie's pens?

(A) 52   (B) 53   (C) 55   (D) 56

7 List the prime factors of 18.

(A) 2, 3   (B) 1, 2, 3   (C) 3, 5   (D) 3,4

8 What is the smallest number that has the factors 4, 24, 28, and 42.

(A) 72   (B) 108   (C) 216   (D) 168

9   List the prime factors of 60.

(A) 2, 3, 5   (B) 2, 3, 4   (C) 1, 3, 5   (D) 2, 3, 7

10   Which of the following is not a factor of the number
$107 \times 18 + 107 \times 42 = ?$

(A) 6   (B) 9   (C) 10   (D) 15

11   List the prime factors of 45.

(A) 2, 3, 11   (B) 2, 3, 7   (C) 3, 5   (D) 1, 2, 3,

12   If the sum of the numbers in this number is 8, What is the smallest
three-digit number that is divisible by 10.

(A) 440   (B) 350   (C) 530   (D) 170

13   What is the greatest common prime factor of 33 and 44.

(A) 3   (B) 4   (C) 5   (D) 11

FACTORS AND MULTIPLES

3.1   Identify Factors

14 Andrea, her older brother, her father, and her grandfather's ages are all factors in the number 195. If Andrea is 13 years old, and her grandfather's age is less than 100 years, how old are her brother, father, and grandfather?

_____

15 What is the greatest common prime factor of 28 and 63?

(A) 3   (B) 7   (C) 5   (D) 11

16 List the prime factors of 75.

(A) 2, 3, 11   (B) 3, 5   (C) 4, 5   (D) 1, 2, 3

17 For the New Year's celebration, the students bought 5 boxes of chocolates with 8 chocolates in each box. Will the students be able to redistribute these boxes so that each box has 10 chocolates?

(A) Yes, 6 boxes   (B) Yes, 8 boxes

(C) Yes, 4 boxes   (D) No

18 For art class, the teacher bought 9 boxes with 12 pencils in each box. If there are 18 students in a class, will the teacher be able to divide the pencils so that each student receives 6 pencils?

(A) Yes   (B) No

19 What is the greatest common prime factor of 18 and 36?

(A) 5   (B) 7   (C) 3   (D) 11

20 There are 42 laps in the drag race. Each member of the team must drive the same number of laps. How many members should be on the team?

(A) 4 members   (B) 7 members

(C) 5 members   (D) 9 members

Next Section: Identify Multiples ›

IDENTIFY MULTIPLES

<u>Multiples</u> of a number can be divided by this number exactly. If you multiply a number by 1,2,3,4,... you calculate its multiples. For example, the multiples of 7 are 7,14,21,28,...

Different numbers can share some of the same multiples. These are called <u>common multiples.</u>

There are infinitely many multiples of a number.

Example: List 10 first multiples of 12 and 18. Write down common multiples.

Solution:
Multiples of 12: 12,24,36,48,60,72,84,96,108,120
Multiples of 18: 18,36,54,72,90,108,126,144,162,180
Common multiples: 36, 72, 108

Identify Multiples   **3.2**

1 Complete the number's first five multiples.

7, _____ , _____ , _____ , _____ .

2 Mrs. Helena has to buy 5 sets of bowls for her restaurant. She is going to buy one set every 3 days. On March 3, she purchased the first set. When will she buy the last set?

(A) 16th March   (B) 12th March   (C) 15th March   (D) 18th March

3 Complete the number's first five multiples.

12, _____ , _____ , _____ , _____ .

4 Sheena plans to buy two packs of stickers every week. How many stickers will Sheena have at the end of 4 weeks?

Sheena will have _____ stickers.

5 Complete the number's first five multiples.

18, _____ , _____ , _____ , _____ .

6 Blessy is playing with car toys. When she arranges them in rows of 8 cars in each row, she gets the prime number of rows that is between 4 and 6. How many cars will be in each row, when Blessy arranges all cars in 10 rows?

A Number of car toys in each row _____ .

FACTORS AND MULTIPLES

3.2   Identify Multiples

7   List the numbers that are multiples of 8.

8, 15, 24, 25, 32, 40, 56, 72, 75

_____

8   There were 12 bikes in the parking lot. Every hour, 4 more bikes arrive. Which of the following figures cannot represent the total number of bikes in the parking lot?

(A) 20   (B) 32   (C) 42   (D) 48

9   Complete the list of numbers 10, 15, 23, 20, 39, 35, 59, 45, 78

5, ____ , ____ , ____ , ____ , ____.

10   Angel thinks of a three-digit number. Her smallest number is a multiple of 3, multiple of 5, and a multiple of 7, but it is not a multiple of 4 or 6. What is Angel's number?

(A) 102   (B) 105   (C) 107   (D) 103

11   What are two common multiples of 2 and 7.

_____ and _____

12 The sum of all digits in a three-digit number is 24. Can this number be a multiple of 4?

A) Yes   B) No

13 What are two common multiples of 3 and 5.
_____ and _____.

14 Thinking of all the 2- digit multiples of 3 that contain the number 5.

_____

15 Write the first five multiples that come next.
17, ____ , ____ , ____ , ____.

16 Lisa's age this year is a multiple of 4, and next year's age will be a multiple of 9. How old is Lisa ? Is there more than one possibility?

_____

17 What are two common multiples of 4 and 9.
_____ and _____.

3.2   Identify Multiples

18 David puts his friends' photos into the album. He can place 3 photos on each page. If the album has 35 pages, how many photos can David put in the album?

David can put _____ photos into the album.

19 Complete the list of numbers 9, 15, 18, 25, 36, 40, 45, 63, 75, 81

9, ____ , ____ , ____ , ____ , ____.

20 Peter is playing with colored cards. He can put all his cards in stacks of 12 or in stacks of 15 cards. What could be the minimum number of cards Peter is playing with?

Peter is playing with _____ sketches.

Next Section:
Prime Factorization

PRIME FACTORIZATION

<u>Prime factorization</u> is finding which prime numbers multiply together to make the original number.

Step 1: Start by dividing the number by the first prime number 2 and continue dividing by 2 until you get a decimal or remainder. Then divide by 3, 5, 7 etc. until the only numbers left are prime numbers.

Step 2: Write the number as a product of prime numbers.

Example

Find the prime factorization of 200.

Solution: Divide 200 by 2:

$200 = 2 \times 100 = 2 \times 2 \times 50 = 2 \times 2 \times 2 \times 25$

Divide 25 by 5:

$200 = 2 \times 2 \times 2 \times 25 = 2 \times 2 \times 2 \times 5 \times 5 = 2^3 \times 5^2$.

FACTORS AND MULTIPLES

3.3   Prime Factorization

1   The product of three consecutive natural numbers is 1,716. What are these numbers?

_____

2   What is the smallest two-digit number, that is the product of two different non-unit perfect squares?

_____

3   The prime factorization of the number is $2^4 \times 3 \times 5^4 \times 7$. Which of the following is a factorization of this number?

(A) $40 \times 100 \times 49$

(B) $16 \times 35 \times 14 \times 25$

(C) $12 \times 250 \times 70$

(D) $32 \times 175 \times 35$

4   The factorization of the number is $30 \times 28 \times 144 \times 60$. Which of the following is a prime factorization of this number?

(A) $2^5 \times 3^2 \times 5^2 \times 7 \times 12^2$

(B) $2^7 \times 3 \times 5^2 \times 7 \times 11^2$

(C) $2^6 \times 3 \times 5^2 \times 7 \times 13^2$

(D) $2^5 \times 3 \times 5^2 \times 7 \times 11^2$

5   The music club has a total of ten members.

24	28	21	42	46
50	19	32	38	x

If $(2 \times 3 \times 5 \times 11) \div (2 \times 5)$ is the average age of all members, what is the value of x? x = _____ .

6   What is the prime factorization of the number $2^4 + 4^4$?

_____

7   Blessy bought a new reclining chair for $616. She put it down $112 and the rest was divided into x equal monthly payments. If she had to pay for the reclining chair for more than 10 months but less than 2 years, how much would she have to pay each month?
She paid _____ each month.

8   Lisa drove 68 miles at a constant speed. If she spent a prime number of hours driving this distance, how long did it take her?

_____

FACTORS AND MULTIPLES

Prime Factorization

9 Stefani is going to plant 320 potatoes. She wants to plant them in rows, each containing the same number of potatoes. If her garden bed allows at most 32 rows, what could be the minimum number of potatoes in each row?

_____

10 Which is the smallest three-digit number with only two prime factors in its prime factorization.

(A) 114   (B) 113   (C) 111   (D) 112

11 119 mangoes were spread evenly into fruit baskets. How many mangoes were put into each basket if there were less than 20 fruit baskets?

_____

12 If 2^3=T, 3^2=R, 5^1=A, 7^2=C, 11=O, 7^1=E, 11^2=M, 2^2=K, what is the code for 21,560?

(A) TACO   (B) TAACO

13 Find the prime factorization of numbers: 18 = _____.

    (A) $18 = 9 \times 2$ (B) $18 = 3^2 \times 2$ (C) $18 = 4 \times 3$ (D) $18 = 2^2 \times 3$

14 The volume of a box is 80 cm³. If all the dimensions of the box are natural numbers, what are the different possible dimensions of the box?

_____

15 The area of Mrs. Jennifer's backyard is 1,044 m2. The length of the backyard is the greatest prime number that is less than 30. What could be the dimensions of Mrs. Jennifer's backyard?

    (A) Length=29m, Width = 36 m   (B) Length=27m, Width = 25 m

    (C) Length=52m, Width = 27 m   (D) Length=36m, Width = 29 m

16 Jessy wants to read a 186 - page book in less than a week. How many pages can Jessy read per day? Is there more than one possibility?

_____

3.3   **Prime Factorization**

17 The area of the base of a rectangular box must be in 36 square meters. If the width and the length of the box are both natural numbers, how many possible dimensions can be built for the same box?

_____

18 Find the prime factorization of numbers: $24 =$ _____.

(A) $24 = 2^3 \times 3$ (B) $24 = 3^2 \times 2$ (C) $24 = 8 \times 3$ (D) $24 = 2^2 \times 3$

19 Angel has 1,564 followers on Instagram. Blessy has a times fewer followers on Instagram than Angel does. If a is a prime number greater than 20, how many followers do Blessy have?

(A) Blessy has 45 followers

(B) Blessy has 55 followers

(C) Blessy has 68 followers

(D) Blessy has 65 followers

20 The restaurant owner divides the tips evenly among all waiters at the end of each week. He divides $6,664 this week. If there is the greatest possible prime number of waiters, how much does each waiter get?

(A) 14 waiters, each gets $298

(B) 15 waiters, each gets $302

(C) 12 waiters, each gets $358

(D) 17 waiters, each gets $392

Next Section: Chapter Review >>

3.4   **Chapter Review**

1 List all factors for number 44. Write the list of factors in ascending order.

   (A) 1, 4, 11, 44   (B) 1, 2, 4, 11, 44

   (C) 1, 2, 3, 4, 11, 44   (D) 1, 4, 5, 11, 44

2 Complete the 5 multiples.

17, ____ , ____ , ____ , ____.

3 What is the smallest three-digit number with only two prime factors in its prime factorization.

   (A) 102   (B) 106   (C) 113   (D) 101

4 Jessy forgot the first digit of the password *34568, but remembered that it is divisible by 3 and 11. What was Jessy's password?

   (A) 123457   (B) 234567   (C) 734568   (D) 873957

5 From the list of numbers 9, 15, 27, 25, 36, 40, 45, 56, 63, 72. write down all the multiples of 9.

9, ____ , ____ , ____ , ____ , ____.

6   The tennis club has ten members.

30	32	19	45	40
49	25	30	50	x

If $(2 \times 5^2 \times 7) \div (2 \times 5)$ is the average age of all members, what is the value of x? x = _____.

7   Mike thinks of a 3 digit number that begins with 24, is divisible by 5 and by 7, but is not divisible by 2. What number does Mike think of?

(A) 205   (B) 245   (C) 225   (D) 215

8   List the prime factors of number 24.

(A) 3,4   (B) 1, 2, 3   (C) 3, 5   (D) 2, 3

9   The factorization of the number is 35 × 28 × 169 × 90. Which of the following is a prime factorization of this number?

(A) $2^3 \times 3^2 \times 5^2 \times 7^2 \times 13^2$ (B) $2^7 \times 3 \times 5^2 \times 7 \times 12^2$

(C) $2^6 \times 3 \times 5^2 \times 7 \times 13^2$ (D) $2^5 \times 3 \times 5^2 \times 7 \times 11^2$

FACTORS AND MULTIPLES

10 Angel thinks of a three-digit number. Her number is the smallest number that is a multiple of 3, multiple of 4, and a multiple of 6, but is not a multiple of 5 or 7. What is Angel's number?

(A) 102   (B) 105   (C) 108   (D) 103

11 The prime factorization of the number is $3^3 \times 5^5 \times 7$. Which of the following is a factorization of this number?

(A) 42 × 105 × 47   (B) 15 × 375 × 105

(C) 10 × 270 × 75   (D) 30 × 185 × 45

12 Write down the common multiples of both 4 and 9.
_____ and _____.

13 Reena, her older sister, mother, and grandmother's ages are factors of number 190. If Reena is 10 years old, and her grandmother's age is less than 100 years, how old are her sister, mother, and grandmother?

14 The sum of all digits in a three-digit number is 23. Can this number be a multiple of 4?

(A) Yes   (B) No

15 What is the greatest common prime factor of 22 and 55?

(A) 3   (B) 7   (C) 5   (D) 11

16 Jenny wants to read a 270-page book in less than a week. How many pages can Jessy read per day? Is there more than one possibility?

_____

17 Find the smallest 3-digit number x, for which an odd number x + 123 divisible by 9.

(A) x = 100   (B) x = 102

(C) x = 103   (D) x = 105

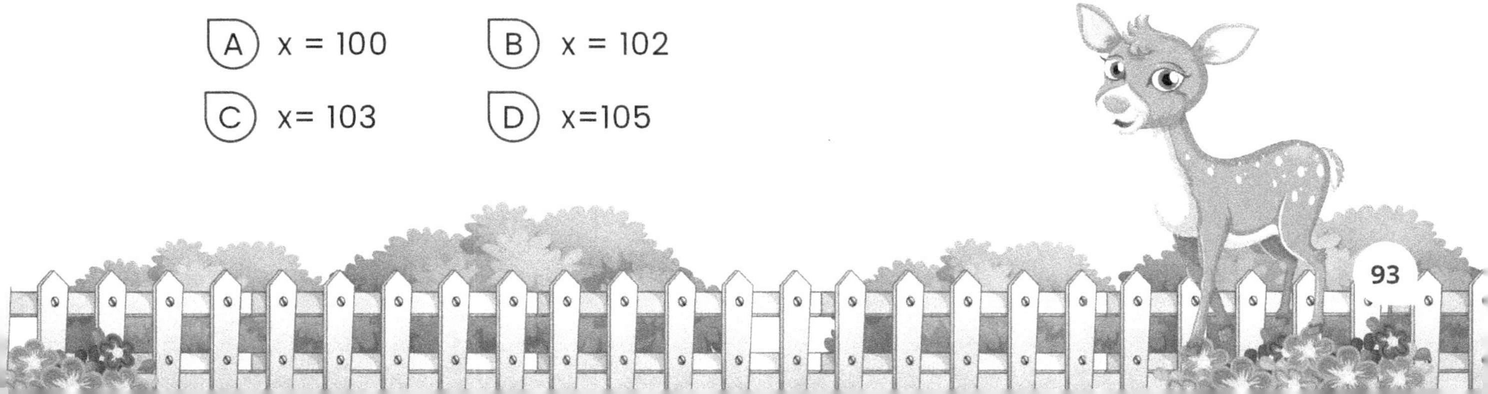

3.4   **Chapter Review**

18 Steffi bought some packs of greeting cards. Each pack contains nearly 12 cards. If the total number of cards Steffi bought was 108, how many packs of greeting cards did she buy?

(A) 8   (B) 6   (C) 9   (D) 12

19 Find the prime factorization of these numbers:
105 = _____.

(A) $105 = 35 \times 7$ (B) $105 = 5 \times 10$

(C) $105 = 3 \times 7 \times 2$ (D) $105 = 3^2 \times 5 \times 7$

20 There are 49 laps in the bike race. Each member of the team must drive the same number of laps. How many members should be on the team?

(A) 4 members   (B) 5 members

(C) 9 members   (D) 7 members

Next Chapter: Exponents >>

CHAPTER 4

EXPONENTS

SHADOW MATCHING GAME

MULTIPLICATION EXPRESSIONS

An expression that represents repeated multiplication of the same factor a is called a power.

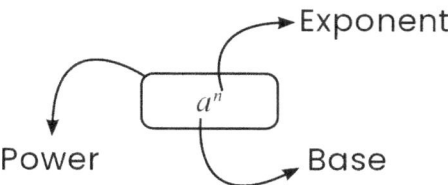

The number a is called the base, and the number n is called the exponent. The exponent corresponds to the number of times the base is used as a factor.

Multiplication

If two powers have the same base then we can multiply the powers. When we multiply two powers, we add their exponents. The rule is

$$a^m \times a^n = a^{m+n}$$

Division

If two powers have the same base then we can divide the powers. When we divide powers we subtract their exponents. The rule is

$$\frac{a^m}{a^n} = a^{m-n}$$

Example: Write as a power $2^4 \times 2^7$.

Solution: $2^4 \times 2^7 = 2^{4+7} = 2^{11}$

EXPONENTS

4.1   **Multiplication Expressions**

1   Fill in the blanks. 5^3

A) Expanded form _____.   B) Standard form _____.

2   Fill in the blanks. 243

A) Expanded form _____.   B) Standard form _____.

3   Fill in the blanks. 9^3

A) Expanded form _____.   B) Standard form _____.

4   Fill in the blanks. 343

A) Expanded form _____.   B) Standard form _____.

5 $6 \times 6 \times 6 \times 6$

The exponent form is _____.

6   Write the expression using an exponent.

$8 \times 8 \times 8 \times 8 \times 8 \times 8 \times 8 \times 8$

(A) 8^8 (B) 8^9 (C) 8^{11} (D) 8^{12}

7   Fill in the blanks. $4^3 - 5^2 = $ _____.

8   Calculate: $10^3 - 9^3 = $ _____.

9   Calculate: $6^3 \div 2^3 = $ _____.

10   Calculate: $6 \times (9^3 + 4^4) = $ _____.

11   Calculate: $8^4 - 6^2 - 3^2 - 4^0 = $ _____

EXPONENTS

4.1　Multiplication Expressions

12 The perimeter of the square is 120 cm. What is its area? Express the area of the square as a power.

(A) 40^2 (B) 30^2 (C) 20^2 (D) 10^2

13 The volume of the cube is 343 cm³. What is the length of the edge?

(A) 5 (B) 6 (C) 7 (D) 8

14 A bike travels at a speed of 3^5 miles per day. How many miles will it travel in 3 days?

(A) 512 miles (B) 789 miles (C) 729 miles (D) 816 miles

15 One watermelon is cut into 9 slices. Each slice is cut into three slices. How many slices are in 27 watermelon? What power is 3 raised to for the answer?

(A) 5 (B) 6 (C) 7 (D) 8

16 Six medium-sized packages are placed in one large package and 36 small packages are placed in a medium-sized package. How many large packages does it take to hold 46,656 small packages? Give your answer as a power.

(A) 6^1 (B) 6^3 (C) 6^5 (D) 6^4

17 Pamela has a rectangular garden whose width is 5^3 cm and whose length is five times longer. What is the area of her garden?

(A) 78,525 cm²   (B) 78,125 cm²

(C) 78,755 cm²   (D) 78,985 cm²

18 A volunteer organization has decided to provide apples for children in orphanages. Each of the 81 volunteers is responsible for 9 children. Each child will get 3 apples. How many apples is the organization providing in total?
Give your answer as a power with the base of 3 or 9.

(A) 3^7 apples   (B) 3^8 apples

(C) 3^6 apples   (D) 3^9 apples

EXPONENTS

4.1   **Multiplication Expressions**

19   Calculate: 2 × 256 − 4 × 64 + 3 × 32 − 5 × 16 + 6 × 1 = ?

(A) 259   (B) 265   (C) 278   (D) 289

20   Chris's age plus the square of Tom's age is 208. Tom's age plus the square of Chris's age is 158. How old is Chris and Tom?

(A)   Chris's age = 19 years, Tom's age = 15 years

(B)   Chris's age = 20 years, Tom's age = 24 years

(C)   Chris's age = 12 years, Tom's age = 14 years

(D)   Chris's age = 21 years, Tom's age = 17 years

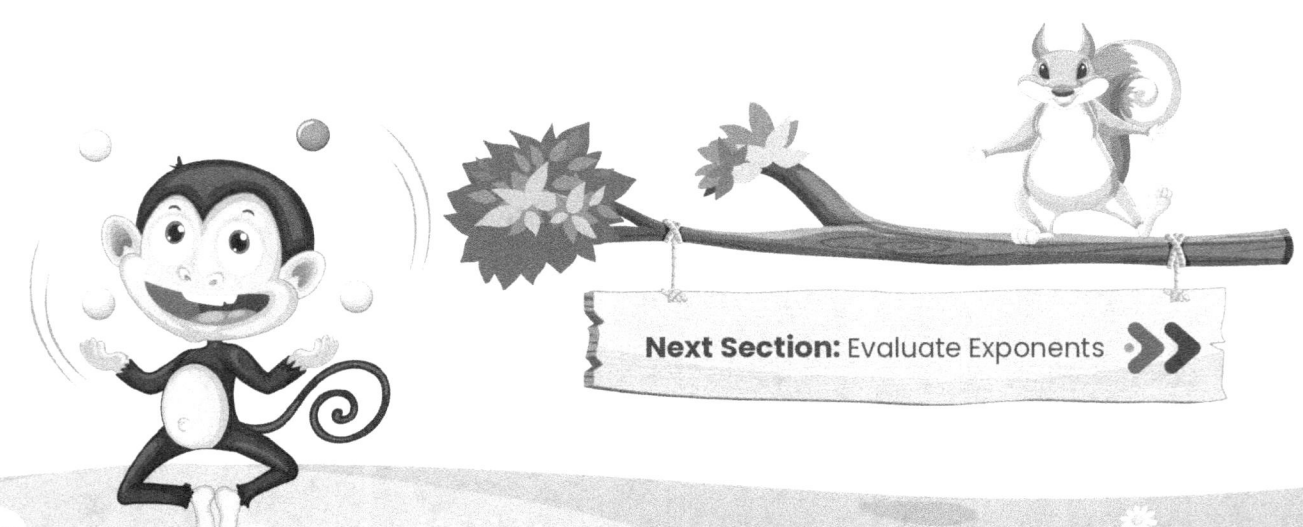

Next Section: Evaluate Exponents ≫

EVALUATE EXPONENTS

Evaluating exponents typically refers to the process of simplifying or solving expressions that involve exponents. An exponent is a mathematical notation indicating that a quantity is to be multiplied by itself a certain number of times.

To determine the value of 2^4, multiply $2 \times 2 \times 2 \times 2$ which would give the result 16.

Some facts about exponents:

- Zero raised to any power is zero (e.g., $0^8 = 0$).

- One raised to any power is one (e.g., $1^{10} = 1$).

- Any number raised to the zero power is one (e.g., $5^0 = 1$).

- Any number raised to the first power is that number (e.g., $5^1 = 5$).

Example: Evaluate $(-2)^6 - (-2)^5$.

Solution:

$(-2)^6 = (-2) \times (-2) \times (-2) \times (-2) \times (-2) \times (-2) = 64$.

$(-2)^5 = (-2) \times (-2) \times (-2) \times (-2) \times (-2) = -32$.

Therefore,

$(-2)^6 - (-2)^5 = 64 - (-32) = 64 + 32 = 96$.

4.2   **Evaluate Exponents**

1   Evaluate. $(-5)^4 = $ _____ .

2   Evaluate. $75^0 = $ _____ .

3   Evaluate. $(-8)^3 + (3)^6$.

(A) 220   (B) 217   (C) 271   (D) 264

4   Evaluate $\left(\frac{1}{4}\right)^3$.

(A) $\frac{1}{43}$ (B) $\frac{1}{84}$ (C) $\frac{1}{16}$ (D) $\frac{1}{64}$

5   Evaluate $\left(-\frac{5}{7}\right)^3$.

(A) $-\frac{125}{343}$ (B) $\frac{125}{343}$ (C) $-\frac{25}{49}$ (D) $\frac{35}{42}$

6   Evaluate. $3^4 \times 4 - 4^3 \times 3 = ?$

(A) 222   (B) 117   (C) 132   (D) 164

7 Select the equivalent answer: $(-4)^4 \times (-\frac{1}{4})^3$

A) 4   B) 1   C) -2   D) -4

8 Select the equivalent answer: $7^{11} \times 7^5$

A) 7^8 B) 7^{16} C) 7^4 D) 7^{11}

9 Elephants grow wider faster than they get heavier. The proportion of increase in length to increase in weight can be written as $\frac{3^6}{3^2}$ per month. Simplify this fraction.

A) 3^8 B) 3^6 C) 3^4 D) 3^{11}

10 The population of India is 10^7, and the population of Australia is 3×10^5. How many more times is the population of India than Australia?

A) $33\frac{1}{3}$ B) $6\frac{4}{3}$ C) $5\frac{2}{3}$ D) $6\frac{5}{3}$

11 Mr. Robert knows his rectangular garden has an area of 225 m². What is the perimeter of Mr. Robert's garden?

A) 55   B) 60   C) 66   D) 64

EXPONENTS

4.2 Evaluate Exponents

12 YouTube blogger has 3^5 followers. The daily number of followers has tripled. How many followers will this blogger have in 7 days?

(A) 3^8 (B) 3^6 (C) 3^4 (D) 3^{12}

13 A solar panel accumulates 4 kilowatts of energy each day. How much energy does 4 solar panels accumulate over 16 days?

(A) 256   (B) 260   (C) 266   (D) 264

14 There are 6^3 residents in each of the 6^2 buildings. How many residents live in each building?

(A) 7756   (B) 7770   (C) 7776   (D) 7764

15 Jim and Aaron went to the market. Jim had $ 216 to spend. Jim had 6 times as much as Aaron to spend. How much money did Aaron have to spend? Express your answer as power.

(A) 6^4 (B) 6^6 (C) 6^8 (D) 6^3

16 In four days, the worker collects 4^5 kg of apples. How many kilograms of apples will the worker collect in 64 days?

(A) 4^4 (B) 4^6 (C) 4^7 (D) 4^3

17 A square with side a length of x^2 in has the area of 625 in^2. What is the area of the square with side length of x in?

   (A) 56 in^2 (B) 25 in^2 (C) 16 in^2 (D) 36 in^2

18 There are 64 people in the audience. Each of them holds a bouquet of 8 roses. How many roses are there in the audience?
Express your answer with power.

   (A) 8^4 (B) 8^6 (C) 8^7 (D) 8^3

19 Steve has a rectangular garden with dimensions 15 m by 20 m. He cuts the garden's length and width by 20% each. What is the area of the new Steve's garden?

   (A) 256 m^2 (B) 250 m^2 (C) 240 m^2 (D) 236 m^2

20 If $5^{5-x}=625$, what is the value of $\left(\frac{1}{5}\right)^{1-x}$?

   (A) 5   (B) 0   (C) $\frac{1}{5}$ (D) 1

Next Section: Missing Exponent

MISSING EXPONENT

To find the missing exponent:

- We have to get the same base on both sides.

- Once we get the same base, exponents can be equated and we can find the value of the missing exponent.

Example: Find the missing exponent $64 = 2^x$

Solution: Since, $64 = 2^x$, we have $2^x = 2^6$, hence $x = 6$

To find the missing base:

- We have to get the same exponent on both sides.

- Once we get the same exponent, bases can be equated and we can find the value of the missing base.

Example: Find the missing base $27 = x^3$

Solution: Since, $27 = x^3$, we have $3^3 = x^3$, hence $x = 3$.

1 Find the missing base. $4^x = 256$.

(A) $x = 1$ (B) $x = 4$ (C) $x = 3$ (D) $x = 5$

2 Find the missing exponent. $9^x = 3^6$.

(A) $x = 1$ (B) $x = 4$ (C) $x = 3$ (D) $x = 5$

3 Find the missing exponent. $81^x = 9^2$.

(A) $x = 2$ (B) $x = 4$ (C) $x = 3$ (D) $x = 5$

4 Find the missing exponent. $x^2 = 169$.

(A) $x = 12$ (B) $x = 14$ (C) $x = 13$ (D) $x = 15$

5 Find the missing exponent and base for the given numbers
If the number is 625, the missing exponent in 5^x, x is _____ and the missing base in x^2, x is _____.

(A) Missing exponent $x = 12$, Missing base $x = 3$

(B) Missing exponent $x = 4$, Missing base $x = 16$

(C) Missing exponent $x = 4$, Missing base $x = 25$

(D) Missing exponent $x = 7$, Missing base $x = 49$

EXPONENTS

4.3 Missing Exponent

6 Find the missing exponent and base for the given numbers

If the number is 6561, the missing exponent in 9^x, x is _____ and the missing base x^8, x is _____.

(A) Missing exponent $x = 12$, Missing base $x = 3$

(B) Missing exponent $x = 4$, Missing base $x = 3$

(C) Missing exponent $x = 4$, Missing base $x = 25$

(D) Missing exponent $x = 7$, Missing base $x = 49$

---

7 Find x.

$17 \times 289 = 17^x$.

(A) $x = 2$ (B) $x = 4$ (C) $x = 3$ (D) $x = 5$

---

8 Find the missing exponent and base for the given numbers

If the number is $\frac{1}{324}$ the missing exponent in $\left(\frac{1}{18}\right)^x$, x is _____ and the missing base is x^2, x is _____.

(A) Missing exponent $x = 6$, Missing base $x = 2$

(B) Missing exponent $x = 4$, Missing base $x = \frac{1}{4}$

(C) Missing exponent $x = 2$, Missing base $x = \frac{1}{18}$

(D) Missing exponent $x = 7$, Missing base $x = \frac{1}{7}$

9 Find x.

$2 \times 256 \times 4 = 2^x$.

(A) $x = 8$ (B) $x = 10$ (C) $x = 6$ (D) $x = 5$

10 One-third of a school tennis court has an area of 81 m². If this section of the tennis court is a square, what are the dimensions of the whole tennis court?

(A) Width = 9 m and Length = 36 m

(B) Width = 3 m and Length = 9 m

(C) Width = 4 m and Length = 12 m

(D) Width = 5 m and Length = 15 m

11 One kilometer is $10x$ times longer than one millimetre. What is the value of x?

(A) $x = 8$ (B) $x = 10$ (C) $x = 6$ (D) $x = 5$

12 The general coastline of Malaysia is approximately x^4 kilometers. The general coastline of Italy is approximately $42x^2$ kilometers, or 16800 kilometers. How long is Malaysia's coastline?

(A) 1,50,000   (B) 1,60,000   (C) 1,60,600   (D) 1,60,660

4.3   Missing Exponent

13 A rectangle has dimensions of $4x^2$ ft long and $5x$ ft wide. If the area of the rectangle is 10,240 ft², what is the length and the width of the rectangle?

(A) Length: 256 feet, Width 40 feet   (B) Length: 226 feet, Width 48 feet

(C) Length: 286 feet, Width 50 feet   (D) Length: 260 feet, Width 45 feet

14 Bertrand has five square tiles, each measuring a length of x^2 cm. He calculates that he can cover an area of 12,500 cm². How long does each tile last?

(A) 20   (B) 23   (C) 28   (D) 50

15 There are 1,764 contestants lined up for a match in a square formation. How many contestants were in each column?

(A) 40   (B) 42   (C) 48   (D) 45

16 Each term in the sequence 3, 9, 27, 81, … is four times the previous term. What is the ninth term of the sequence?

(A) 59049   (B) 59059   (C) 59069   (D) 59079

17   Children place chess board pieces in separate cells on a board. The first child put one piece, the second child – two pieces, the third child – twice as many as the second, and so on. If the size of the board is 9 cells by 9 cells, which child will finish laying out the pieces?

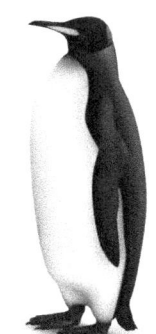

- (A) 8th child will finish
- (B) 9th child will finish
- (C) 7th child will finish
- (D) 6th child will finish

18   If $20^k = 400^2$, what is the value of k^2 ?

- (A) 20
- (B) 22
- (C) 24
- (D) 16

19   The area of the cube surface is 1536 cm². What is the volume of this cube?

- (A) 4049 cm³
- (B) 4096 cm³
- (C) 4069 cm³
- (D) 4079 cm³

20   If $c^3 d^2 = 25000$, what is the value of c and d ?

- (A) c=8 and d=5
- (B) c=9 and d=4
- (C) c=10 and d=6
- (D) c=10 and d=5

Next Section: Powers of Tens ❯❯

POWERS OF TENS

Powers of 10 are commonly used in scientific notation, which is a way of writing very large or very small numbers using powers of 10.

Powers of 10 are

$$10^0 = 1$$

$$10^1 = 10, \quad 10^{-1} = \frac{1}{10}$$

$$10^2 = 100, \quad 10^{-2} = \frac{1}{100}$$

$$10^3 = 1000, \quad 10^{-3} = \frac{1}{1000}$$

$$10^4 = 10000, \quad 10^{-4} = \frac{1}{10000}$$

Scientific notation is a form of powers10 notation that expresses a number between 1 and 10 times a power of 10. The power of 10 indicates the placement of the decimal point.

When expressing a number in scientific notation, remember the following rules:

- Express the number as a number between 1 and 10 times a power of 10.

- If the decimal point is moved to the left in the original number, make the power of 10 positive.

- If the decimal point is moved to the right in the original number, make the power of 10 negative.

- The power of 10 always equals the number of places the decimal point has been shifted to the left or right in the original number.

Example: Express the number 5,300,000 in scientific notation.

$$5{,}300{,}000 = 5.3 \times 1{,}000{,}000 = 5.3 \times 10^6$$

1   Write the following numbers as the power of 10

10000000

(A) 10^4 (B) 10^5 (C) 10^7 (D) 10^3

2   Write the following numbers as the power of 10. $\frac{1}{1000}$

(A) 10^{-4} (B) 10^{-5} (C) 10^{-7} (D) 10^{-3}

3   Express numbers in scientific notation: 50

(A) 5×10^0 (B) 5×10^5 (C) 5×10^7 (D) 5×10^1

4   Express the numbers in scientific notation: 0.00085

(A) 8.5×10^{-2} (B) 8.5×10^{-3} (C) 8.5×10^{-4} (D) 8.5×10^{-5}

5   Write the numbers in standard form: 3.33×10^3

(A) 0.33   (B) 3330   (C) 33.3   (D) 0.003

6   Write the numbers in standard form: 7.22321×10^5

(A) 7223.21   (B) 72232.1   (C) 0.722321   (D) 722321

EXPONENTS

4.4   **Powers of Tens**

7 Perform the following operations and express your answer in scientific notation: $5.8 \times 10^2 + 0.006 \times 10^3$

(A) 58.6   (B) 5860   (C) 586   (D) 0.586

8 Perform the following operations and express your answer in scientific notation: $88.05 \times 10^5 + 6.54 \times 10^{-1} + 5 \times 10^0$

(A) 88,05,005.654   (B) 88,05,05.654

(C) 88,05,05654   (D) 93,05,00.654

9 Calculate and write in scientific notation:
$5200 \div 10^5 + 4.25$

(A) 4.205   (B) 4.302   (C) 4302   (D) 56.25

10 The mass of a substance is 5.2×10^{11} grams. If one gram is equal to 10^{-8} kilograms, what is the mass of the substance in kilograms?

(A) 5.2×10^2 (B) 5.2×10^3 (C) 5.2×10^4 (D) 5.2×10^5

11 The microscope magnifies the size of the object at 7×10^3 times. If the diameter of the microbe is 2.4×10^{-6} cm, then what is the diameter of the microbe after magnification with the microscope?

(A) 0.168×10^3 (B) 1.68×10^3

(C) 16.8×10^3 (D) 16.8×10^{-3}

12 An internet company offers internet service with a cap of 1,000 GB for $50 per month. What is the price per GB?

(A) $5   (B) $0.5   (C) $0.05   (D) $0.005

13 A square section of the field has a length of 4.8×10^6 cm. What is the area of this section of fields written in scientific notation?

(A) 23.04×10^{12} (B) 2304×10^{12} (C) 23.04×10^{-12} (D) 230.4×10^{12}

14 One nanometer is equivalent to 10^{-9} m. What is the scientific notation for 50 nanometers?

(A) 510^{-8} (B) 5×10^{-9} (C) 5×10^{-10} (D) 510^{-12}

15 One light year is about 8×10^{15} miles. The Earth is about 6×10^{-11} light years from the Moon. How far away, in miles, is the Earth from the Moon?

(A) 48×10^{-8} (B) 48×10^5 (C) 48×10^4 (D) 48×10^{-12}

16 The circumference of the sun is about 55,800 miles. Express this number in scientific notation.

(A) 5.58×10^4 (B) 5.58×10^5 (C) 5.58×10^6 (D) 5.58×10^8

4.4   **Powers of Tens**

17 Knights of King Alexander made an initial contribution to the Treasury in size of 8×10^5 gold coins. Express this number in standard form.

(A) 8000 gold coins

(B) 80000 gold coins

(C) 800000 gold coins

(D) 8000000 gold coins

18 Find the mistakes in the calculation:

$(10 \times 10^{25}) \div (5 \times 10^5) = (10 \div 5) \times (10^{25} \div 10^5) = 2 \times 10^5$

(A) $(10 \times 10^{25}) \div (5 \times 10^5) = (10 \div 5) \times (10^{25} \div 10^5) = 2 \times 10^{22}$

(B) $(10 \times 10^{25}) \div (5 \times 10^5) = (10 \div 5) \times (10^{25} \div 10^5) = 2 \times 10^{15}$

(C) $(10 \times 10^{25}) \div (5 \times 10^5) = (10 \div 5) \times (10^{25} \div 10^5) = 2 \times 10^{20}$

(D) $(10 \times 10^{25}) \div (5 \times 10^5) = (10 \div 5) \times (10^{25} \div 10^5) = 2 \times 10^{26}$

19 If $\frac{100^{15}}{100^7} \div 10^{-3} = \left(\frac{1}{10}\right)^x$, what is the value for x?

(A) $x = -8$

(B) $x = -11$

(C) $x = -9$

(D) $x = -7$

20 The state of Colorado covers an area of 2.2×10^6 square miles. Express this number in standard form.

(A) 22000 square miles

(B) 220000 square miles

(C) 2200000 square miles

(D) 22000000 square miles

Next Section: Chapter Review >>

EXPONENTS

4.5   Chapter Review

1   Fill in the blanks. 5^3

     (A) Expanded form _____.   (B) Standard form _____.

2   Calculate: $9^2 - 5^2 - 2^4 - 10^1$ _____.

3   One cake is cut into 16 slices. Each slice is cut into 4 slices. How many slices are in 64 cakes? What power is 4 raised to for the answer?

     (A) 5   (B) 6   (C) 7   (D) 8

4   Emma has a rectangular garden whose width is 6^3 cm and whose length is 6 times longer. What is the area of her garden?

     (A) 2,79,936 cm²   (B) 2,79,836 cm²

     (C) 2,79,536 cm²   (D) 2,79,736 cm²

5   The volume of the cube is 729 cm³. What is the length of the edge?

     (A) 9 cm   (B) 6 cm   (C) 7 cm   (D) 8 cm

6   Evaluate: $(-9)^3 + (2)^8$ _____

7   Select the equivalent answer: $7^{25} \times 7^{-10}$

(A) 7^{22} (B) 7^{15} (C) 7^{12} (D) 7^{9}

8   In 5 days, the worker collects 5^4 kg of apples. How many kilograms of apples will the worker collect in 25 days?

(A) 5^5 (B) 5^6 (C) 5^7 (D) 5^3

9   If $6^{6-x} = 1296$, what is the value of $\left(\frac{1}{6}\right)^{1-x}$?

(A) 6   (B) 0   (C) $\frac{1}{6}$ (D) 1

10   YouTube blogger has 4^6 followers. The daily number of followers has tripled. How many followers will this blogger have in 5 days?

(A) 4^8 (B) 4^6 (C) 4^4 (D) 4^{11}

11   Find the missing exponent. $16^x = 4^4$

(A) $x = 1$ (B) $x = 4$ (C) $x = 3$ (D) $x = 2$

4.5   Chapter Review

12
Find the missing exponent and base for the given numbers
If the number is 1296, the missing exponent in 6^x, x is _____ and the missing base in x^2, x is _____ .

(A) Missing exponent $x = 12$, Missing base $x = 3$

(B) Missing exponent $x = 4$, Missing base $x = 36$

(C) Missing exponent $x = 4$, Missing base $x = 25$

(D) Missing exponent $x = 7$, Missing base $x = 49$

13
Find x.
$18 \times 5832 = 18^x$

(A) $x = 2$ (B) $x = 4$ (C) $x = 3$ (D) $x = 5$

14
One-third of a college campus has an area of 121 m². If this area of the college campus is a square, what are the dimensions of the whole college campus?

(A) Width = 11 m and Length = 33 m

(B) Width = 3 m and Length = 9 m

(C) Width = 4 m and Length = 12 m

(D) Width = 5 m and Length = 15 m

15 The area of the cube surface is 1944 cm². What is the volume of this cube?

   (A) 5832 cm³   (B) 5842 cm³   (C) 5862 cm³   (D) 5872 cm³

16 If $c^3 d^2 = 11664$, what is the value of c and d ?

   (A) c = 8 and d = 5   (B) c = 9 and d = 4
   (C) c = 10 and d = 6   (D) c = 10 and d = 5

17 Express numbers in scientific notation: 0.000095

   (A) 9.5×10^{-2} (B) 9.5×10^{-3} (C) 9.5×10^{-4} (D) 9.5×10^{-5}

18 The mass of a substance is 8.2×10^{15} grams. If one gram is equal to 10^{-7} a kilogram, what is the mass of the substance in kilograms?

   (A) 8.2×10^8 (B) 8.2×10^3 (C) 8.2×10^4 (D) 8.2×10^5

19 An internet company offers internet service with a cap of 1,000 GB for $80 per month. What is the price per GB?

   (A) $8   (B) $0.8   (C) $0.08   (D) $0.008

20 The state of Columbus covers an area of 4.2×10^5 square miles. Express this number in standard form.

(A) 42000 square miles

(B) 420000 square miles

(C) 4200000 square miles

(D) 42000000 square miles

Next Chapter: Expressions, Equations and Inequalities

CHAPTER 5

EXPRESSIONS, EQUATIONS, AND INEQUALITIES

VARIABLE EXPRESSIONS

A variable expression is an expression that contains one or more variables, which are letters or symbols that represent unknown values or quantities.

An algebraic expression is a mathematical phrase that contains numbers, variables, and algebraic operators (such as addition, subtraction, division, multiplication, etc.).

A term is a number, a variable, the product of two or more variables, or the product of a number, and a variable. An algebraic expression is formed by a single term or by a group of terms. For example, in the expression $3x + 6$, the two terms are $3x$ and 6.

The numbers or variables that are multiplied to form a term are called its factors. Example, $5x$ is a term with factors 5 and x.

A coefficient is the numerical factor of a term containing constants and variables.

A constant is a term, that always has a definite value.

Variable

Constant

Coefficient

$7 - 11y$

Example: For the expression $13x - 5$, write down all terms, coefficients, and constant.

Solution: Terms: $13x$ and -5

Coefficients: 13

Constant: -5

EXPRESSIONS, EQUATIONS, AND INEQUALITIES

5.1   Variable Expressions

1   The expression for the sum of x and 5 is written as _____.

   (A) $x + 5$ (B) $x - 5$ (C) $5x$ (D) $x \div 5$

2   Write the expression. One-third of the sum x and 6

   (A) $\frac{1}{3}(x + 6)$ (B) $\frac{1}{3}(x - 6)$ (C) $\frac{1}{3}+(x + 6)$ (D) $\frac{1}{3}(x \div 6)$

3   Complete the table, by filling in the blank cells.

Expressions	Terms	Co-efficient	Constants
$6x^2 + 8$			

(A)

Expressions	Terms	Co-efficient	Constants
$6x^2 + 8$	$6, x^2, 8$	6	8

(B)

Expressions	Terms	Co-efficient	Constants
$6x^2 + 8$	$6x^2, 8$	6	8

(C)

Expressions	Terms	Co-efficient	Constants
$6x^2 + 8$	$6, x^2, 8$	1	6

(D)

Expressions	Terms	Co-efficient	Constants
$6x^2 + 8$	$6x^2, 8$	1	-6

Variable Expressions   **5.1**

4 Write the expression. The quotient of $x + 8$ and 9.

(A) $\frac{1}{9}(x+8)$ (B) $\frac{(x-8)}{9}$ (C) $\frac{1}{9}+(x+8)$ (D) $\frac{(x+8)}{9}$

5 Write the expression. Four decreased by half of x _____.

(A) $\frac{1}{4}(x+2)$ (B) $4+\frac{1}{2}x$ (C) $4-\frac{1}{2}x$ (D) $4(\frac{x}{2})$

6 Evaluate the expression. $2x^2 - 4x + 8$, when $x = 3$

(A) 20   (B) 25   (C) 18   (D) 14

7 Evaluate the expression. $t^2 - 7u + 5ut$, when $t = 60$ and $u = 40$.

(A) 15320   (B) 15520   (C) 15820   (D) 15380

8 Lisa has h books. She gave 8 books to Steward. Choose the expression that shows how many books Lisa now has.

(A) h+8   (B) h−8   (C) 8h   (D) h÷8

EXPRESSIONS, EQUATIONS, AND INEQUALITIES

5.1 Variable Expressions

9 Robert sold 11 more balloons in the first week than in the second week. He sold three times as many balloons in the third week. as in the second week. Write an expression for the total number of balloons sold by Robert in three weeks.

(A) $(x + 11) + x + 3x$ balloons (B) $(x + 11) + x - 3x$ balloons

(C) $(x + 11) + x + x$ balloons (D) $(x - 11) + x + 3x$ balloons

10 Evaluate the expression. $x^3y - y^3x$, when $x = 5, y = 4.$

(A) 80 (B) 120 (C) 100 (D) 180

11 John works as a driver and is paid $8.50 per hour. Create an expression to represent the amount of money John earned while working h hours.

(A) h + 8.50 (B) h - 8.50 (C) 8 . 50h (D) h ÷ 8.50

12 You and eight friends plan a party. Each of your friends contributes the same amount of money, y , for food and decorations. You contribute $5 more than your friends share. Evaluate the expression in dollars if each of your friends contributed $20.

(A) $185 (B) $195 (C) $175 (D) $205

13 Harriett bought a box with 12 strawberries for $k . Write an expression to determine the cost of each strawberry in the box.

(A) $(k+12)   (B) $(k−12)   (C) $(12k)   (D) $($\frac{k}{12}$)

14 A rectangle has side lengths of 6 cm and d − 4 cm. Write an expression that represents the perimeter of the rectangle, if d = 12 cm.

(A) 28 cm   (B) 38 cm   (C) 48 cm   (D) 58 cm

15 Eda is on the page 83 of her book now. She reads x pages per hour. Write an expression representing the number of pages Eda will have read after y hours.

(A) 83 + xy (B) 83 − xy (C) 83 xy (D) $\frac{83}{xy}$

16 A chef pays a cook a flat fee of $45, plus $10 for every additional hour he cooks. Write an expression for the total amount the cook will be paid for working additional h hours. Evaluate this expression for 5 additional hours of cooking.

(A) $85   (B) $95   (C) $75   (D) $105

EXPRESSIONS, EQUATIONS, AND INEQUALITIES

5.1 Variable Expressions

17 The shortest side of a triangle is 8 cm shorter than the longest side. The longest side of the triangle is 5.5 cm longer than the middle side. If x cm is the length of the middle side, write the expression to represent the perimeter of the triangle.

(A) $(x+5.5)-8-x+(x+5.5)$ cm

(B) $(x+5.5)-8+x+(x+5.5)$ cm

(C) $(x+5.5)-8+x-(x+5.5)$ cm

(D) $(x-5.5)-8+x+(x-5.5)$ cm

18 At the restaurant, the cost of lunch is 60% of the cost of dinner. Let x be the cost of dinner. What is the cost of l lunch?

(A) $\$(l + 0.6x)$

(B) $\$(l \times 0.6x)$

(C) $\$(l - 0.6x)$

(D) $\$(l \div 0.6x)$

19 The sum of twice the number a and 4 is b. What is the difference between twice the number b and 6 in terms of a ?

(A) 2(2a + 4) + 6

(B) 2(2a − 4) − 6

(C) 2(2a + 4) − 6

(D) 2(2a + 8) − 6

20 State whether the statements are True or False.
An expression with two terms is called a binomial.

(A) True

(B) False

Next Chapter: Equivalent Expressions ≫

EQUIVALENT EXPRESSIONS

Equivalent expressions are expressions that are the same, even if they look different. If you plug the same variable value into equivalent expressions, they will each give you the same value when solved.

Properties of algebraic expressions:
·Commutative properties: $a + b = b + a$, $ab = ba$
·Associative properties: $(a + b) + c = a + (b + c)$, $(ab)c = a(bc)$
·Distributive property: $a (b + c) = ab + ac$, $(a + b) c = ac + bc$

Example: Prove that the algebraic expression $x (x - 2)$ is equivalent to expression $-2x + x^2$.

Solution: First, use distributive property:
$$x(x-2) = x \cdot x - x \cdot 2$$
Now, use the commutative property twice:
$$x \cdot x - x \cdot 2 = x^2 - 2x = -2x + x^2$$

5.2 **Equivalent Expressions**

1 Apply properties to get rid of brackets. $x(x - 4) + 5$.

A) $x^2 - 4x - 5$

B) $x^2 - 4x + 5$

C) $x^2 - 4x^2 + 5$

D) $x^2 - 4x + 5x$

2 Apply properties to get rid of brackets. $m(5 - m) + m^3 \times 4m$.

A) $4m^4 - m^2 + 5m + 5$

B) $4m^4 - m^2 + 5m$

C) $4m^3 - m^2 + 5m$

D) $4m^4 - m^2 + 5m^2$

3 Combine the like terms. $b^3 - 4b^3 + 7b^2 - 2 - 5b^2 + 8$.

A) $3b^3 + 2b^2 + 6$

B) $-3b^3 + 2b^2 + 6$

C) $-3b^3 + 2b^2 - 6$

D) $-3b^3 - 2b^2 + 6$

4 Combine the like terms. $-b - 5b^2 + 8b + 9b^2 - 11 + 8$.

A) $4b^2 + 7b - 3$

B) $4b^2 + 7b + 3$

C) $4b^2 - 7b - 3$

D) $-4b^2 + 7b + 3$

5 Kira and Linda are putting cookies in gift boxes. Kira is putting x cookies in each gift box and Linda is putting y cookies in each gift box. When they are finished, Kira has 82 gift boxes and 5 extra cookies, and Linda has 88 gift boxes and 7 extra cookies. Write an expression in a standard form that represents the number of cookies the girls started with.

(A) $82x + 88y + 12$ (B) $82x + 88y + 2$

(C) $82x + 88y - 12$ (D) $82x - 88y + 12$

6 A rectangle has a length of x cm and width of $(x - 4)$ cm. Write an expression in standard form that represents the area of the rectangle.

(A) $2x - 4$ cm^2 (B) $x^2 - 4$ cm^2 (C) $x^2 - 4x$ cm^2 (D) $x^2 + 4x$ cm^2

7 A rectangular prism is h in wide, 8 inches longer than wider and 6 inches higher than longer. Write an expressions in the standard form representing the volume of the prism. Evaluate the value of the volume when a prism is 15 wide.

(A) 10005 in^3 (B) 12345 in^3 (C) 10065 in^3 (D) 10908 in^3

8 Aaron made a + 2 three-point shots and b two-point shots. Robert made a three-point shot and b + 4 two-point shots. Write a standard form for the total number of points scored by two basketball players.

_____ .

EXPRESSIONS, EQUATIONS, AND INEQUALITIES

5.2   Equivalent Expressions

9   Bridgett sold a + 8 kg of oranges for $a per kg. Write an expression in a standard form representing the amount of money Bridgett earned.

A (a^2+10a) B (a^2-8a) C (a^2+15a) D (a^2+8a)

10   Becky is ordering pizza from "Pizza House". She ordered 4c-5 pepperoni pizza slices and 15-2c salami pizza slices. How many pizza slices did Becky order from "Pizza House"?

A 2(c+5)   B 2(c+7)   C 2(c-5)   D 2(2c+5)

11   Mike bought pencils and erasers. He bought 200 - 2(30 - 6n) pencils, where 2n is the number of erasers Mike bought. How many pencils and erasers did Mike buy altogether? _____.

12   Gabriella is planting a garden. She is going to plant 2d daisies and of d-2 roses. She will plant lilies to to match the number of daisies and roses combined. Write an expression, in standard form, representing the number of plants Gabriella is going to plant.

A 6d-4   B 6d+4   C 6d-5   D d-4

13 Peter is buying fruit for his holiday party. First, he bought $2x$ mangoes, $4y$ nectarines, and $3z$ pomegranates. Then he bought as many nectarines as he bought mangoes and pomegranates. Write an expression representing the total number of fruits Peter bought for his holiday party.

Evaluate the value of this expression if $x = 15$, $y = 20$, $z = 25$.

_____

14 Maddy is paid a flat fee of $ 60 per week and additional $ 9.50 per hour. His company deducts 25% of his pay each week for taxes. Write an expression in standard form representing the total of Maddy's earnings in 3 weeks if he works h hours per week.

_____

15 Kennedy says that the expressions $3y + 11 - 5$ and $6 + 3y$ are equivalent because they have the same value at $y = 2$. Is Kennedy correct?

  Ⓐ   Yes, Kennedy is correct.   Ⓑ   No, Kennedy is incorrect.

5.2 **Equivalent Expressions**

16 A shark can swim at speeds of up to m miles per hour. Humans can swim one-fourth as fast as sharks. Write an expression that could be used to find how much further a shark can swim in an hour than a human.

(A) $\frac{3}{4}$ m miles

(B) $\frac{3}{4}$ ma miles

(C) $\frac{4}{3}$ ma miles

(D) $\frac{3}{4}$ m²a miles

17 Jace is 4 years younger than Lincoln is. If Lincoln is x years old, write an expression representing Jace's and Lincoln's total age in a years. If Lincoln is 18 years old, what will be Jace's and Lincoln's total ages in 4 years?

(A) 20 years   (B) 40 years   (C) 30 years   (D) 50 years

18 The length of the rectangle is 10 cm greater than the width of the rectangle. Which expression cannot represent the perimeter of the rectangle?

(A) $2(2x+10)$ (B) $4x+20$ (C) $2(x+(x+10))$ (D) $2(2x+20)$

19 The length of the rectangle is 12 cm smaller than the width of the rectangle. Which expression cannot represent the perimeter of the rectangle?

(A) $4x-16$ (B) $2(2x-8)$ (C) $2(x+(x-8))$ (D) $2(2x-4)$

20 Jim has d dimes and n nickels. Tom has thrice the amount Jim has in total. Write an expression in a standard form representing the amount of money Jim and Tom have altogether.

(A) 40d+20n pennies   (B) 30d+20n pennies

(C) 50d+10n pennies   (D) 30d+10n pennies

Next Section: Solving Equations

SOLVING EQUATIONS

An <u>equation</u> is a mathematical sentence containing an equal's sign. This sentence tells us that two expressions mean the same thing, or represent the same value. Equations can have <u>constants</u>, which are values that are known, and variables, which are unknown values typically expressed with letters.

Example of equations:

$$x - 4 = 10$$
$$6 - 3x = 1$$
$$4x + 3 = 2 - 5x$$

Equations are used to solve real-life word problems.

Example: Seven times a number is equal to 210

Solution: Let x be unknown number. Three times a number is $7x$. Since three times a number is equal to 210, then

$$7x = 210$$
$$x = \frac{210}{7} = 30.$$
$$x = 30$$

1   Solve the equation. $15x - 5 = 10$.

$\quad$ (A) $x = 1$ $\qquad$ (B) $x = 2$ $\qquad$ (C) $x = 3$ $\qquad$ (D) $x = 4$

2   Solve the equation. $x - 2 = 4$.

$\quad$ (A) $x = 6$ $\qquad$ (B) $x = 2$ $\qquad$ (C) $x = 3$ $\qquad$ (D) $x = 4$

3   Solve the equation. $\dfrac{1}{3} - x = 9x$.

$\quad$ (A) $x = \dfrac{1}{30}$ $\qquad$ (B) $x = \dfrac{2}{30}$ $\qquad$ (C) $x = 10$ $\qquad$ (D) $x = \dfrac{4}{30}$

4   Solve the equation using distributive property.
$4(x + 2) - 3(x + 3) = 12$.

$\quad$ (A) $x = 16$ $\qquad$ (B) $x = 12$ $\qquad$ (C) $x = 13$ $\qquad$ (D) $x = 14$

5   Solve the equation using distributive property.
$6(x + 5) - 4(x + 5) = 20$.

$\quad$ (A) $x = 6$ $\qquad$ (B) $x = 5$ $\qquad$ (C) $x = 3$ $\qquad$ (D) $x = 4$

6   Solve the equation using distributive property.
$9(1 - 3x) + 7(2 + 5x) = 3(x + 8) + 30$.

$\quad$ (A) $x = 2.55$ $\qquad$ (B) $x = -2.55$ $\qquad$ (C) $x = 1.55$ $\qquad$ (D) $x = 6.2$

5.3   **Solving Equations**

7 Solve the equation using distributive property.
$5(3 + x) - 8(2x + 6) = 5(x + 5) - 10.$

(A) $x = -6$ (B) $x = -5$ (C) $x = -3$ (D) $x = -4$

8 Solve the equation with fractional coefficients. $\frac{x+6}{4} - \frac{x+2}{3} = \frac{1}{12}$

(A) $x = 10$ (B) $x = 9$ (C) $x = 8$ (D) $x = 7$

9 How many solutions does the equations have?
$6 - 4x + x = 2 - 2x - x - 8$

(A) No solution   (B) One Solution   (C) Infinite Solution

10 How many solutions does the equations have?
$25 + 4x - 2x = 5 + x + x + 20$

(A) No solution   (B) One Solution   (C) Infinite Solution

11 Tom and Tony like to eat cookies. This evening, Tom ate x cookies and Tony ate 9 cookies. If they ate a total of 16 cookies, write an equation to describe this situation. How many cookies did Tom eat?

(A) 17 cookies.   (B) 7 cookies.   (C) 10 cookies.   (D) 12 cookies.

Solving Equations   **5.3**

12 How many solutions do the equations have? $\dfrac{4x-2}{3} = \dfrac{5x-20}{3}$

(A) No solution (B) One Solution (C) Infinite Solution (D) None

13 Steve buys some doughnuts and pays $40.50. Each doughnut cost $4.50. Write an equation to and find the number of doughnuts bought. Find the number of doughnuts bought.

(A) 9 doughnuts.   (B) 7 doughnuts.
(C) 15 doughnuts.   (D) 12 doughnuts.

14 Lisa went shopping $200 in her pocket. She bought several cups for $5 each and a shelf for $25. After all her purchases, Lisa had $45 left. Write an equation and solve it to find the number of cups Lisa bought.

(A) 29 cups.   (B) 26 cups.   (C) 20 cups.   (D) 22 cups.

15 Lincoln had 10 apples. He gives $\frac{1}{3}$ of the apples to each of his cousins and had 4 apples left. Write an equation to find the number of Lincoln's cousins. How many cousins does Lincoln give apples to?

(A) 9 friends.   (B) 26 friends.   (C) 18 friends.   (D) 22 friends.

5.3   **Solving Equations**

16 Donna had $100 to spend at the clothing store. She bought pants, which cost three times as much as a shirt. What was the price of the shirt?

(A) $100   (B) $126   (C) $25   (D) $96

17 Olivia's parents gave her an allowance of $120. Knowing that she would go on a trip in the summer, Olivia set aside $20 each week. Olivia saved for how many weeks if she went on the trip with $380?

(A) 10 weeks   (B) 13 weeks   (C) 16 weeks   (D) 20 weeks

18 Harden is x years old. In 6 years, she will be thirty-five years old. Write an equation to represent this situation. How old is Harden now?

(A) 29   (B) 23   (C) 26   (D) 20

19 The sum of two consecutive numbers is 321. What is the smallest of these numbers?

(A) $x = 126$ (B) $x = 160$ (C) $x = 158$ (D) $x = 180$

20 Bennie had $76 to spend at the market. She bought a hot dog and some candy. The hot dog cost 3 times as much as the candy. What was the price of the hot dog?

A) $57   B) $62   C) $75   D) $96

Next Chapter:
Solving Inequalities

SOLVING INEQUALITIES

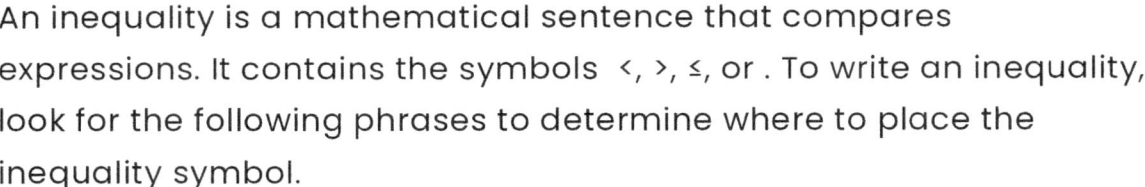

An inequality is a mathematical sentence that compares expressions. It contains the symbols <, >, ≤, or . To write an inequality, look for the following phrases to determine where to place the inequality symbol.

<u>Inequality key words:</u>
- More than, greater than means >;
- Less than, fewer than means < ;
- No more than, at most means ;
- No less than, at least means ≥.

Example: Number a is greater than a number b but no more than number c. Write an inequality representing number a.

Solution: Number a is greater than number b means a > b.
Number a is no more than number c means a ≤ c.
This can be written as double inequality b < a ≤ c.

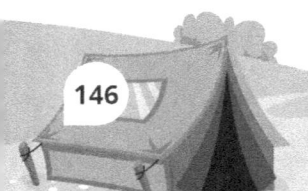

1 Write the following as an algebraic inequality:

x is at most 12

(A) $x < 12$ (B) $x \geq 12$ (C) $x \leq 12$ (D) $x = 12$

2 Write the following as an algebraic inequality:

a is less than 15.5

(A) $a > 15.5$ (B) $a < 15.5$ (C) $a \leq 15.5$ (D) $a = 15.5$

3 Write the following as an algebraic inequality:

The sum of x and 5 is fewer than −4

(A) $x + 5 < -4$ (B) $x + 5 > -4$ (C) $x + 5 \leq -4$ (D) $x = -9$

4 Which of these represent the following as an algebraic inequality?

Ten times a number z is more than or equal to 1000

(A) $10z < 1000$ (B) $10z \geq 1000$ (C) $10z \leq 1000$ (D) $10z > 1000$

5 Tell whether the given value of x is a solution to the inequality.

$x - 2 > 4$, $x = 7$.

(A) Yes   (B) No

EXPRESSIONS, EQUATIONS, AND INEQUALITIES

5.4   Solving Inequalities

6   Choose an inequality for the situation below. A game is designed for ages 5 and up.

(A) $x < 5$ (B) $x \geq 5$ (C) $x \leq 5$ (D) $x > 5$

7   Write an inequality for the situation below. The sum of a $20 ticket and other expenses must be no more than $50.

(A) $20 + x \geq 50$ (B) $20 + x \leq 50$ (C) $20 + x > 50$ (D) $20 + x < 50$

8   An online bookstore offers free shipping for orders of $40 or more. If you have already spent $14 shopping online for books. Write an inequality representing the additional amount you must spend to get free shipping.

(A) $14 + x \geq 40$ (B) $14 + x \leq 40$ (C) $14 + x > 40$ (D) $14 + x < 40$

9   A taxi charges a $5.20 flat rate in addition to $0.80 per mile. James has no more than $15 to spend on a ride. Write an inequality representing the number of miles James can ride.

(A) $5.20 + 0.80x \geq 15$ (B) $5.20 + 0.80x \leq 15$
(C) $5.20 + 0.80x > 15$ (D) $5.20 + 0.80x < 15$

10 It takes a teacher more than 30 minutes, but less than 3 hours to prepare for a lesson. Choose a double inequality to determine the time spent by a teacher to prepare for 5 lessons.

(A) $150 \leq x \leq 900$ (B) $30 \leq x \leq 900$

(C) $150 \leq x \leq 180$ (D) $30 \leq x \leq 180$

11 Solve the inequality algebraically. $x - 5 > -2$.

(A) $x < 3$ (B) $x > 3$ (C) $x < 7$ (D) $x > -7$

12 Solve the inequality algebraically. $-\frac{2-x}{4} \geq 4$.

(A) $x \geq 18$ (B) $x \geq -18$ (C) $x \geq 16$ (D) $x \geq -16$

13 Solve the inequality algebraically. $2.5x - 5 \leq 7.5$.

(A) $x \leq 5$ (B) $x \leq -5$ (C) $x \leq 6$ (D) $x \leq -6$

14 Solve the inequality algebraically. $4x - 13 \leq 19$.

(A) $x \leq 13$ (B) $x \leq 19$ (C) $x \leq 8$ (D) $x \leq 4$

EXPRESSIONS, EQUATIONS, AND INEQUALITIES

5.4   Solving Inequalities

15 Write an inequality to model the situation below.

To buy a new bag, Becky has to save more than $45.

(A) $x < 45$ (B) $x \geq 45$ (C) $x \leq 45$ (D) $x > 45$

16 Peter took 2 physics exams. On the first exam, he scores an 85. He needs to have an average above 90. Write an inequality that represents the situation. What score does he need to get on his second exam?

(A) $x > 95$ (B) $x < 95$ (C) $x = 95$ (D) $x \leq 95$

17 At an exhibition, Chris can purchase any dress for $7. The most she can spend is $42. Solve the inequality to find the number of dresses Chris can buy.

(A) 5   (B) 7   (C) 6   (D) 8

18 Lily and Jasmine are planting a garden. The ratio of lilies to jasmines in the garden is 5:1. If there is no more than 360 flowers in total, find the inequality that represents the possible number of lilies.

_____

19 Linda has $6,000 it in her bank account. She must keep a balance of at least $1,000 to avoid a fee. She plans to write five of the same checks for her workers, each in the same amount. What is the greatest amount of money each of her workers could get this week?

(A) $x > 1000$ (B) $x < 1000$ (C) $x = 1000$ (D) $x \leq 1000$

20 Solve the inequality: $15 - x > 27 - 7x$.

(A) $x < 2$ (B) $x > -2$ (C) $x < 4$ (D) $x > -4$

Next Section: Chapter Review

EXPRESSIONS, EQUATIONS, AND INEQUALITIES

5.5   Chapter Review

1   The expression for the sum of x and 6 is written as _____.

Ⓐ $x + 6$ Ⓑ $x - 6$ Ⓒ $6x$ Ⓓ $x \div 6$

2   Evaluate the expression. $3x^2 - 6x + 10$, when $x = 5$.

Ⓐ 50   Ⓑ 55   Ⓒ 58   Ⓓ 54

3   Antony works as a gatekeeper and is paid $11.50 per hour. Write an expression for the amount of money Antony earned working b hours.

Ⓐ b+11.50   Ⓑ b−11.50   Ⓒ 11.50b   Ⓓ b÷11.50

4   A rectangle has side lengths of 8 cm and d − 16 cm. Write an expression representing the perimeter of the rectangle. Find the perimeter of the rectangle if d = 32 cm.

Ⓐ 28 cm   Ⓑ 38 cm   Ⓒ 48 cm   Ⓓ 58 cm

5   Mike is on the page 53 of his book. He reads x pages per hour. Write an expression representing the number of pages Mike will have read after y hours.

Ⓐ $53 + xy$ Ⓑ $53 - xy$ Ⓒ $53xy$ Ⓓ $\dfrac{53}{xy}$

6 Apply properties to get rid of brackets. $x(x - 7) + 14$.

(A) $x^2-7x-14$ (B) $x^2-7x+14$ (C) $x^2-7x-15$ (D) $x^2-7x+15$

7 A rectangle has a length of x cm and width of $(x + 5)$ cm. Write an expression in standard form that represents the area of the rectangle.

(A) $2x+5$ cm^2 (B) x^2+5 cm^2 (C) x^2-5x cm^2 (D) x^2+5x cm^2

8 Jim made a+3 three-point shots and b two-point shots. Tom made a three-point shots and b+5 two-point shots. Write an expression in standard form for the total number of points two basketball players got.

_____.

9 Lincoln bought pens and a glue stick. He bought 120 - 2(40 - 4n) pencils, where 4n is the number of glue sticks Lincoln bought. How many pens and glue sticks did Lincoln buy altogether

_____.

5.5   Chapter Review

10   Allen is paid a flat fee $80 per week and additional $11.50 per hour. His company deducts 35% from his pay each week for taxes. Write an expression in a standard form representing the total of Allen's earnings in 4 weeks if he works h hours per week.

_____.

11   Solve the equation. $40x + 5 = 85$.

(A) $x = 1$ (B) $x = 2$ (C) $x = 3$ (D) $x = 4$

12   Solve the equation using the distributive property.
$5(1 + 2x) + 6(1 + 4x) = 4(x + 6) + 20$.

(A) $x = 1.1$ (B) $x = -1.1$ (C) $x = 2.15$ (D) $x = -2.15$

13   How many solutions do the equations have?
$5 - 11x + x = 2 - 4x - x - 7$.

(A) No solution   (B) One Solution   (C) Infinite Solution

14 Jenny's parents gave her an allowance $80. Knowing that she would go on a trip in the summer, Jenny set aside $15 each week. How long did Jenny save money if she went camping with $305?

(A) 10 weeks (B) 13 weeks (C) 15 weeks (D) 20 weeks

15 Each wrap costs $6, and Jack buys some number of wraps and pays $66. Write an equation to find the number of wraps Jack bought. What is the number of wraps bought?

(A) 9 wraps. (B) 7 wraps. (C) 15 wraps. (D) 11 wraps

16 The sum of two consecutive numbers is 521. What is the smallest of these numbers?

(A) $x = 226$ (B) $x = 260$ (C) $x = 258$ (D) $x = 280$

17 Represent the following as an algebraic inequality.
x is at most 25

(A) $x < 25$ (B) $x \geq 25$ (C) $x \leq 25$ (D) $x = 25$

18 Choose an inequality for the situation.
A book is available for ages 9 and up

(A) $x < 9$ (B) $x \geq 9$ (C) $x \leq 9$ (D) $x > 9$

5.5   **Chapter Review**

19   Write an inequality for the situation.

The sum of the $30-ticket and the other expenses must be no more than $60.

(A) $30 + x \geq 60$ (B) $30 + x \leq 60$ (C) $30 + x > 60$ (D) $30 + x < 60$

20   Solve the inequality algebraically. $6x - 12 \leq 18$.

(A) $x \leq 12$ (B) $x \leq 18$ (C) $x \leq 6$ (D) $x \leq 5$

Next Chapter:
Area, Volume and Nets

CHAPTER 6

AREA, VOLUME, AND NETS

SHADOW MATCHING GAME

AREA OF TRIANGLES

The area of a triangle is the measure of the region enclosed by the three sides of the triangle. The formula for the area of a triangle can be expressed in terms of the base and height of the triangle

Consider right triangle $\triangle ABC$. Copy this triangle and rotate it by 180°. This triangle together with the initial triangle forms a rectangle with area $a \times b$, so the area of each triangle is

$$A = \frac{1}{2} \times a \times b$$

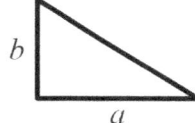 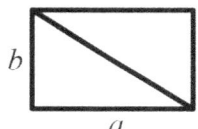

Consider right triangle $\triangle ABC$ with base $AC = a$ and height $BD = h$. This height $A = \frac{1}{2} \times a \times b$ divides the triangle into two right triangles $\triangle ABD$ and $\triangle CBD$. Copy these two triangles and rotate them by 180deg. All triangles together form a rectangle with area $a.h$, so the area of an initial triangle is

$$A = \frac{1}{2} \times a \times h$$

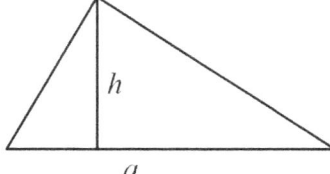 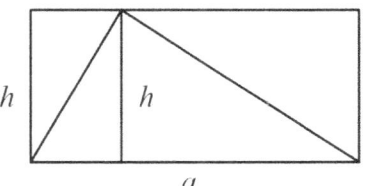

AREA, VOLUME, AND NETS

6.1   Area of Triangles

1 If the base of a triangle 15 cm and the height is 12 cm. Find the area of the triangle.

- A) 90 cm²
- B) 75 cm²
- C) 100 cm²
- D) 95 cm²

2 If the height of a triangle 16 cm and the area of the triangle is 40 cm2, find the base of the triangle.

- A) 5 cm
- B) 10 cm
- C) 15 cm
- D) 20 cm

3 Find the area of the triangle.

- A) 100 m²
- B) 90 m²
- C) 95 m²
- D) 200 m²

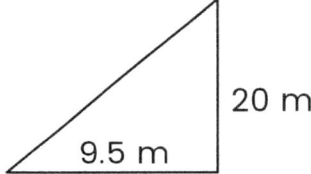

20 m

9.5 m

4 Find the area of the triangle.

- A) 151.2 cm²
- B) 154.6 cm²
- C) 162. 6 cm²
- D) 178.6 cm²

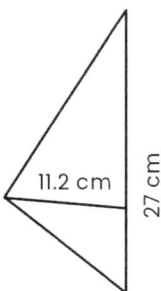

11.2 cm   27 cm

5 Find the area of the triangle.

- A) 77 mm²
- B) 56 mm²
- C) 44 mm²
- D) 28 mm²

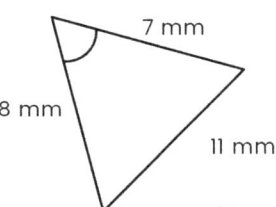

7 mm

8 mm

11 mm

Area of Triangles   6.1

6 Find the area of the triangle.

(A) 315 m²   (B) 375 m²

(C) 445 m²   (D) 495 m²

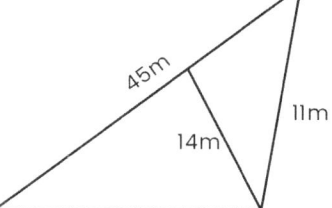

7 Find the area of the triangle.

(A) 86.5 cm²   (B) 94.5 cm²

(C) 101.5 cm²   (D) 126.5 cm²

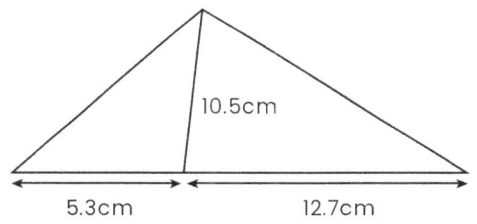

8 Olivia cut a cloth into a triangular shape. If the cloth has a base of 4.8 m and a height of 2.2 m, What is the area of the cloth?

(A) 5.8 m²   (B) 5.12 m²   (C) 5.28 m²   (D) 5.36 m²

9 Dana has a triangular shaped piece of cardboard with a height of 22 cm and a base of 24 cm. She plans to cover the front with a piece of colored paper. How much-colored paper does Dana need?

(A) 286 cm²   (B) 294 cm²   (C) 201 cm²   (D) 264 cm²

6.1   **Area of Triangles**

10 Mary needs to order triangle-shaped tiles for the floor that has a base of 26 feet and a height of 28 feet. What is the area of the tiles she needs?

(A) 364 ft²   (B) 296 ft²   (C) 438 ft²   (D) 198 ft²

11 The base and the height of the triangle are in the ratio 2:3. If the area of the triangle is 75 m², what is the length of the base of the triangle?

(A) 8 cm   (B) 10 cm   (C) 12 cm   (D) 14 cm

12 The height of the triangle is 90 % of the base. If the base of the triangle is 15 cm, what is the area of the triangle?

_____

13 The height of the triangle is 17 cm. The base of the triangle is y longer. If the area of the triangle is 153 cm², what is the base of the triangle?

_____

Area of Triangles   **6.1**

14 An equilateral triangle has a perimeter of 96 mm. The height of the triangle measures 21 mm. What is the area of the triangle?

    (A) 312 mm²   (B) 336 mm²

    (C) 358 mm²   (D) 374 mm²

15 Jack wants to paint a triangle-shaped wall. The base of the wall is 428 cm long. It has an area of 84,744 cm².
What is the height of the wall?

    (A) 864 cm   (B) 532 cm   (C) 784 cm   (D) 396 cm

16 In the equilateral triangle XYZ, point W divides the side XZ in the ratio 2:5. If the area of XYZ is 24 cm², what is the area of XYW?

    (A) 1 cm²   (B) 3 cm²

    (C) 6 cm²   (D) 9 cm²

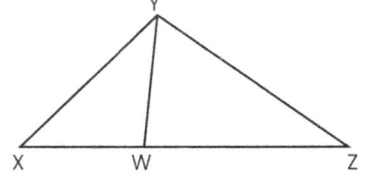

17 Larry cut a square sheet of cardboard with a side length of 14 cm diagonally into two equal parts. What is the area of each of these parts?

6.1   Area of Triangles

18 If the base is 30 cm and the area of the triangle is 330 cm², find the height of the triangle.

(A) 22 cm   (B) 28 cm   (C) 34 cm   (D) 36 cm

19 A cake is shaped like a triangle. The base of the cake is 50 cm, and the height is 40 cm. What is the area of the cake?

(A) 700 cm²   (B) 800 cm²   (C) 900 cm²   (D) 1000 cm²

20 What is the area of the shaded triangle?

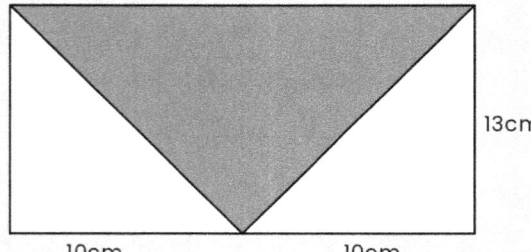

13cm

10cm   10cm

_____

Next Section: Area of Quadrilaterals and Polygons

AREA OF QUADRILATERALS AND POLYGONS

The area of a quadrilateral and polygon is the measure of the region enclosed by its four sides.

To find the area of the parallelogram, we can cut it across one of its diagonals into two triangles and find the area of each triangle.

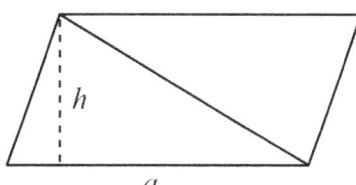 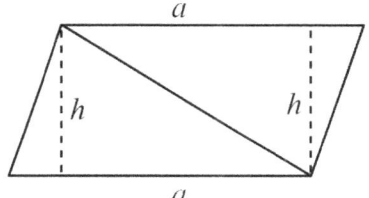

The area of the parallelogram is the sum of the areas of two congruent triangles.

$$A = \frac{1}{2} \times a \times h + \frac{1}{2} \times a \times h = a \times h$$

To find the area of the trapezoid, we can cut it across one of its diagonals into two triangles and find the area of each triangle.

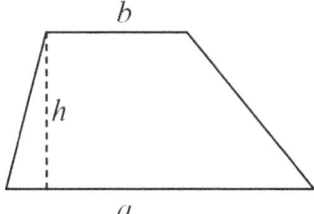 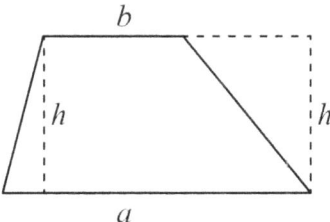

The area of the parallelogram is the sum of the areas of two formed triangles.

$$A = \frac{1}{2} \times a \times h + \frac{1}{2} \times b \times h = \frac{a+b}{2} \times h$$

AREA OF QUADRILATERALS AND POLYGONS

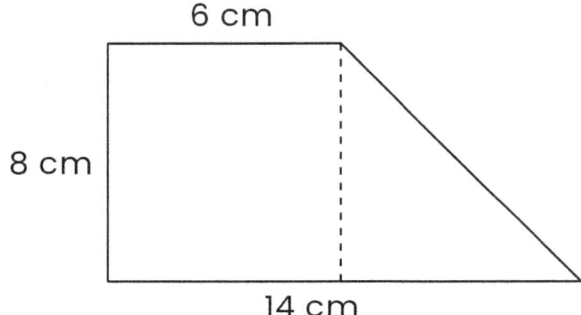

Solution: The area of this quadrilateral consists of the area of the rectangle 6 cm by 8 cm and the area of the right triangle with legs 8 cm and 14 - 6 = 8 cm. Hence,

$$A_{quadrilateral} = 8 \times 6 + 12 \times 8 \times 8 = 48 + 32 = 80 \text{ cm}^2$$

Area of Quadrilaterals and Polygons   6.2

1 Find the area of each shape by decomposing it into rectangles or triangles.

(A) 38 square units   (B) 46 square units

(C) 54 square units   (D) 58 square units

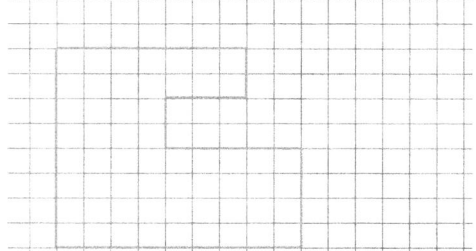

2 Find the area of each shape by decomposing it into rectangles or triangles.

(A) 78 square units   (B) 84 square units

(C) 98 square units   (D) 102 square units

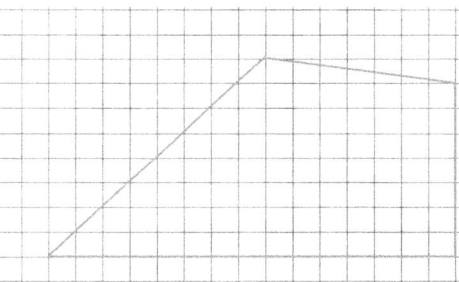

3 The area of a parallelogram with a height of 8 meters is 96 square meters. What is the base length of the parallelogram?

(A) 2 m   (B) 6 m   (C) 12 m   (D) 28 m

4 Find the area of each shape by decomposing it into rectangles or triangles.

(A) 110 square units   (B) 120 square units

(C) 130 square units   (D) 140 square units

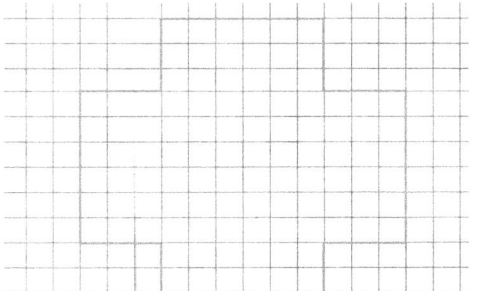

6.2 **Area of Quadrilaterals and Polygons**

5 The area of a quadrilateral with a width of 12 meters is 204 square meters. What is the length of the quadrilateral?

(A) 17 m   (B) 19 m   (C) 21 m   (D) 23 m

6 Find the area of the quadrilateral.

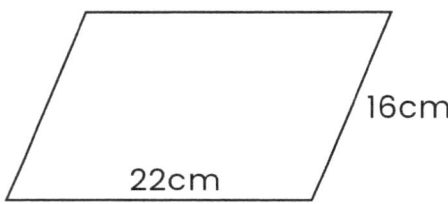

16cm

22cm

(A) 109 cm²   (B) 169 cm²

(C) 268 cm²   (D) 352 cm²

7 The length and the width of the quadrilateral are 19.5 cm and 11.5 cm. Find the area of the quadrilateral?

(A) 176.10 cm2   (B) 224.25 cm2   (C) 272.25 cm2   (D) 195.25 cm2

8 Find the area of the quadrilateral.

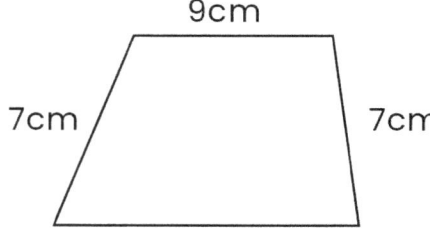

9cm

7cm   7cm

15cm

(A) 67 cm²   (B) 72 cm²

(C) 84 cm²   (D) 91 cm²

Area of Quadrilaterals and Polygons   6.2

9 The area of a rhombus with is 44 square centimeters with a height of 4 cm. What is the length of the side of the rhombus?

(A) 9 cm   (B) 11 cm   (C) 16 cm   (D) 22 cm

10 The area of a rhombus is 100 square centimeters with a length of 10 cm. What is the height of the rhombus?

(A) 40 cm   (B) 30 cm   (C) 20 cm   (D) 10 cm

11 Find the area of a rhombus whose height is 12 m and length is 15 m.

(A) 170 m²   (B) 180 m²   (C) 190 m²   (D) 200 m²

12 What is the area of the figure?

(A) 132 square units   (B) 147 square units

(C) 174 square units   (D) 198 square units

6.2 Area of Quadrilaterals and Polygons

13 What is the area of the square?

5cm

5cm [square] 5cm

5cm

_____

14 Find the numerical area of the rectangle shown in the diagram below.

$3x - 6$

$3x - 3$

$14 - x$

(A) 108 units²   (B) 114 units²

(C) 126 units²   (D) 138 units²

15 What is the area of the figure?

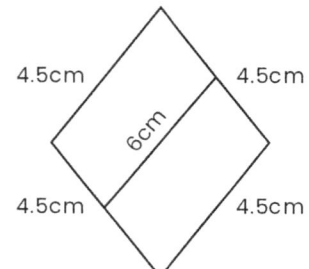

4.5cm   4.5cm

6cm

4.5cm   4.5cm

16 Find the area of the trapezoid?

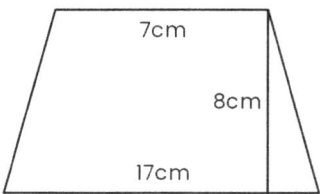

7cm

8cm

17cm

_____   _____

17 The area of a parallelogram is 189 square meters with a base of 9 meters. What is the height of the parallelogram?

(A) 19 m   (B) 21 m   (C) 23 m   (D) 27 m

18 Find the area of a parallelogram whose height is 20.5 m and the base is 22.5 m.

(A) 344.5 m²   (B) 222.4 m²   (C) 461.25 m²   (D) 765.2 m²

19 Find the area of rectangle.

7cm

11cm

_____

20 Find the area of the square whose side is 11 mm.

_____

Next Chapter: The Volume of Rectangular Prisms

THE VOLUME OF RECTANGULAR PRISMS

A rectangular prism is a three-dimensional shape with six faces, all of which are rectangles. The volume of a rectangular prism is the amount of space it occupies in three-dimensional space.
The formula for calculating the volume of a rectangular prism is:

Volume = length * width * height

When finding the volume of a rectangular prism with fractional edge lengths, you have to find the number of cubes with fractional edge lengths that can fill the prism.

Example: Find how many $\frac{1}{4}$ cm cubes fit into rectangular prism shown below. What is the volume of the prism?

Solution:

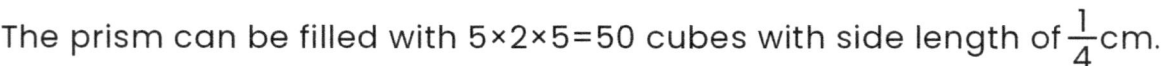

Width $1\frac{1}{4} = \frac{5}{4} = 5 \times \frac{1}{4}$ cm

Length $\frac{1}{2} = \frac{2}{4} = 2 \times \frac{1}{4}$ cm

Height $1\frac{1}{4} = \frac{5}{4} = 5 \times \frac{1}{4}$ cm

The prism can be filled with 5×2×5=50 cubes with side length of $\frac{1}{4}$ cm.

One 14cm cube has the volume of $\frac{1}{4} \times \frac{1}{4} \times \frac{1}{4} = \frac{1}{64}$ cm³, so the volume of the prism is $50 \times \frac{1}{64} = \frac{25}{32}$ cm³

The Volume of Rectangular Prisms **6.3**

1 Fill in the blanks in the table.

Length of the prism	Width of the prism	Height of the prism	Cube side	Number of cubes	Volume of the prism (cm²)
2cm	3cm	$\frac{1}{2}$ cm	$\frac{1}{2}$ cm		

2 Fill in the blanks in the table.

Length of the prism	Width of the prism	Height of the prism	Cube side	Number of cubes	Volume of the prism (cm²)
4cm	8cm	2cm	2cm		

3 Fill in the blanks in the table.

Length of the prism	Width of the prism	Height of the prism	Cube side	Number of cubes	Volume of the prism (cm²)
1.6m		6m	0.6m	80	

4 Fill in the blanks in the table.

Length of the prism	Width of the prism	Height of the prism	Cube side	Number of cubes	Volume of the prism (cm²)
	10mm	25mm	4mm	125mm	

6.3   **The Volume of Rectangular Prisms**

5   Find the volume of the rectangular prism shown below.

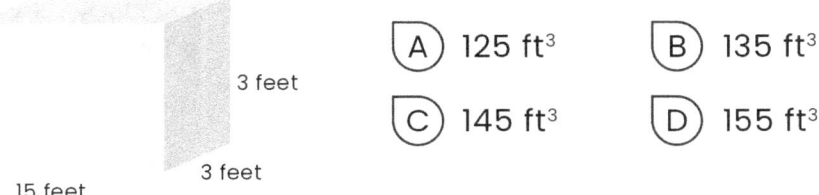

3 feet

3 feet

15 feet

(A) 125 ft³   (B) 135 ft³

(C) 145 ft³   (D) 155 ft³

6   Find the volume of the rectangular prism shown below.

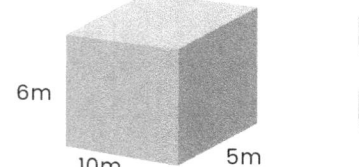

6m

10m   5m

(A) 200 m³   (B) 250 m³

(C) 300 m³   (D) 350 m³

7   Find the volume of the rectangular prism shown below.

5cm

30cm   10cm

(A) 1500 cm³   (B) 1600 cm³

(C) 1700 cm³   (D) 1800 cm³

8   Find the missing value for each rectangular prism.

Volume = 13.6 cm³
Base = 27.2 cm²
Height: _____.

(A) 3 cm²   (B) 2 cm²

(C) $\frac{2}{3}$cm²   (D) $\frac{1}{2}$cm²

9   Find the missing value for each rectangular prism.

Volume = 6 mm³

Base = 33 mm²

Height: _____

(A) $\frac{3}{11}$ mm²   (B) $\frac{2}{11}$ mm²

(C) $\frac{11}{3}$ mm²   (D) $\frac{11}{2}$ mm²

10   Find the missing value for each rectangular prism.

Volume = 40 m³

Height = 5 m²

Base: _____

(A) 10 m²   (B) 8 m²

(C) 12 m²   (D) 4 m²

11   Find the missing value for each rectangular prism.

Volume = $18\frac{2}{6}$ mm³

Height = $11\frac{2}{3}$ mm²

Base: _____

(A) $1\frac{4}{7}$ mm²   (B) $1\frac{5}{3}$ mm²

(C) $1\frac{3}{2}$ mm²   (D) $1\frac{2}{5}$ mm²

12   Find the volume of the rectangular prism shown below.

20mm

15mm

6mm

(A) 1200 mm²   (B) 1400 mm²

(C) 1600 mm²   (D) 1800 mm²

6.3 The Volume of Rectangular Prisms

13 Find and compare the volumes of the two rectangular prisms

Length	Width	Height	Volume
8m	$4\frac{1}{2}$ m	$8\frac{1}{2}$ m	
5m	4m	4m	

14 A rectangular prism can fit 448 small identical cubes. If the volume of the prism is 7 cm³, what is the side length of each cube?

A) $\frac{1}{2}$ cm   B) $\frac{1}{4}$ cm   C) $\frac{1}{6}$ cm   D) $\frac{1}{8}$ cm

15 A rectangular prism can fit 5 large identical cubes. If the volume of the prism is 135 cm³, what is the side length of each cube?

A) 1 cm   B) 7 cm   C) 3 cm   D) 9 cm

16 Fill the missing number into the table

Length of the prism	Width of the prism	Height of the prism	Cube side	Number of cubes	Volume of the prism (cm²)
	2mm	4mm	2mm	20mm	

17 Two rectangular prisms have a combined volume of 43.2 m³. The volume of the prism A is twice the volume of prism B. Determine the volume of prism B.

(A) 13.2 m³   (B) 13.4 m³   (C) 14.2 m³   (D) 14.4 m³

18 Two rectangular prisms have a combined volume of 27 cm³. The volume of the prism A is twice the volume of the prism B. Determine the volume of the prism A.

(A) 9 cm³   (B) 18 cm³   (C) 21 cm³   (D) 36 cm³

19 A rectangular prism can fit 625 small identical cubes. If the volume of the prism is 5 m³, what is the side length of each cube?

(A) $\frac{1}{3}$ m   (B) $\frac{1}{7}$ m   (C) $\frac{1}{5}$ m   (D) $\frac{1}{9}$ m

20 A rectangular prism can fit 7 large identical cubes. If the volume of the prism is 2,401 mm³, what is the side length of each cube?

(A) 3 mm   (B) 7 mm   (C) 5 mm   (D) 2 mm

Next Section:
Represent 3-D Figures

REPRESENT 3-D FIGURES

3-D figures typically refer to the ability to visualize and draw three-dimensional objects on a two-dimensional surface. A 3-D figure is an object that has length, width, and height, such as a cube, sphere, or cylinder.

To represent a 3-D figure, we can use various methods, such as drawing a net, creating a solid model using materials like clay or paper, or using computer software to create a virtual model. A net is a 2-D representation of a 3-D object that can be cut out and folded to create the actual 3-D object.

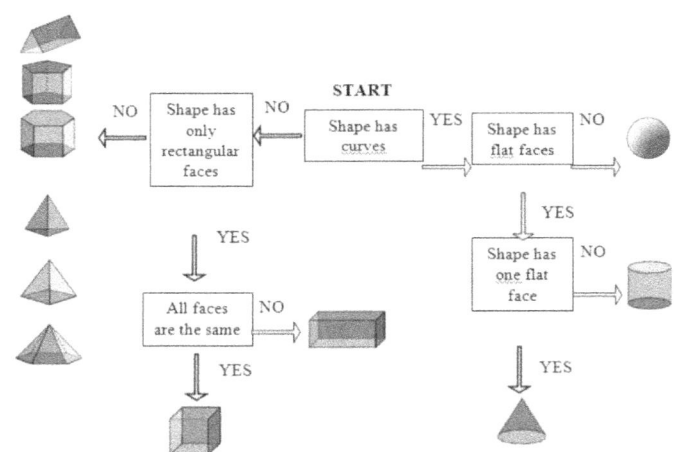

Example: Use the picture to answer the questions.

Name of the shape: _____.

Number of vertices: _____.

Number of edges: _____.

Number of faces: _____.

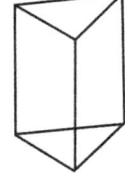

Solution:

Name of the shape: Triangular prism

Number of vertices: 6

Number of edges: 9

Number of faces: 5

1 Find the following for the triangular prism.

Number of faces _____.

Number of edges _____.

Number of vertices _____.

2 Find the following for the rectangular pyramid.

Number of faces _____.

Number of edges _____.

Number of vertices _____.

3 Which of the following net is a triangular pyramid net?

A 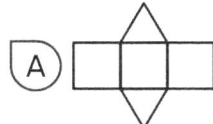   B    C 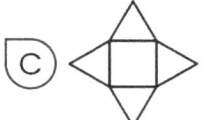   D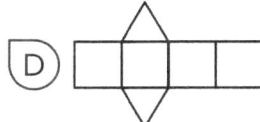

4 Which of the following net is a cuboid's net?

A 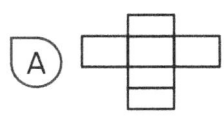   B 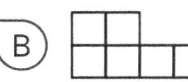   C 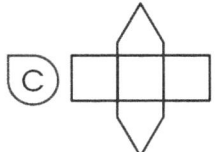   D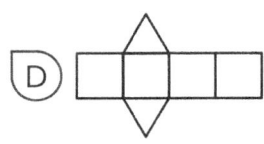

6.4   Represent 3-D Figures

5 Which of the following net is not a cylinder net?

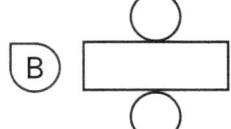

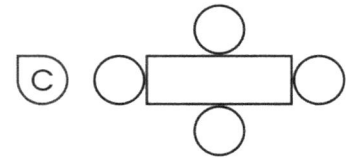

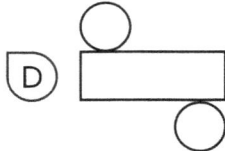

6 Mary drew a net of a 3-D shape. Which 3-D shape can she obtain from this net?

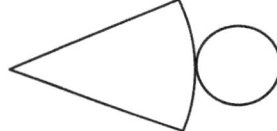

- (A) Sphere
- (B) Cone
- (C) Circle
- (D) Hemisphere

7 Lucy drew a net of a 3-D shape. Which 3-D shape can she obtain from this net?

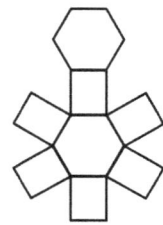

- (A) Pentagonal prism
- (B) Octagonal prism
- (C) Triangular prism
- (D) Hexagonal prism

8 Answer Yes or No. Is this a net of a rectangular pyramid?

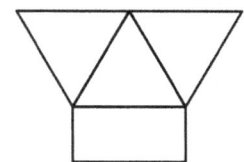

- (A) Yes
- (B) No

9   Draw the remaining parts to form a triangular pyramid's net.

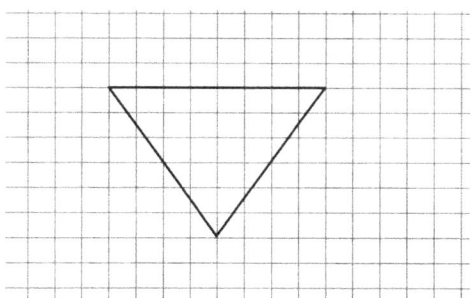

10   Diana drew a net of a 3-D shape. Which 3-D shape can she obtain from this net?

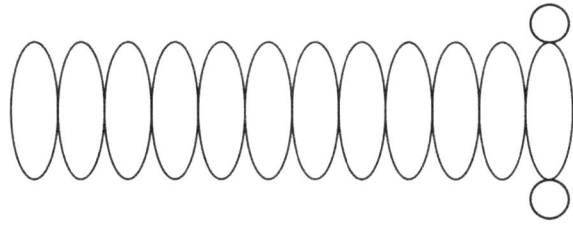

A) Sphere   B) Cone

C) Circle   D) Hemisphere

11   When the net is folded up, which sides will touch? 3 and _____.

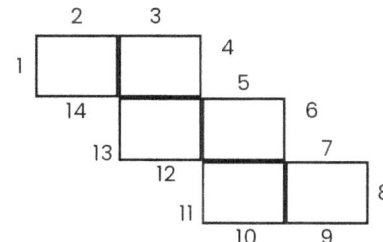

A) 7   B) 9

C) 8   D) 6

6.4   **Represent 3-D Figures**

12   When the net is folded up, which sides will touch? 12 and _____.

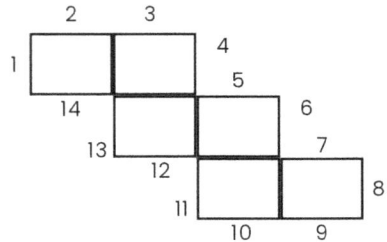

(A) 8   (B) 9

(C) 10   (D) 11

13   When the net is folded up, which sides will touch? 1 and _____.

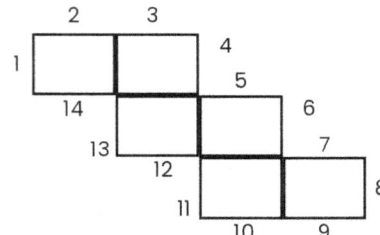

(A) 10   (B) 14

(C) 4   (D) 13

14   When the net is folded up, which sides will touch? 11 and _____.

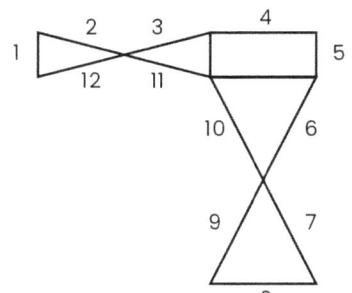

15   When the net is folded up, which sides will touch? 8 and _____.

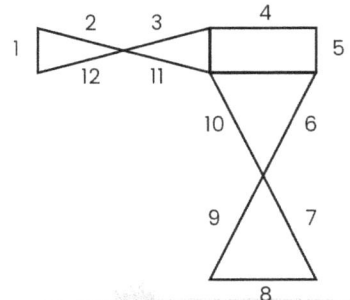

16   When the net is folded up, which sides will touch? 2 and _____.

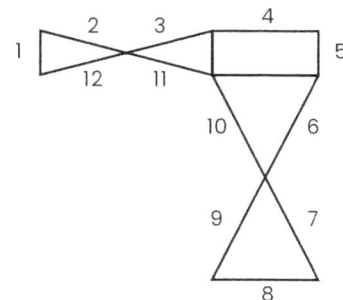

17   Draw the remaining parts to form a trapezoidal prism's net.

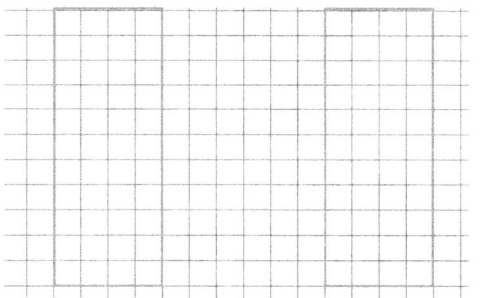

18   Find the following for the hexagonal pyramid

Number of faces _____.

Number of edges _____.

Number of vertices _____.

6.4   **Represent 3-D Figures**

19 Jerry drew a net of the square pyramid. Is he correct? If not, redraw the correct net of the square pyramid.

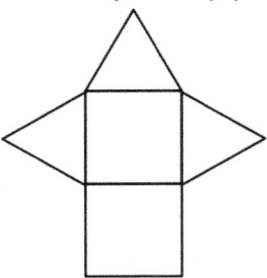

20 Answer Yes or No. Can the following net make a cube net?

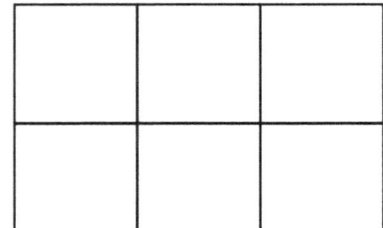

    Ⓐ Yes   Ⓑ No

Next Chapter: Surface Area ≫

SURFACE AREA

The surface area of a 3-D object is the total area of all its faces. This means that one way to find the surface area of a solid is to find the area of its net.

Example:

Find the surface area of a rectangular prism with a length of a units, width of b units and height of c units.

Solution:

The surface area of a rectangular prism is the area of the six rectangles that cover it. However, we don't have to find the area of all six faces because we know that the top and bottom faces are the same, the front and back faces are the same, and the left and right faces are the same.

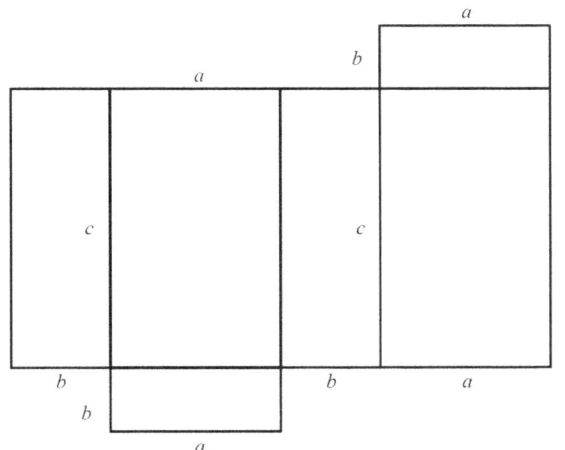

Hence, the surface area of the rectangular prism is twice the sum of the area of the front, left, and top faces.

Therefore, SA = 2(ab + ac + bc) un^2.

6.5 Surface Area

1 Which expression represents the surface area of this cube?

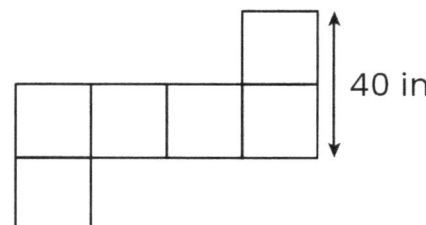

40 in

- (A) 10×4×6
- (B) 20×20×6
- (C) 40×6
- (D) 20×6

2 Graph a triangle with vertices (3, 2), (5, 5), and (8, 1).

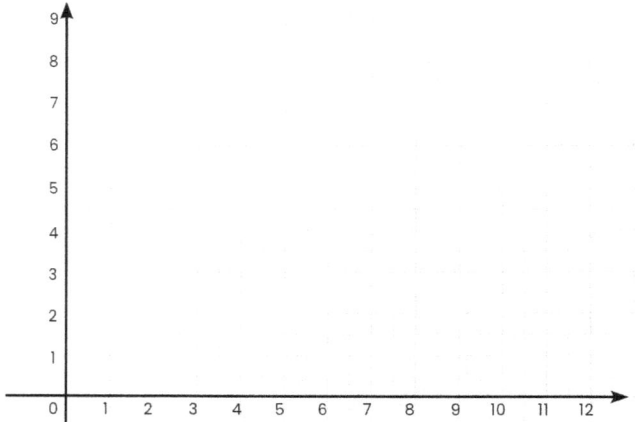

3 John states that the net below shows a three-dimensional shape with a surface area smaller than 360 square feet. Do you agree with John? Explain your reasoning.

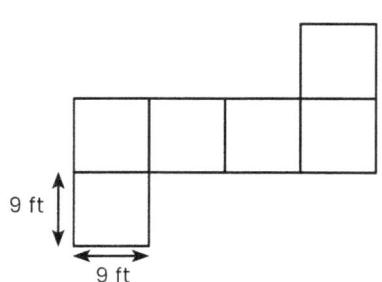

9 ft

9 ft

Surface Area   **6.5**

4   Graph a triangle with vertices (7, 3), (4,5), and (2, 1).

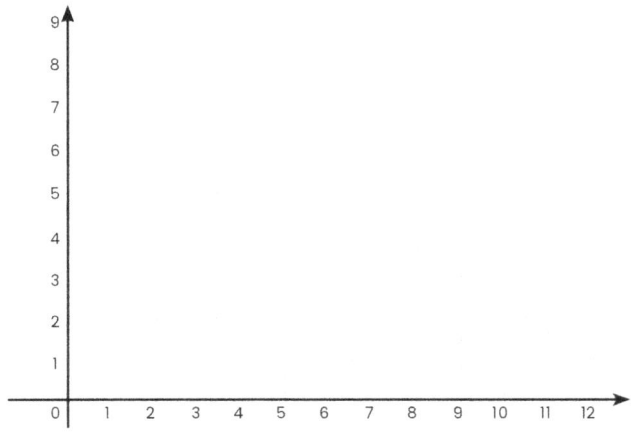

5   Mary states that the net below shows a three-dimensional shape with a surface area smaller than 360 square feet. Do you agree with Mary?

6   What is the surface area of 3-D shape represented by its net?

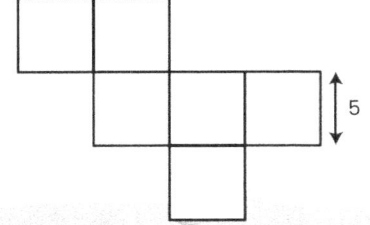

(A) 150 unit²   (B) 125 unit²

(C) 175 unit²   (D) 225 unit²

6.5   Surface Area

7   What is the surface area of 3-D shape represented by its net?

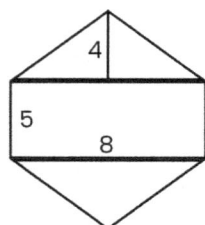

- (A) 32 unit²
- (B) 40 unit²
- (C) 48 unit²
- (D) 20 unit²

8   For each 3-D shape draw a net and find their surface area.

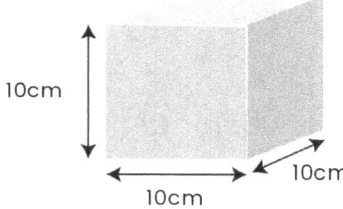

10cm

10cm   10cm

- (A) 400 unit²
- (B) 600 unit²
- (C) 200 unit²
- (D) 800 unit²

9   Draw the net and find the surface area of the 3-D shape given below.

5

15   3

- (A) 125 unit²
- (B) 175 unit²
- (C) 225 unit²
- (D) 270 unit²

10   A rectangular prism has a width of 6 units, a length of 12 units, and a height of 16 units. Can the following expression be used to calculate the total surface area of the pyramid? Yes or No?

$$2(6 \times 12 + 6 \times 16 + 12 \times 16) \text{ units}^2$$

11 A square pyramid has a base length of 2 inches. The height of each triangular face is 4 inches. Can the following expression be used to calculate the total surface area of the pyramid? Yes or No?

$$((2 \times 2) + 4(2 \times 4)) \text{ in}^2$$

_____

12 A square pyramid has a base length of 7 inches. The height of each triangular face is 11 inches. Can the following expression be used to calculate the total surface area of the pyramid? Yes or No?

$$(7 \times 7) + 2(7 \times 11) \text{ in}^2$$

_____

13 Angela bought a gift box for her friend's birthday. The box is 13 cm long, 11 cm wide, and 9 cm high. What is the surface area of the box?

Ⓐ 707 cm²   Ⓑ 718 cm²   Ⓒ 736 cm²   Ⓓ 742 cm²

14 Casey is drawing a pyramid in a piece of cardboard. The length of each edge of the base is , and the height of each triangular face is How much space will Casey need to draw the pyramid?

Ⓐ 220 cm²   Ⓑ 240 cm²   Ⓒ 280 cm²   Ⓓ 290 cm²

AREA, VOLUME, AND NETS

6.5 Surface Area

15 The base of the square pyramid has an area of 100 cm². If the surface area is 140 cm², what is the length of the slant height (height of triangular face)?

    (A) 1 cm   (B) 2 cm   (C) 4 cm   (D) 7 cm

16 The surface area of a cube is 384 cm². What is the length of the sides of the cube?

    (A) 4 cm   (B) 6 cm   (C) 8 cm   (D) 10 cm

17 The surface area of this cuboid is 400 cm². What is the value of x?

8

x

14

    (A) 16 cm   (B) 8 cm

    (C) 14 cm   (D) 4 cm

18 The material used to make a box costs $ 1.20 per square centimeter. The boxes have the same volume but a different surface area. How much does a company save by choosing to make 16 of Box 1 instead of 16 of Box 2?

	Length	Width	Weight
Box 1	15 cm	13 cm	7 cm
Box 2	19 cm	18 cm	5 cm

19 What is the surface area of the 3-D shape represented by its net.

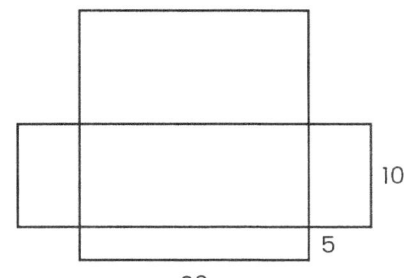

10
5
20

(A) 100 unit^2 (B) 700 unit^2
(C) 500 unit^2 (D) 200 unit^2

20 The surface area of a cube is 384 cm^2. What is the length of the sides of the cube?

(A) 4 cm (B) 6 cm (C) 8 cm (D) 10 cm

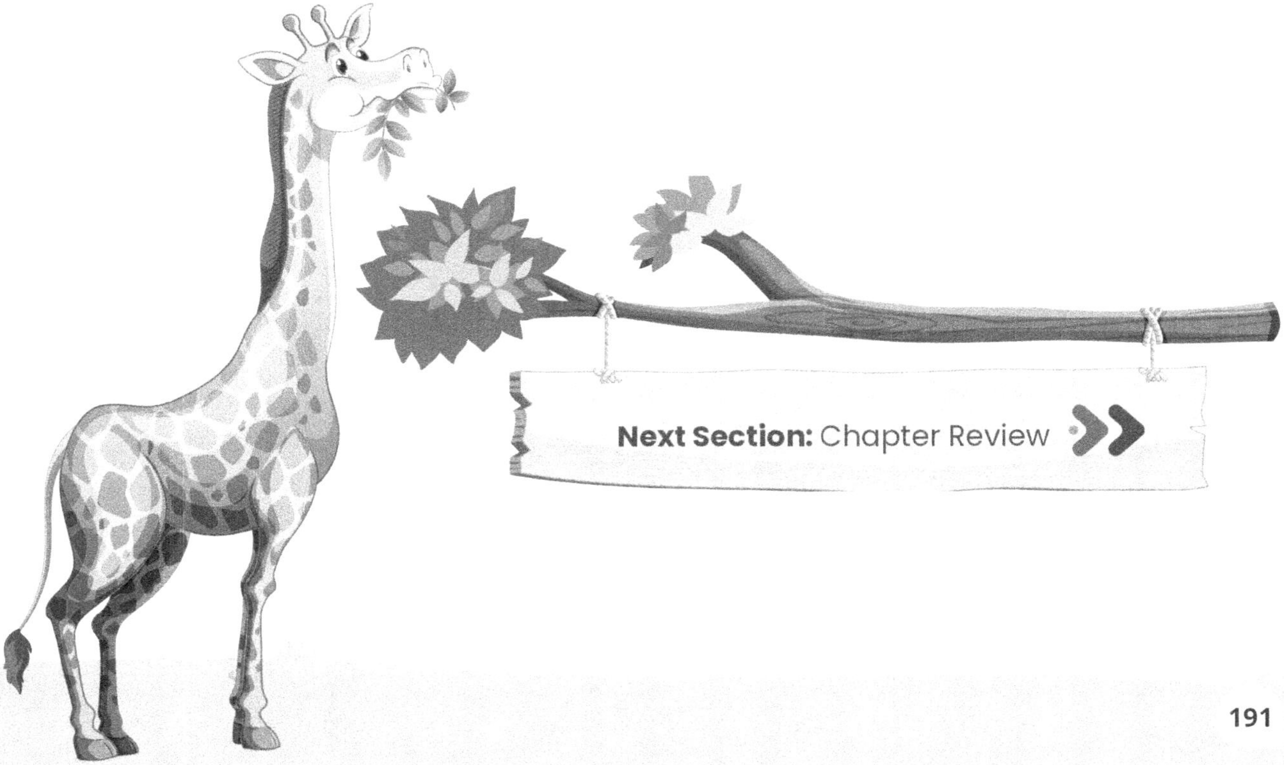

Next Section: Chapter Review

AREA, VOLUME, AND NETS

6.6   Chapter Review

1   If the base of a triangle is 25 cm and the height is 22 cm. Find the area of the triangle.

     (A) 225 cm²   (B) 250 cm²   (C) 275 cm²   (D) 300 cm²

2   The ratio of the base and the height of the triangle are in the ratio is 5:6. If the area of the triangle is 240 m², What is the length of the base of the triangle?

     (A) 20 cm   (B) 30 cm   (C) 40 cm   (D) 50 cm

3   Find the area of the triangle

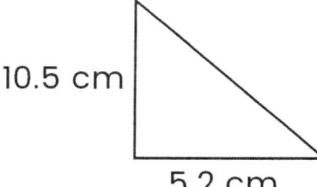

10.5 cm

5.2 cm

     (A) 25.7 cm²   (B) 27.3 cm²
     (C) 29.5 cm²   (D) 31.9 cm²

4   The area of a parallelogram with a height of 11 meters is 242 square meters. What is the base length of the parallelogram?

     (A) 18 m   (B) 19 m   (C) 21 m   (D) 22 m

5   Find the area of a rhombus whose height is 7 m and length is 14 m.

     (A) 86 m²   (B) 98 m²   (C) 106 m²   (D) 128 m²

6 What is the area of the triangle ADB?

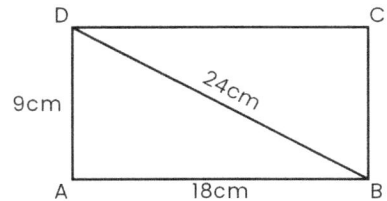

- A 62 cm²
- B 73 cm²
- C 81 cm²
- D 94 cm²

7 What is the area of the following diagram?

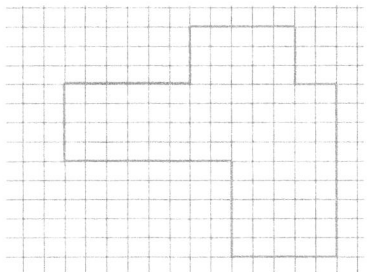

- A 92 unit²
- B 102 unit²
- C 126 unit²
- D 138 unit²

8 What is the volume of the rectangular prism?

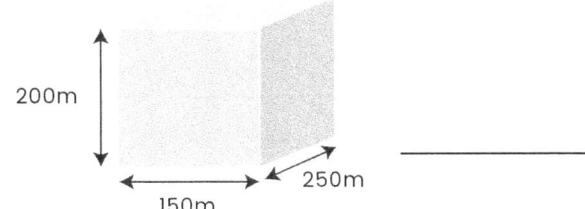

_____

9 The cardboard box in the shape of a rectangular prism, has a length of 16 cm and a width of 10 cm that can fit 4,480 half-centimeter cubes. What is the height of the box?

- A $3\frac{1}{2}$ cm
- B $4\frac{1}{7}$ cm
- C $5\frac{2}{9}$ cm
- D $6\frac{2}{7}$ cm

6.6 Chapter Review

10 A cardboard box in the shape of a rectangular prism, has a length of 13 cm, a width of 6 cm, and a height of $\frac{7}{3}$. What is the volume of the box?

(A) 62 cm²   (B) 73 cm²   (C) 81 cm²   (D) 94 cm²

11 Fill in the blanks in the table.

Length of the prism	Width of the prism	Height of the prism	Cube side	Number of cubes	Volume of the prism (cm²)
2cm		5cm	1cm	60cm	

12 Find the volume of the rectangular prism shown below

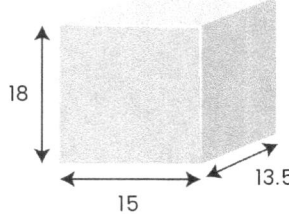

18   15   13.5

_____

13 Find the missing value for each rectangular prism.

Volume = 21 mm³

Base = 63 mm²

Height: _____.

(A) $\frac{2}{5}$ mm²   (B) $\frac{1}{3}$ mm²

(C) $\frac{3}{7}$ mm²   (D) $\frac{1}{9}$ mm²

14 A rectangular prism can fit 1,750 identical cubes. If the volume of the prism is 14 cm³, what is the side length of each cube?

(A) $\frac{1}{7}$ cm   (B) $\frac{3}{4}$ cm   (C) $\frac{5}{6}$ cm   (D) $\frac{1}{5}$ cm

15 If one face of the cube has an area of 92 cm², what is the surface area of this cube?

(A) 336 cm²   (B) 474 cm²   (C) 552 cm²   (D) 682 cm²

16 The surface area of the square pyramid is 426 in². The base has an area of 289 in². What is the length of the base?

(A) 17 in   (B) 25 in   (C) 33 in   (D) 45 in

17 Graph a triangle with vertices (9, 4), (7, 5), and (5, 0).

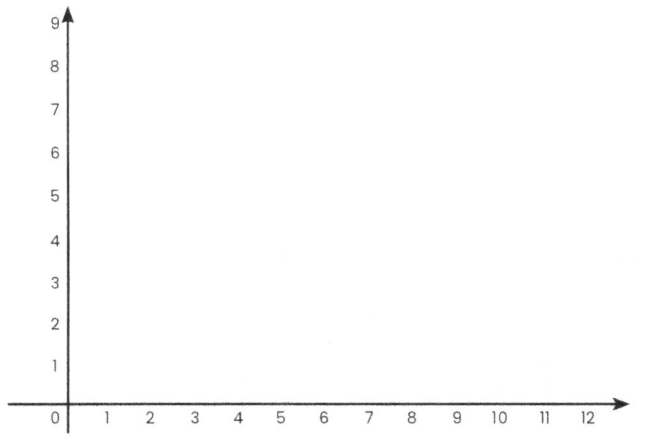

6.6 Chapter Review

18 The surface area of this cuboid is 428 cm². What is the value of z?

z

4 cm

19 cm

(A) 4 cm   (B) 6 cm

(C) 8 cm   (D) 12 cm

19 For the cube find the following

Number of faces _____.

Number of edges _____.

Number of vertices _____.

20 Sam drew a net of a 3-D shape. Which 3-D shape can he obtain from this net?

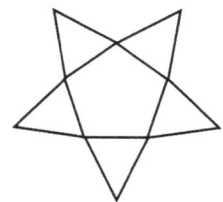

(A) Hexagonal pyramid   (B) Pentagonal prism

(C) Pentagonal pyramid   (D) Hexagonal prism

Next Chapter: Collecting and Interpreting Data

CHAPTER 7

COLLECTING AND INTERPRETING DATA

SHADOW MATCHING GAME

STATISTICAL VARIABILITY

Statistical variability refers to the degree to which data points in a set of data vary or differ from each other. This is typically measured using statistical measures such as range, mean absolute deviation, and variance.

The least data value is called minimum (Min), and the greatest data value is called maximum (Max).

The range is the difference between maximum and minimum, so

$$\text{Range} = \text{Max} - \text{Min}$$

Quartiles are values that divide the data set into four equal parts (the upper and lower quartiles are the medians of the upper half and lower half of a set of data, respectively). One-fourth of the data lie below the lower quartile Q_1 and one-fourth of the data lie above the upper quartile Q_3. So, one-half of the data lies between the lower quartile Q^1 and upper quartile Q_3. This is called the interquartile range (IQR - the range of the middle half of the data). Hence,

$$\text{IQR} = Q_3 - Q_1$$

An outlier is a data value that is either much greater or much less than the median. If a data value is more than 1.5 times the value of the IQR beyond the quartiles, it is an outlier.

The median is often denoted as Q_2 and called the second quartile.

STATISTICAL VARIABILITY

One way to think about the variability in data is to examine how far the data values are from their mean. If x is the mean of the data, the mean absolute deviation (MAD) is a measure of the variability of n values from their mean:

$$MAD = \sum x - xn$$

Example: Find the mean absolute deviation (MAD) for the data set 3,6,5,4,8,5,9,8

Solution:

First, find the mean:

$$x = \frac{3+6+5+4+8+5+9+8}{8} = \frac{48}{8} = 6$$

Now, fill in the following table:

x	$|x - \bar{x}|$
3	$|3 - 6| = 3$
6	$|6 - 6| = 0$
5	$|5 - 6| = 1$
4	$|4 - 6| = 2$
8	$|8 - 6| = 2$
5	$|5 - 6| = 1$
9	$|9 - 6| = 3$
8	$|8 - 6| = 2$

Therefore,

$$MAD = 3 + 0 + 1 + 2 + 2 + 1 + 3 + 28 = \frac{14}{8} = \frac{7}{4} = 1.75 \ .$$

1 A pizza shop sells 4 different size pizzas. The median value of the pizza is $ 3.16. What are the prices for the different size pizzas?

(A) $ 1.09+$ 1.78+$ 2.98+$ 2.34   (B) $ 2.51+$ 2.98+$ 3.57+$ 3.94

(C) $ 2.09+$ 1.18+$ 3.98+$ 2.04   (D) $ 2.12+$ 0.98+$ 1.28+$ 3.33

2 This dot plot shows the weight of watermelons.

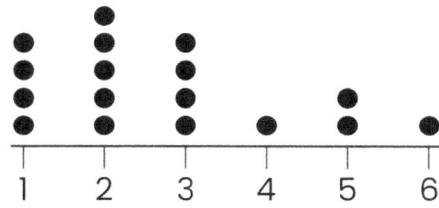

Which statement describes the shape of this graph?

(A) The data has more than one peak.   (B) The data is normally distributed.

(C) The graph is skewed left.   (D) The graph is skewed right.

3 Franklin made this bar graph to represent the number of red roses in each flower bouquet. What is the mean number of red roses ?

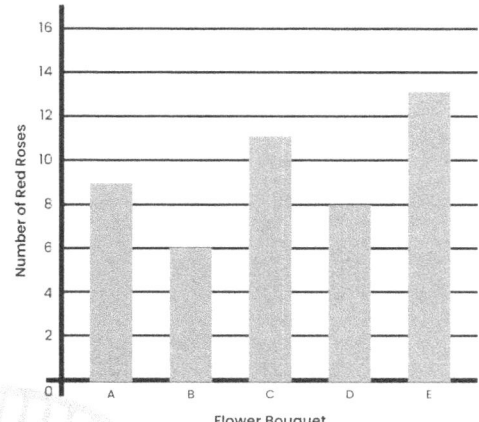

Flower Bouquet

7.1   Statistical Variability

4   Mr.Smith made this bar graph to represent the number of students from grade 1 to grade 6. What is the mean number of students?

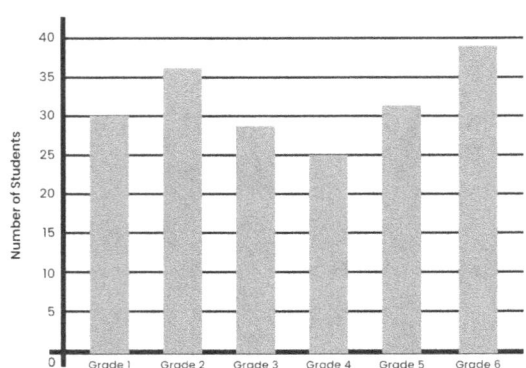

(A) 31.67   (B) 33.08

(C) 37.21   (D) 38.11

5   Find the minimum from the data list below.
25, 67, 45, 98, 24, 15, 82, 65, 36, and 45

(A) 45   (B) 24   (C) 36   (D) 67

6   Find the maximum from the data list below.
89, 101, 356, 327, 189, 120, 489, 380, and 346

(A) 999   (B) 89   (C) 489   (D) 101

7   Find the range from the given data list.
2, 13, 8, 34, 27, 89, 46, 73, 50, and 28.

Statistical Variability   7.1

8 Find the IOR from the given data list.

11, 5, 19, 14, 32, 21, 19, 6, 11, 43, and 17.

_____

9 Find the MAD from the data list.

23, 1, 16, 17, 9, 11, 21, 13, 35, 27, 12, 3, and 21.

(A) $11\frac{2}{13}$ (B) $16\frac{1}{13}$ (C) $21\frac{5}{13}$ (D) $35\frac{7}{13}$

10 Which shop sold the greatest number of cakes?

Shop	Number of cakes sold
A	18, 23, 21, 34, 5, 41, 29, 43, 44
B	20, 25, 23, 36, 7, 43, 31, 45, 46
C	9, 13, 31, 27, 42, 39, 28, 27, 11
D	11, 15, 29, 25, 39, 22, 37, 12, 8

_____

11 Which grade has the greatest IQR?

Grade	Number of students
I	21, 43, 26, 45, 23, 61, 16, 11, 23, 12
II	32, 27, 19, 5, 9, 31, 31, 45, 46, 20
III	13, 21,6, 6, 7, 43, 24, 17, 35, 41
IV	9, 4, 13, 19, 25, 21, 36, 31, 30, 29

_____

7.1 **Statistical Variability**

12 Which grade has the least MAD?

Grade	Number of students
I	12, 34, 26, 45, 32, 61, 16, 11, 23
II	27, 19, 15, 9, 31, 21, 45, 26, 20
III	21, 9, 17, 7, 32, 24, 17, 35, 14
IV	4, 13, 19, 25, 13, 43, 31, 10, 17

_____

13 Which list has the greatest range?

Grade 5 = 38, 15, 49, 51, 25, 30, 10, 72, 12, 22.

Grade 6 = 48, 24, 19, 36, 26, 26, 39, 47, 39, 57.

(A) Grade 5

(B) Grade 6

14 Which list has the least range?

Grade 1 = 62, 17, 39, 20, 50, 26, 56, 69, 42, 10, 9.

Grade 2 = 32, 18, 46, 29, 6, 29, 31, 43, 52, 17, 14.

(A) Grade 1

(B) Grade 2

15 Which list has the greatest IOR?

Cake = 54, 37, 19, 20, 44, 28, 51, 29, 22, 30.

Pizza = 42, 28, 43, 39, 16, 23, 21, 53, 13, 27.

(A) Cake

(B) Pizza

16 Which list has the least MAD?

Grade 3 = 31, 56, 12, 8, 5, 21, 12, 54, 37, 22, 23.

Grade 5 = 24, 28, 43, 32, 16, 8, 2, 12, 1, 16, 30.

(A) Grade 3   (B) Grade 5

17 What is the range of the whole aquarium?
Large fish = 54, 37, 9, 20, 44, 28, 11, 29, 22, 30.
Small fish = 38, 15, 49, 51, 25, 30, 10, 72, 12, 22.

18 What is the range of the listed data?

Fruits	Number of Fruits
Apple	885
Mango	568
Orange	989
Cherry	921
Strawberries	710

19 What is the mean of the given data

Vegitables	Number of Vegitables
Tomoto	80
Carrot	102
Onion	58
Potato	72

7.1 Statistical Variability

20 What is the MAD of the list?

Grade	Number of Students
Grade 4	45
Grade 5	37
Grade 6	51
Grade 7	34
Grade 8	48

A) 34   B) 43

C) 42   D) 58

Next Section:
Mean and Median

MEAN AND MEDIAN

Median

The median is the value in the middle of an ordered list of data. This value means that 50% of the data is greater than or equal to it and that 50% of the data is less than or equal to it. When there is an even number of data values, the median is the arithmetic average of the two values in the middle.

Mean

The mean is the arithmetic average: the sum of the values in a data set divided by the number of data values in the set. The mean measures center on the sense that it is the hypothetical value that each data point would equal if the total of the data values were redistributed equally.

Mode

The mode is the most commonly observed value in a set of data. If no number in the list is repeated, then there is no mode for the list.

Example: Find the mean, median, and mode for the following list of values: 13, 17, 13, 15, 12, 17, 13, 22, 13

Solution:

First, rewrite the list in numerical order: 12, 13, 13, 13, 13, 15, 17, 17, 22.

MEAN AND MEDIAN

The mean is the usual average, so add all numbers and divide the sum by the number of numbers:

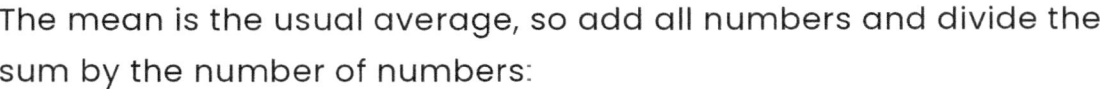

$$\text{Mean} = \frac{12+13+13+13+13+15+17+17+22}{9} = \frac{135}{9} = 15$$

The median is the middle value. There are nine numbers in the list, so four numbers stay to the left from the median, four numbers stay to the right from the median and the median is in the middle:

12, 13, 13, 13, 13, 15, 17, 17, 22

Therefore, The median = 13

The mode is the number that is repeated more often than any other, so mode = 13

1 What is the mean of this data set?
7, 11, 8, 15, 5, 18, 6, 2.

(A) 13   (B) 9   (C) 14   (D) 3

2 What is the median of this data set?
7, 4, 4, 6, 1, 7, 1, 8, 2.

(A) 1   (B) 7   (C) 2   (D) 4

3 The median of this data set of 15. What is the value of the missing number?
21, 15, 4, 23, 11, 17, 27, 8.

(A) 11   (B) 17   (C) 15   (D) 21

4 Zara bought chocolates for her children. The list shows the number of chocolates each child ate:
1, 1, 4, 4, 6, 8, 3, 5, 7, 1.
What is the mean number of chocolate eaten?

(A) 4   (B) 1   (C) 3   (D) 5

7.2   Mean and Median

5   Emma made carrot juice for her family. The list shows the number of carrots she used for each cup of carrot juice.

16, 8, 15, 7, 19, 3, 1, 12, 6, 17, 4.

What was the median number of carrots used?

(A) 7   (B) 8   (C) 12   (D) 15

6   What is the mode of this data set?

11, 6, 4, 10, 4, 1, 7, 4, 2, 9.

(A) 2   (B) 6   (C) 1   (D) 4

7   In the list of numbers 12, 14, 12, 11, 15, 17, 12, if the number 12 is removed. Which of the following measures does not change?

(A) Mean   (B) Median   (C) Mode   (D) None of them

8   In the list of numbers 11, 16, 13, 8, 10, 16, 17 if the numbers 16 and 10 are replaced by numbers 17 and 8. Which of the following measures changes?

(A) Mean   (B) Median

(C) Mode   (D) None of them

9 Janie got the following scores on her math tests: 85, 91, 72, and 86. She wants an 82 or better overall average. What is the minimum score she must get on the last test in order to achieve her goal?

(A) 76   (B) 82   (C) 84   (D) 91

10 If the number 19 added to the list of numbers 18, 11, 20, 30, 19. Which of the following must be true about the median of the list?

(A) It will increase from 19 to 21   (B) It will not change

(C) It will decrease from 19 to 18   (D) It will increase from 19 to 20

11 The table below shows the distribution of marks obtained on an English test in a grade 6. What is the median score?

Marks	Number of Students
35	3
27	2
58	1
65	6
32	4
76	7
85	2
50	6
63	3
78	1
71	7

7.2   Mean and Median

12 By comparing means, which fruit sold the least in the following four months?

Fruits	January	February	March	April
Orange	$62	$72	$54	$79
Mango	$56	$62	$63	$81
Apple	$81	$78	$70	$62
Blueberry	$87	$58	$62	$80

(A) Orange   (B) Mango   (C) Apple   (D) Blueberry

13 Rank the fruits in order of most sold to least sold by comparing their means.

Fruits	January	February	March	April
Orange	$55	$67	$51	$83
Mango	$63	$52	$69	$78
Apple	$71	$60	$75	$68
Blueberry	$85	$66	$74	$88

(A) Orange, Mango, Apple, Blueberry   (B) Blueberry, Apple, Mango, Orange

(C) Mango, Blueberry, Orange, Apple   (D) Orange, Apple, Mango, Blueberry

14 John has six colored balls. The number of balls in each color is given below. What is the median?

Ball	Red	Blue	White	Black	Green	Violet
	65	57	60	57	28	38

15 During class, a survey was taken asking how many pencils each student had. The results were: 2, 3, 1, 2, 1, 0, 4, 3, 3, 2, 1, 1, 2, 4, 2, 3, 0. Which of the measurements (mean, median, and mode) is the greatest?

(A) Mean   (B) Median   (C) Mode   (D) None of them

16 Eleven people were asked how many hours they traveled each week for work. The responses were 12, 6, 10, 9, 8, 10, 5, 15, 11, 10, 7
Which of the measurements (mean, median, and mode) is the smallest?

(A) Mean   (B) Median   (C) Mode   (D) None of them

17 The table below shows the distribution of marks obtained on a science test in a grade 5. What is the difference between the median and the mean ?

Marks	Number of Students
35	3
27	2
58	1
65	6
32	4
76	7
85	2
50	6
63	3
78	1
71	7

_____

7.2   **Mean and Median**

18 A list contains three numbers, the greatest number is 14 more than the smallest number. The mean and the median of this list of numbers is 16. What is the value of x?

(A) $x = 6$ (B) $x = 7$ (C) $x = 9$ (D) $x = 8$

19 The sum of three consecutive integers is 510. If the least number is m and the largest number is n, what is the mean of m and n?

The mean of m and n = _____.

20 The mean of 16 numbers is 36. The mean of another 14 numbers is 21. What is the mean of all the 30 numbers?

Mean of all the 30 numbers = _____.

Next Section: Use Dot Plots, Box Plots, and Histograms to Represent Data ≫

USE DOT PLOTS, BOX PLOTS, AND HISTOGRAMS TO REPRESENT DATA

A dot plot is a graphical display used in statistics that uses dots to represent data. Dot plots work very well for data with a small number of values. They would not work well for large sets of data, because a dot would need to be plotted for each value.

To create a dot plot, we start by drawing a horizontal line with categories or numbers written under it. Then, we drew a dot above the line representing given values, so the total number of dots is equal to the total number of values.

The **box plot** is

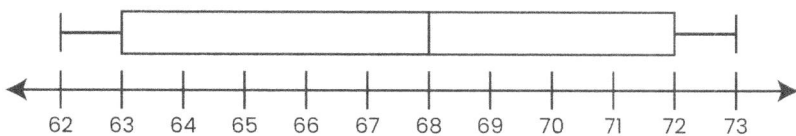

To make a histogram of data, you first need to choose a bin width. As a rule, try to choose an interval that will give you from 5 to 10 bins. Next, find the number of data values in each bin. These values are called frequencies. Note that a bin contains the left boundary value, but not the right.

For example, the bin from 11 to 13 includes the values 11, 11.5, 12, and 12.5, but not 13. Now, draw the axes. Scale the horizontal axis to show bins. Scale the vertical axis to show frequency values. Finally, draw in bars to show the frequency values in your tab.

USE DOT PLOTS, BOX PLOTS, AND HISTOGRAMS TO REPRESENT DATA

Example: This data set gives pulse rates, in beats per minute, for a group of 20 people:

64 62 73 64 65 72 72 73 64 63 70 72 66 62 73 72 63 72 70 62

Draw a histogram for this data.

Solution: We know that Min = 62 and Max = 73, so it would be reasonable to consider 5 bins with a length of 2.

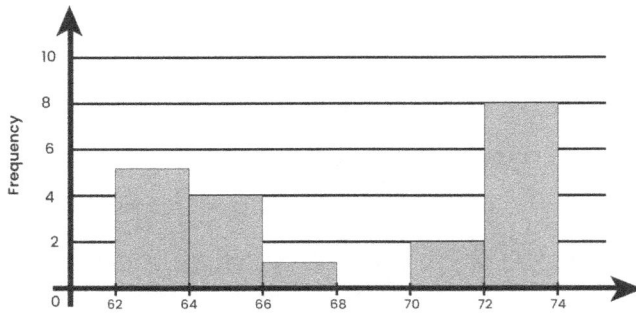

Box plots and histograms works very well for big data sets.

**Use Dot Plots, Box Plots, and Histograms
to Represent Data**   **7.3**

1   Which data set is represented by this dot plot?

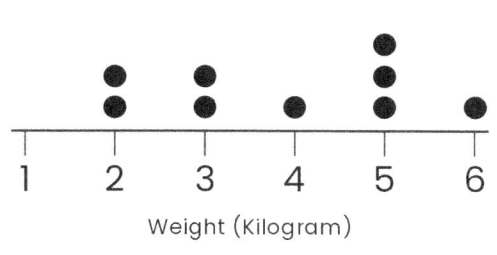

Weight (Kilogram)

(A) (2, 3, 4, 5, 6)

(B) (2, 2, 3, 3, 4, 5, 5, 5, 6)

(C) (2, 2, 1, 3, 1)

(D) (4, 5, 5, 8, 7)

2   What values are used to create this dot plot?

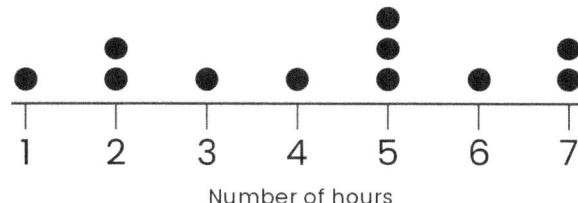

Number of hours

_____

3   Which data set is represented by this box plot?

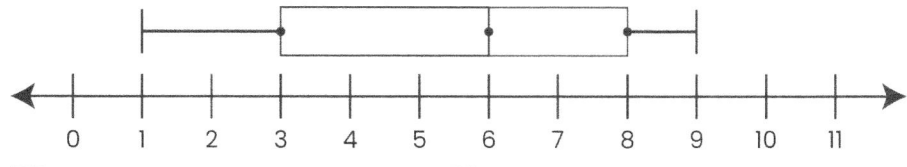

(A) (8, 1, 0, 2, 6, 8, 6)   (B) (1, 3, 6, 8, 9)

(C) (9, 1, 8, 3, 7, 5, 6)   (D) (9, 0, 8, 1, 7, 3, 6, 5, 4, 3)

7.3 Use Dot Plots, Box Plots, and Histograms to Represent Data

4 Which data set is represented by this histogram?

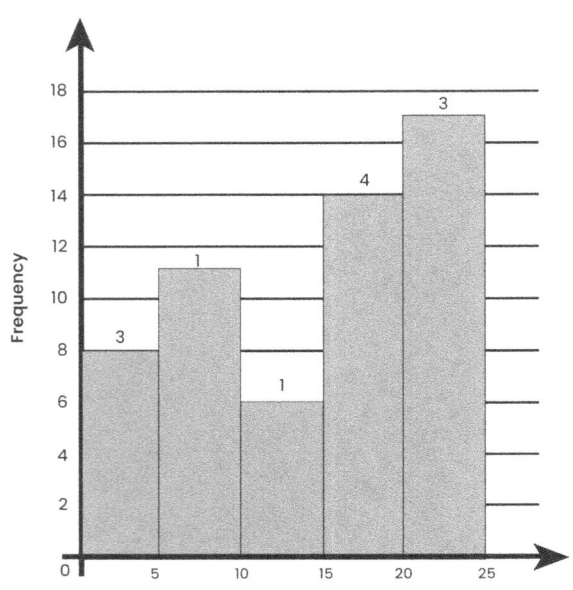

A (1, 3, 4, 5, 11, 15, 16, 18, 19, 20, 23, 24)

B (0, 5, 10, 15, 20, 25, 0, 1, 3, 1, 1, 5)

C (1, 1, 3, 5, 5. 11, 16, 19, 20, 24)

D (1, 3, 24, 23, 1, 3, 15, 16, 18, 19, 20)

5 Create dot plots for the following data.
4, 6, 2, 4, 8, 10, 4, 2, 2, 8, 10.

_____

6 Create box plots for the following data.
9, 13, 13, 15, 17, 17, 19, 21, 23, 26, 26.

_____

Use Dot Plots, Box Plots, and Histograms
to Represent Data   **7.3**

7 Create histograms for the following data.
3, 3, 3, 5, 5, 7, 9, 10, 11, 13,14, 15, 17, 17 (with 8 bins)

_____

8 The dot plot below shows a list of data. How many values are on this list?

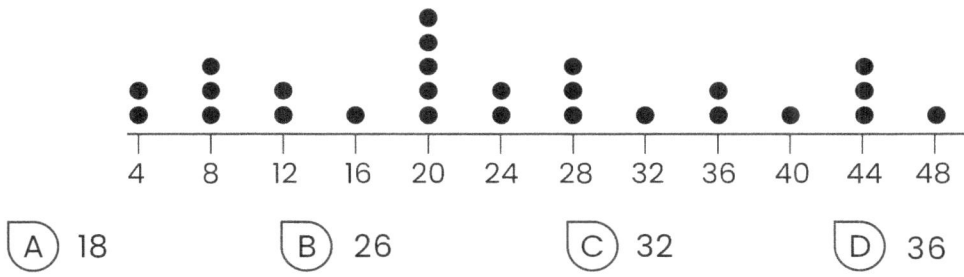

(A) 18   (B) 26   (C) 32   (D) 36

9 What is the mode in a set of numbers represented by the dot plot below?

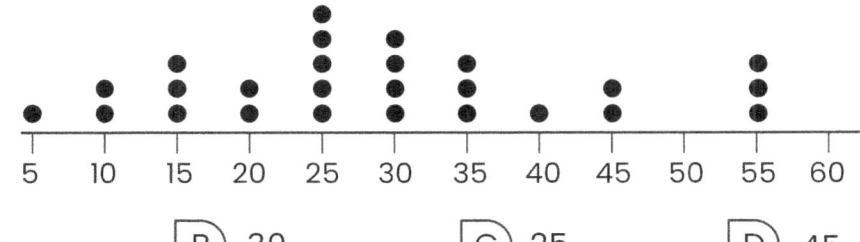

(A) 15   (B) 30   (C) 25   (D) 45

7.3 Use Dot Plots, Box Plots, and Histograms to Represent Data

10 Roy asked his friends how many hours they usually slept during holidays. He collected the following data set.

6, 7, 5, 6, 6, 7, 8, 9, 8, 10, 8, 7, 10, 9, 9, 7, 6, 8, 9.

What is the mean of the collected data?

(A) $7\frac{12}{19}$ (B) $8\frac{11}{19}$ (C) $9\frac{8}{19}$ (D) $10\frac{5}{19}$

11 The data below shows the scores of 6th grade students in math.

68, 79, 83, 99, 100, 80, 95, 78, 58, 63, 49, 93, 86.

What are the minimum and maximum marks scored?

Min = _____.

Max = _____.

12 Bella asked her students how much time they usually study during a test. She collected the following data set.

5, 6, 4, 3, 4, 5, 2, 7, 6, 5, 7, 5, 4, 6, 3, 6, 5, 7.

What is the mode of the collected data?

Mode = _____.

13 What is the first quartile in a set of numbers represented by the box plot below?

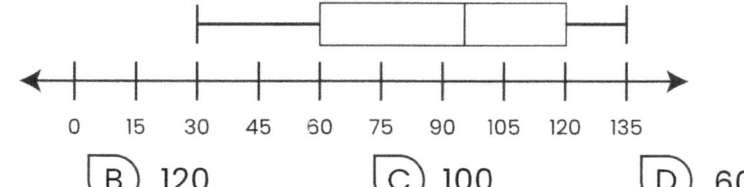

(A) 30 (B) 120 (C) 100 (D) 60

14 What is the mode score in the histogram below?

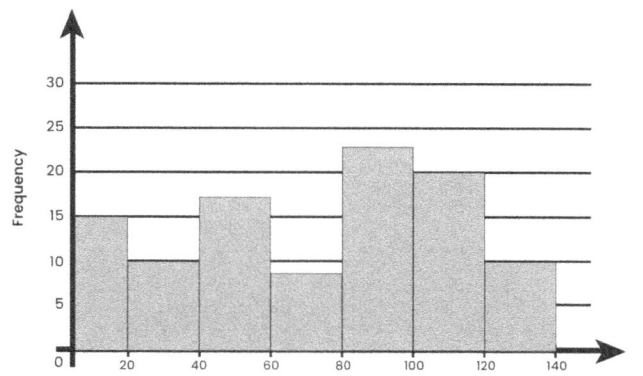

(A) 80-100

(B) 40-60

(C) 100-120

(D) 0-20

15 Smith asked his friends to estimate the number of minutes they spend playing each day. The following data shows the results of his survey. 45, 52, 38, 49, 35, 25, 30, 40, 25, 35, 25.
Draw a dot plot for the collected data.

7.3 Use Dot Plots, Box Plots, and Histograms to Represent Data

16 The histogram below shows the survey results on how much time, in minutes, people spent walking each day.Which of the following statements is true? How many people answered the question?

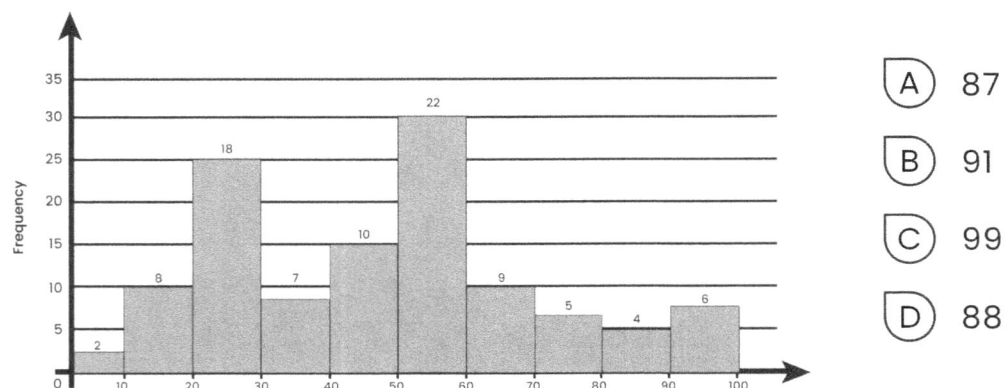

A) 87

B) 91

C) 99

D) 88

17 A pizza shop surveyed their customers, All customers were asked to rate the quality of their service with a rating from 0 to 10. The first 25 people who responded had the following results.

5, 8, 9, 6, 10, 8, 5, 9, 10, 4, 6, 3, 6, 3, 10, 8, 9, 6, 7, 8, 5, 9, 8, 4, 7

Draw a dot plot for this data.

18 A fruit shop surveyed their customers, All customers were asked to rate the quality of fruit in the shop with a rating from 0 to 10. The first 15 people who responded had the following results.
2, 8, 1, 9, 3, 7, 4, 6, 5, 10, 2, 4, 6, 8, 10.
Draw a box plot for this data.

_____

19 Twenty-five 6th grade students were asked to estimate how many hours a week they spend on gardening. This dot plot represents their reported number of hours spent gardening per week. What is the largest number of hours a student spends on gardening per week?

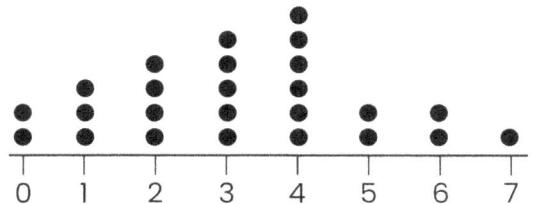

A) 2

B) 3

C) 4

D) 5

7.3   **Use Dot Plots, Box Plots, and Histograms to Represent Data**

20 The histogram below shows the measured speeds of 30 motorbikes at the entrance to the city, all taken by an electronic radar. The maximum allowed speed is 70 km/h. What is the number of motorbikes exceeding allowable speed?

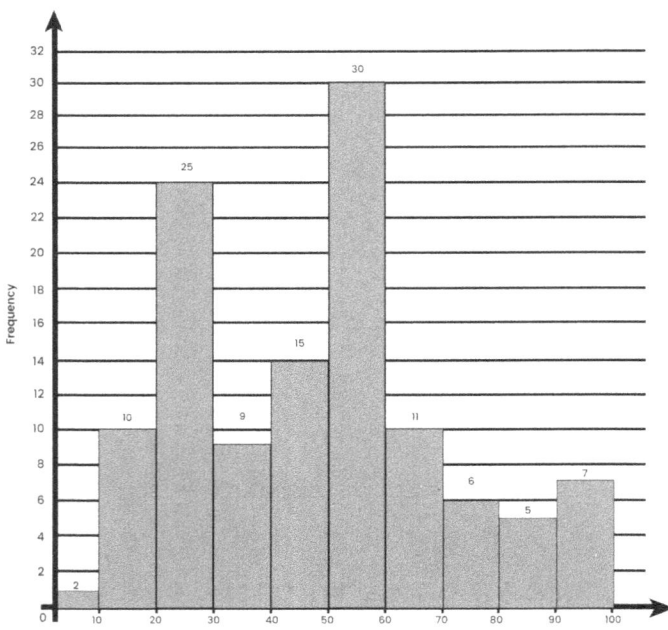

A) 18

B) 29

C) 30

D) 45

Next Section: Chapter Review

1   Find the maximum from the given data list.
101, 98, 124, 89, 23, 268, 213, 183, 165, 209.

(A) 23   (B) 268   (C) 209   (D) 101

2   Find the MAD from the given data list.
16, 21, 16, 19, 23, 17, 19, 12, 23, 20.

(A) $12\frac{1}{10}$ (B) $15\frac{7}{10}$ (C) $20\frac{3}{10}$ (D) $18\frac{6}{10}$

3   Which list has the smallest IOR?
Apple =10, 24, 98, 36, 81, 45, 72, 55, 60, 71, 9
Orange =75, 19, 28, 73, 30, 69, 61, 50, 11, 29, 18

(A) Apple

(B) Orange

4   What is the range of all the whole balls?
Red =45, 27, 31, 40, 44, 26, 11, 29, 22, 35
White =36, 21, 26, 19, 23, 7, 39, 12, 23, 20

7.4   **Chapter Review**

5   What is the mean of the given data

Animals	Number of Animals
Dog	45
Lion	36
Sheep	90
Tiger	51
Cat	38
Elephant	64

A) 48   B) 52

C) 54   D) 62

6   In the list of numbers, 16, 21, 18, 13, 15, 21, 22 numbers 21 and 15 are replaced by numbers 22 and 13. Which of the following measures changes?

A) Mean   B) Median   C) Mode   D) None of them

7   A basketball team took a survey asking how many jerseys each player had. The results were: 2, 1, 2, 3, 2, 4, 3, 2, 3, 4, 3, 5, 4, 5, 2 Which of the measurements (mean, median, and mode) is the smallest?

A) Mean   B) Median   C) Mode   D) None of them

Chapter Review 7.4

8 The table below shows the distribution of scores obtained during a handwriting competition. What is the difference between the median and the mean ?

Marks	Number of Students
25	8
78	6
55	7
65	9
80	9
95	3
98	1
72	8

(A) 4   (B) 5

(C) 6   (D) 7

9 A list contains three numbers. The greatest number is 24 more than the smallest number. The mean and the median of this list of numbers is 26. What is the value of z?

(A) $z = 11$ (B) $z = 12$ (C) $z = 13$ (D) $z = 14$

10 The sum of five consecutive integers is 800. If the least number among them is p and the largest number among them is q, what is the mean of p and q?

The mean of p and q = _____.

11 What is the range of this data set?
−7, −5, −10, −3, −11, −13, −9, −6.

(A) −10   (B) 10   (C) −8   (D) 8

7.4   **Chapter Review**

12 What is the mode of this data set?
20, 17, 21, 16, 25, 13, 15, 17, 27, 7, 36, 19.

(A) 11   (B) 21   (C) 17   (D) 36

13 If the number 39 is to be added to the list of numbers 38, 31, 40, 50, 39. Which of the followings must be true about the median of the list?

(A) It will increase from 39 to 41   (B) It will not change

(C) It will decrease from 39 to 48   (D) It will increase from 39 to 40

14 Which of the following data sets has the mode of 7?

(A) (2, 4, 6, 8, 10)   (B) (1, 3, 5, 7, 9, 11)

(C) (1, 4, 5, 8, 7, 9, 9, 8)   (D) (11, 9, 2, 7, 6, 8, 7, 4)

15 What is the five-number summary represented on the box plot below?

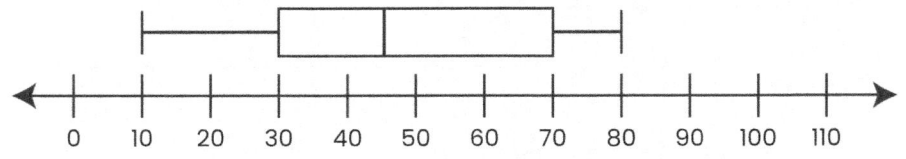

(A) (10, 30, 45, 70, 80)   (B) (10, 20, 30, 40, 50)

(C) (30, 40, 50, 60, 70)   (D) (10, 30, 40, 50, 70, 80)

16 The box plot below represents a list of data values. Which of the following statements is true?

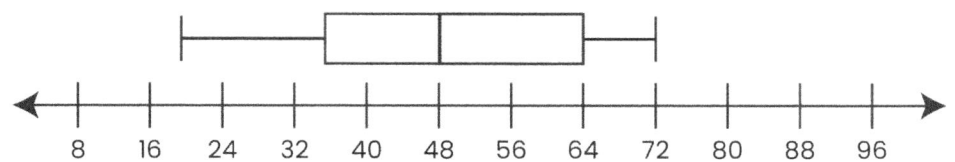

8 16 24 32 40 48 56 64 72 80 88 96

Ⓐ Median =55   Ⓑ Q_1=36   Ⓒ Range =48   Ⓓ Q_3=72

17 The owner of the pizza shop counted the number of pizzas sold in the last fifteen days. The results are listed below:

15, 27, 39, 19, 44, 36, 51, 30, 50, 45, 55, 62, 16, 11, 40

What is the IQR of the number of pizzas sold?

_____

18 What values are used to create this dot plot?

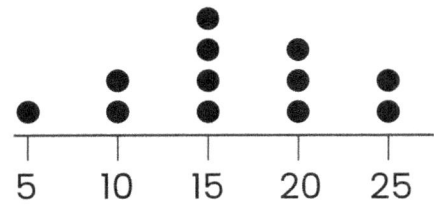

5   10   15   20   25   _____

7.4 Chapter Review

19 Create box plots for the following data.
2, 5, 8, 10, 13, 16.

---

20 Athletes took a survey about how much time, in minutes, they spent exercising each day. The histogram below shows the survey results. Which of the following statements is true?
How many people answered the question?

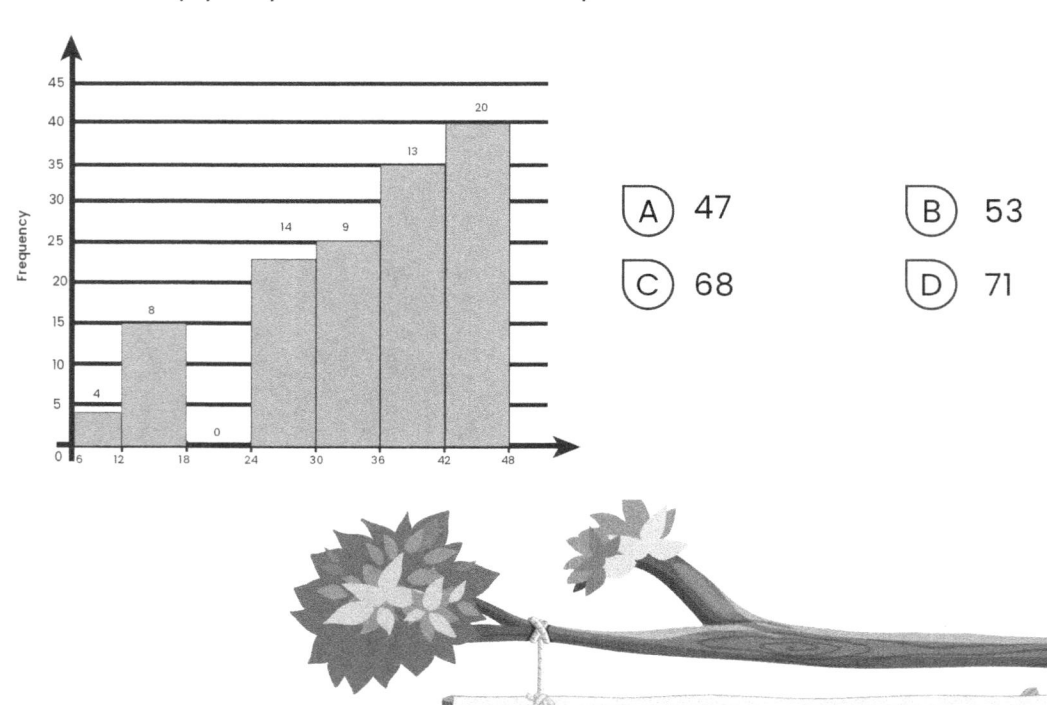

(A) 47

(B) 53

(C) 68

(D) 71

Next Chapter:
Comprehensive Assessment 1 & 2 ≫

COMPREHENSIVE ASSESSMENT

1 Tom travels 396 miles to his friend's house. If the trip takes 5.5 hours by car and he travels at a constant speed, how fast was he driving?

(A) 72 miles per hour
(B) 75 miles per hour
(C) 69 miles per hour
(D) 58 miles per hour

2 There are 36 chocolates in the box. Lisa took $\frac{2}{4}$ of the chocolates. If 1 serving is $\frac{1}{12}$ of the entire box of chocolates, how many servings does Lisa have?

(A) 8
(B) 7
(C) 6
(D) 9

3 Use the table below to find the cost of oranges per pound at a store.

Number of oranges (lb)	Cost (Dollars)
3	5.25
7	12.25
9	15.75

_____

4 Rita runs the 100-meter dash in 8.93 seconds. Teena runs a 200-meter dash in twice the amount of time as Rita runs the 100-meter dash.

(A) 4.92 sec
(B) 18.02 sec
(C) 13.4 sec
(D) 17.86 sec

233

5 A car salesman is selling motorcycles and cars. The ratio of cars sold to motorcycles sold is 10 to 4. There are a total of 240 wheels on the vehicles sold. How many motorcycles were sold?

_____

6 Mike goes hiking every 12 day and rides his bike every 10 day. Today, he goes hiking and rides his bike. What is the shortest number of days that will pass before going hiking and biking on the same day?

(A) 18   (B) 80   (C) 20   (D) 60

7 Which values are missing from this ratio table?

Apples	4	12	20	?
Strawberries	8	24	?	48

Apples = _____ ; Strawberries = _____.

8 How do you find the absolute value of a number? Select the correct answer below.

(A) Subtract the opposite of the number

(B) Add the opposite of the number

(C) Count how far the number is from zero on a number line

(D) Determine the opposite value of the number.

9 A television station reports 6 new stories every 15 minute. At this rate, how many new stories will they report each hour?

(A) 5   (B) 7   (C) 12   (D) 24

10 David wants to paint his room. He needs at least 5 gallons of paint to cover all the walls. Which inequality represents the amount of paint, p, David should buy?

(A) $p \geq 5$ (B) $p < 5$ (C) $p \leq 5$ (D) $p > 5$

11 Mercy and Jessy are musicians. Mercy learns 3 songs every 4 day. Jessy learns 5 songs every 6 day. Who learns the most songs after 3 weeks? Explain your reasoning.

_____

12 Terrell makes two stacks with these boxes. He stacks eight 10 inch boxes on top of each other. How many 16 inch boxes will he need to stack to reach this height?

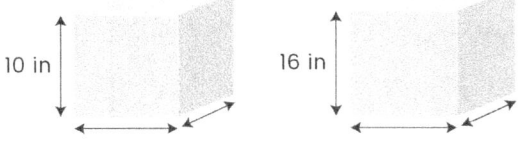

10 in   16 in

(A) 6   (B) 5

(C) 7   (D) 8

235

13 Robin is planning a trekking trip with his friends. This table shows the amount of time he plans to spend trekking during the trip.

Day	Amount of time for trekking (hours)
Friday	4.25
Saturday	7.75
Sunday	6.5

During the three days, Robin and his friends plan to cover 28 miles while trekking at a constant rate. What is the average rate, in miles per hour they should travel to trek 28 miles? Round your answer to the nearest tenth and explain your reasoning.

_____

14 When examining a credit statement, Angel has a balance of zero. What does this mean in terms of her credit cards?

(A) She owes the credit company money.

(B) She has zero dollars to spend on her credit card.

(C) The company owes her money.

(D) She does not owe the credit company money.

15 Jerry has a shirt with red and blue stripes. The number of red stripes is 4 times the number of blue stripes. There are 35 red and blue stripes on Jerry's shirt. How many red and blue stripes are on Jerry's shirt?

16 Jessica uses 4.5 cups of flour to bake 13 muffins, and 2.5 cups of flour to bake 1 cake. She bakes 52 muffins and 4 cakes for a school bake sale. How much flour does Jessica use?

(A) 28   (B) 30   (C) 42   (D) 48

17 Before the Christmas holiday, students bought 7 bouquets of 10 roses in each. Will the students be able to redistribute these roses into bouquets so that each bouquet has 14 roses?

(A) Yes, 12 bouquets   (B) Yes, 5 bouquets
(C) Yes, 9 bouquets   (D) No

18 The ratio of sketches to crayons in a box is 4:8. If there are 48 sketches and crayons combined inside the box, how many sketches are there?

_____

19 Mrs. Jaquelin has to buy 4 sets of plates for her kitchen. She is going to buy one set every 5 day. She purchased the first set on June 2nd. When will she buy the last set?

(A) 9th June   (B) 12th June   (C) 22th June   (D) 20th June

20 Merlin bought a new sofa for $836. She paid a deposit of $ 104 and the remaining balance was divided into x equal monthly payments. If she had to pay for the sofa for more than 10 months but less than 2 years, how much would she have to pay each month?

_____

21 What is the value of this expression? $9 + 19(7 + 2) - \dfrac{7^2}{7}$

A) 132   B) 173   C) 158   D) 145

22 What is the area of the figure, in square feet?

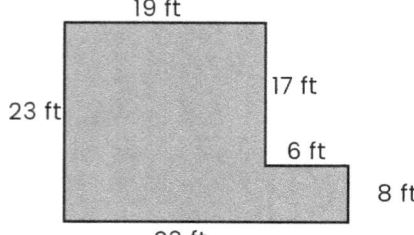

19 ft

17 ft

23 ft

6 ft

8 ft

23 ft

_____

23 The teacher bought 8 pencil boxes of 15 pencils each for the students. If there are 20 students in a class, will the teacher be able to divide pencils so that each student receives 6 pencils?

A) Yes   B) No

24 The area of quadrilateral $wtyv$ is 176 cm². What is the length, in cm, of ty?

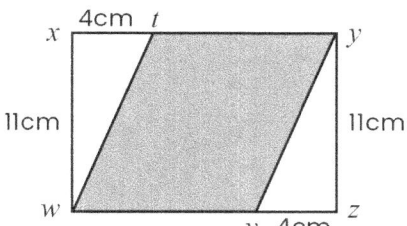

_____

25 What is the coefficient of d? 5+ 8d + 59.

_____

26 How many cubes with side lengths of an $\frac{1}{2}$ inch will fill the prism?

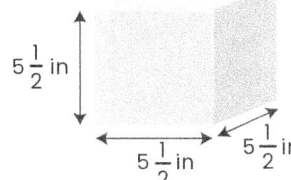

Ⓐ 1,331   Ⓑ 729

Ⓒ 832   Ⓓ 692

27 Using the distributive property, which expression is equivalent to
$$r + 6 + 6r + 8 = ?$$

Ⓐ 6r+14   Ⓑ 7(r+2)

Ⓒ 7r+8   Ⓓ 4 (2r+3)

28 A small cube has side lengths of $\frac{1}{2}$ inch.

True or False: The expression $\left(5\frac{1}{2}\times6\times4\frac{1}{2}\right)$ can be used to determine the number of cubes that can fit inside the larger rectangular prism.

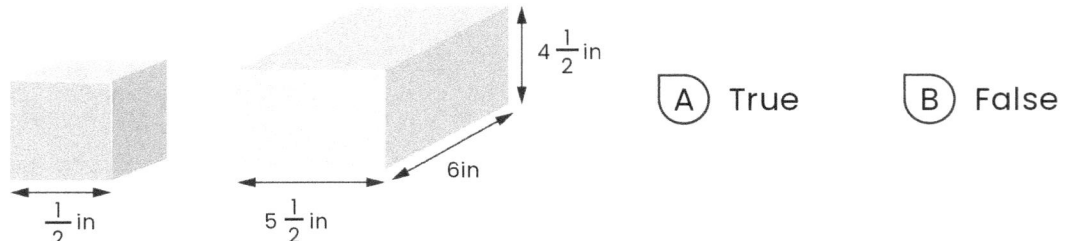

$4\frac{1}{2}$ in

6in

$\frac{1}{2}$ in

$5\frac{1}{2}$ in

(A) True   (B) False

29 Which ordered pair would create a square on this coordinate plane?

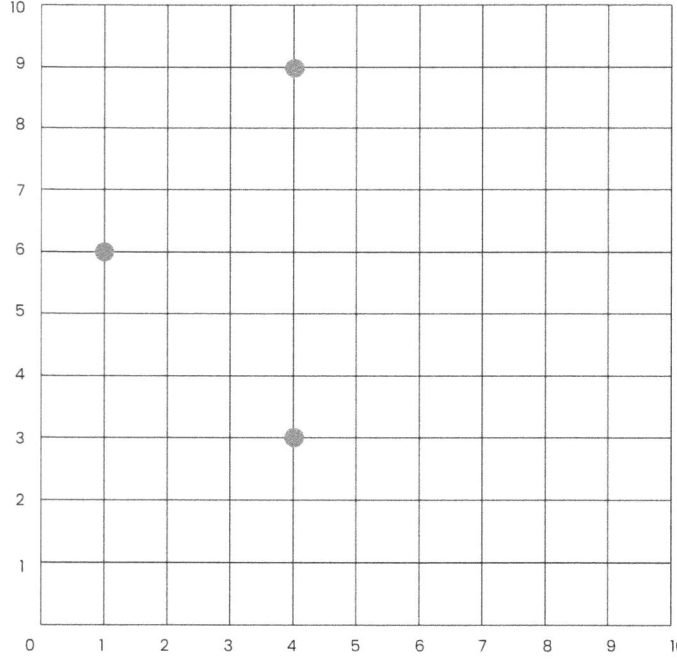

(A) (8, 6)

(B) (8, 5)

(C) (7, 6)

(D) (7, 4)

30 Is the inequality 18 (5 – t) > 5 true for t = 3?

(A) True

(B) False

31 Silvia creates a hexagon on this coordinated plane with an area of 12 square units. Where should the last 2 points be placed?

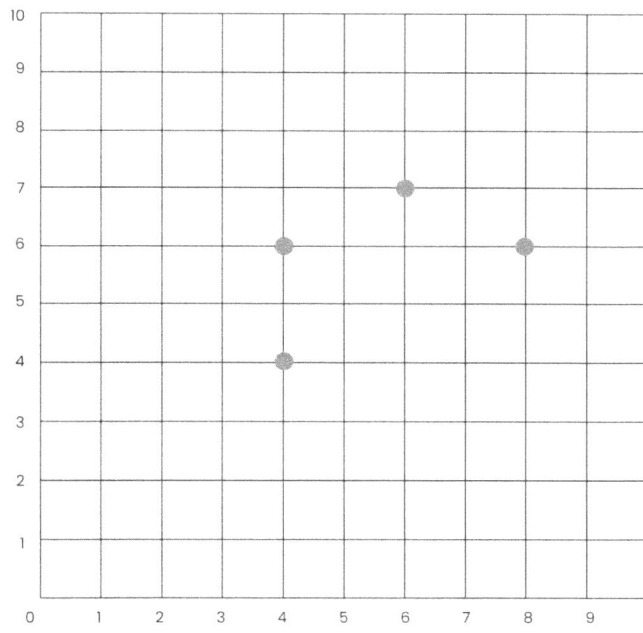

(A) (2, 5) and (3, 7)

(B) (5, 2) and (7, 3)

(C) (6, 3) and (8, 4)

(D) (5, 1) and (4, 2)

32 Andrea creates this skateboard ramp using 2 wooden boards. What is the length of each board, in feet?

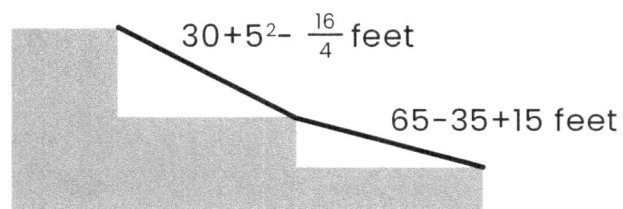

$30+5^2- \frac{16}{4}$ feet

$65-35+15$ feet

33 Determine the value of the expression below when n = 7.

25 + 12n.

34 Jessica is wrapping this box. She has a piece of wrapping paper that is 12 inches by 14 inches. Does Jessica have enough wrapping paper to cover the entire box?

Explain your reasoning.

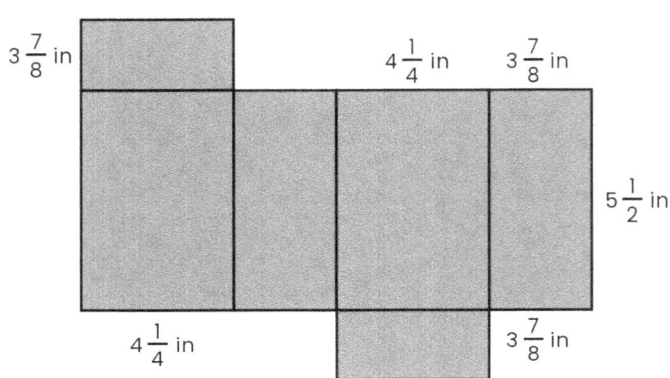

$3\frac{7}{8}$ in $4\frac{1}{4}$ in $3\frac{7}{8}$ in

$5\frac{1}{2}$ in

$4\frac{1}{4}$ in $3\frac{7}{8}$ in

35 Peter earned $20.88 each hour on the job. He spends $120 of the money he made to buy a new phone. This equation models the amount of money he has left, which x represents hours.

20.88x – 120 – 339.36

How many hours did Peter work?

36 Use the distributive property to write an expression equivalent to the expression. 6x + 7 – 2x + 9.

_____

37 Tim is a member of an internet music service. The music service charges a fee for each song he downloads. This table shows the cost y of downloading x songs.

Number of songs x	Cost (Dollars) y
3	3.97
6	5.95
9	8.92
21	21.80

Write an equation to represent this situation.

_____

38 Which data set is represented by this dot plot?

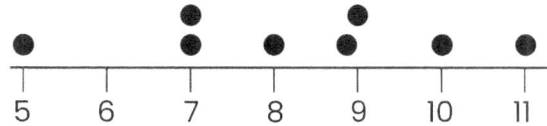

(A) {5, 6, 7, 8, 9, 10, 11}   (B) {5, 7, 8, 9, 0, 11}

(C) {5, 6, 7, 7, 8, 9, 9, 10, 11}   (D) {5, 7, 7, 8, 9, 9, 10, 11}

39 This net represents a box. Justin uses this expression to represent the surface area of the box. 6 × 6 × 14 × 4.

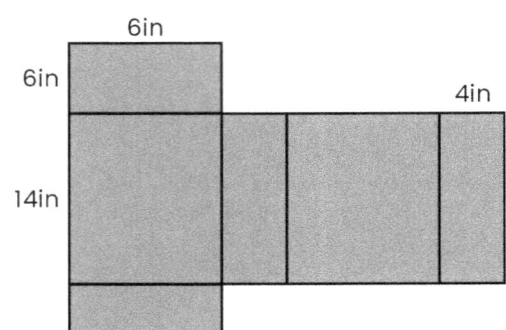

6in

6in

4in

14in

Jerzy writes this expression to represent the surface area of the box. 2(6 × 6) + 4(14 × 4). Which person, Justin or Jerzy, or neither, is correct? Explain your reasoning.

_____

40 Kathrine has the following data:

22, p, 15, 13, 17, 16, 20, 13, 17, 13, 13.

If the value of p is 14, what is the median of this data set?

_____

41 This box plot shows the amount of time 10 people spend at the gym each month.

Time spent at the gym each month (minutes)

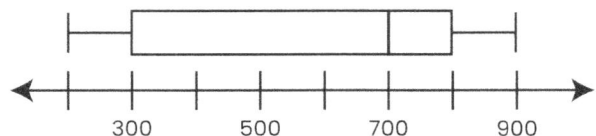

300   500   700   900

(A) Most of the group spend more than 800 minutes at the gym.

(B) The spread of the data ranges between 200 and 900 minutes.

(C) The spread of the data ranges between 300 and 800 minutes.

(D) Most of the group spends less than 500 minutes at the gym.

42 What values were used to create this dot plot?

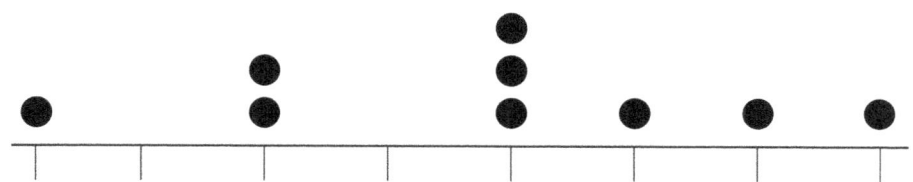

_____

43 Determine whether or not the question is a statistical question.
Answer true or false.

Question: Who is Jenny's favorite movie star?

(A) True   (B) False

44 What is the range of this data set?

−4, −2, −4, −9, −8, −7, −6, −5, −3.

(A) 7   (B) 9   (C) 8   (D) 3

45 This dot plot shows the birth weight of newborn babies.

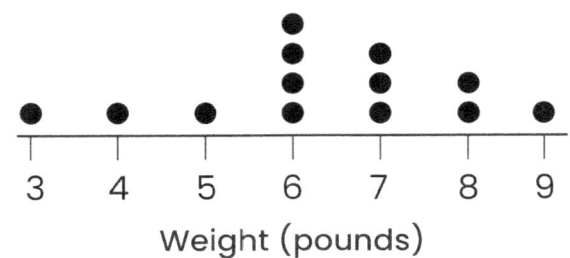

3
4
5
6
7
8
9
Weight (pounds)

Ⓐ The data has more than 1 peak.

Ⓑ The data is normally distributed.

Ⓒ The graph I skewed left.

Ⓓ The graph is skewed right.

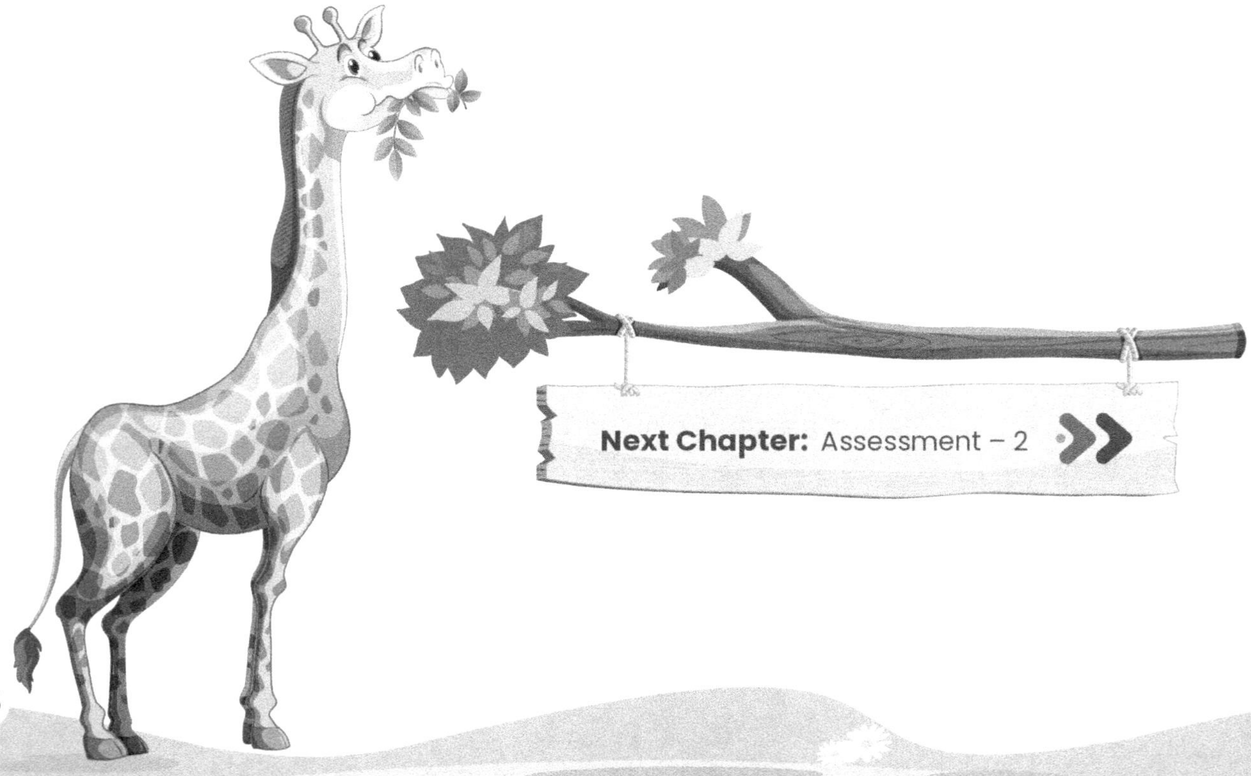

Next Chapter: Assessment – 2

COMPREHENSIVE ASSESSMENT

1 Five stores charge a different amount for the same candy bar. The mean price of the candy bar is $0.63. Which list could show the price of the candy bar at each store?

(A) $0.63, $0.63, $0.78, $0.99, $0.99

(B) $0.24, $0.39, $0.65, $0.45, $0.40

(C) $0.61, $0.70, $0.51, $0.80, $0.63

(D) $0.61, $0.99, $0.89, $0.75, $0.85

---

2 What is the value of B?

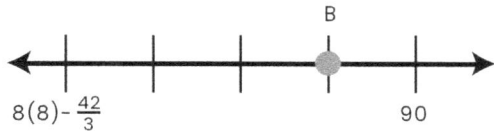

(A) 50   (B) 60   (C) 70   (D) 80

---

3 **True or False: This question is a statistical question:** What is the favorite subject of the sixth-grade students at Mercy Junior High School?

(A) True   (B) False

---

4 Elisa checked the memory on the 8 computers in his office complex. The amounts of memory, in GB, she found are:

5, 4, 6, 2, 9, 9, 5, 4.

What was the range of the amount of memory available?

(A) 6 GB   (B) 7 GB   (C) 8 GB   (D) 9 GB

5 Which mathematical expression represents this word statement?
Half of a number z.

(A) $\dfrac{3}{z}$ (B) $3z$ (C) $z-3$ (D) $\dfrac{z}{2}$

6 Olivia draws this net.
Which shape is represented by the net?

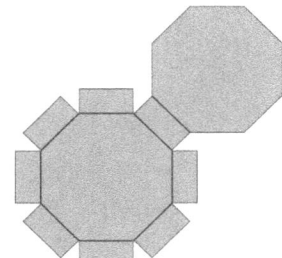

(A) Pentagonal prism   (B) Hexagonal prism

(C) Octagonal prism   (D) Rectangular prism

7 True or False: 6a + 8 is the simplified form of 8a + 2 – 2a – 10 + 1.

(A) True   (B) False

8 Shyam plans to spend x days studying for his tests at school. This table shows the number of hours he plans to study each day.

Test	Number of Hours
Social studies	$2\frac{3}{4}$
Math	3
Science	2
Chinese	$2\frac{1}{9}$
Language Arts	$2\frac{1}{5}$

(A) $(1\frac{2}{3}+x)+(2+x)+(1+x)+(1\frac{1}{8}+x)+(1\frac{1}{4}+x)$ (B) $(2\frac{3}{4}+3+2+2\frac{1}{9}+2\frac{1}{5}+x)$

(C) $(2\frac{3}{4}+3+2+2\frac{1}{9}+2\frac{1}{5})(x)$ (D) $(1\frac{2}{3}x)(2x)(1x)(1\frac{1}{8}x)(1\frac{1}{4}x)$

9 Using the distributive property, which expression is equivalent to
$$6(8x - 9) = ?$$

(A) 48x–13   (B) 8x–9   (C) 48x–9   (D) 48x–54

10 What is the greatest common factor of 68 and 56?

(A) 4   (B) 5   (C) 7   (D) 6

11 Which value makes this equation true?
$$6.5e = 54.6$$

(A) 23   (B) 0.19   (C) 8.4   (D) 37

12 Which value makes this equation true?
$$9x = (9 + 27)$$

(A) 21   (B) 4   (C) 14   (D) 12

13 John has ¾ of a bottle of juice. Each bottle of juice holds 20 ounces. A serving of juice is 10 ounces. How many servings of juice are in John's bottle?

(A) $\frac{1}{4}$ (B) $\frac{2}{3}$ (C) 2   (D) $1\frac{1}{2}$

14 Kim owes Steve $22. Steve owes Kim $32. Which expression can be used to determine the amount of money Steve owes to Kim if he discounts what he owes him?

    (A) (−32)−22   (B) (−22)−32   (C) 32−22   (D) 32−(−22)

15 True or False: If the base area of a rectangular prism is 72 cm² and the height is $\frac{36}{6}$ cm, the volume is 432 cm³.

    (A) True   (B) False

16 Which value is a solution to this inequality?

$$n \times 9 < 54$$

    (A) 3   (B) 6   (C) 5   (D) 7

17 What is the area of this triangle?

12cm

26cm

    (A) 132   (B) 143

    (C) 156   (D) 162

18 What is the least common multiple of 6 and 9?

    (A) 12   (B) 14   (C) 16   (D) 18

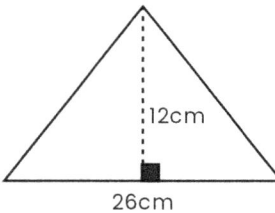

19 Tom hiked 11 km up a mountain. He then hiked 6 km back down the mountain. Which integers represent the distance from the place he started his hike?

(A) +11, –6   (B) –11, +6   (C) +11, +6   (D) –11,–6

20 Which points have a – 6 unit vertical distance between them?

(A) (– 13, 7) and (– 11, 6)   (B) (– 13, 7) and (– 7, 7)

(C) (– 11, 5) and (– 17, 5)   (D) (– 15, 7) and (– 15, 13)

21 Which numbers are missing from this number line?

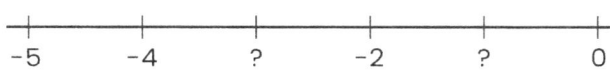

$$-5 \quad -4 \quad ? \quad -2 \quad ? \quad 0$$

(A) –3, –1   (B) –5, 0   (C) –2, 0   (D) –3, 0

22 Rita uses the standard algorithm to divide these numbers. Write the dividend.

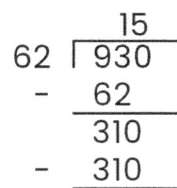

```
        15
  62 | 930
  -   62
      310
  -   310
        0
```

(A) 15   (B) 930

(C) 62   (D) 310

23 The table below shows the data the county released about the number of banks in 7 towns.

True or False: The median number of banks is 5.

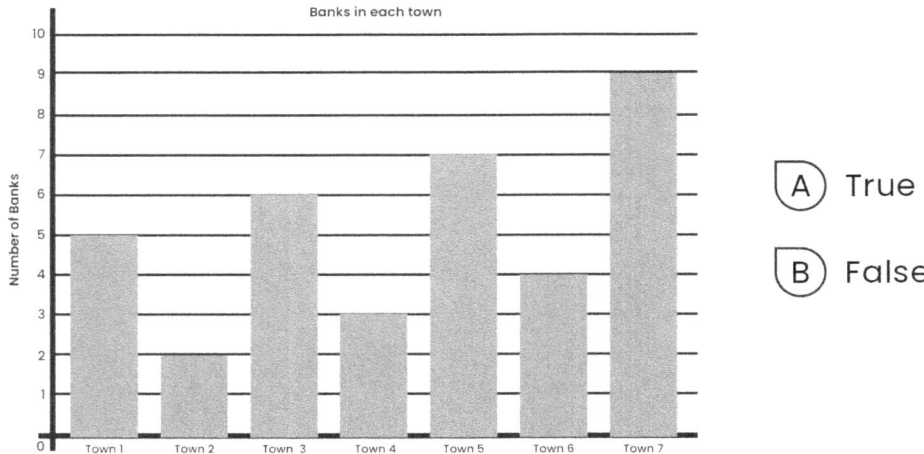

(A) True

(B) False

24 Mercy creates this dot plot to display the weight of the newborn babies at the city hospital. What is the range of this data set?

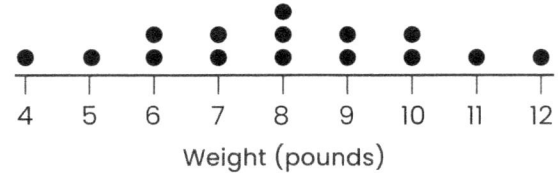

Weight (pounds)

_____

25 There are 50 girls and 40 boys who want to participate in a competition. There are 4 teams in the competition, and each team must have an equal number of girls and boys. What is the greatest number of boys and girls on one team?

26 Three stocks experienced the following changes per share in one day:

Stock A: – 5.5 dollars; Stock B: – 8.5 dollars; Stock C: + 8 dollars

Which stock lost the most money per share?

_____

27 This pyramid has a surface area of 340 square centimeters. Each triangular face has an area of 26 square centimeters. What is the area of the base, in square centimeters?

_____

28 Tom weighs 6 ½ kg more than his younger brother. He writes this equation to compare his weight z to his brother's weight.

$y = z - 6\frac{1}{2}$

Do you agree with Tom's equation? Explain your reasoning.

_____

29 This table shows the relationship between inches and feet. Find the missing values.

Inches	12	18	26	36	45
Feet	1		$2\frac{1}{6}$		

30 Lisa buys 12 crates for $14.52. Each crate costs the same amount of money. How much does each crate cost?

_____

31 The volume of this prism is $102\frac{9}{20}$ cm³.

What is the value of a, in cm?

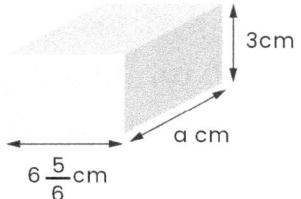

3cm

a cm

$6\frac{5}{6}$cm

_____

32 Seven friends receive the bill at a restaurant. They decide to split the bill equally. How much will each person pay if the bill is $58.80?

_____

33 Immanuel has $513.85 it in his checking account. He withdraws $215.97 and then later deposits $79.12. What is the new balance in Immanuel's checking account?

_____

34 The area of the quadrilateral ABCD is 5 times larger than the area of the triangle AEB. What is the length of AD, in cm?

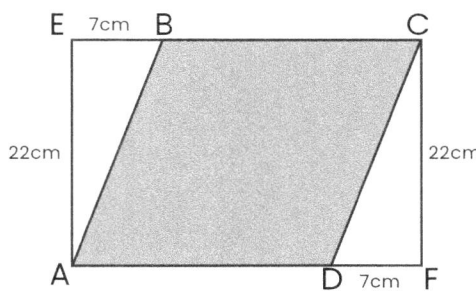

_____

35 Write a word problem and draw a model to represent this equation. $8\frac{1}{4} \div \frac{5}{4} = 6\frac{3}{5}$.

_____

36 A group of 28 strawberry plants produces 1,120 strawberries. Each plant produces the same number of strawberries. Use the standard algorithm of division to determine how many strawberries each plant produces.

_____

37 Graph a triangle with vertices (5,1), (3, 6), and (7, 8).

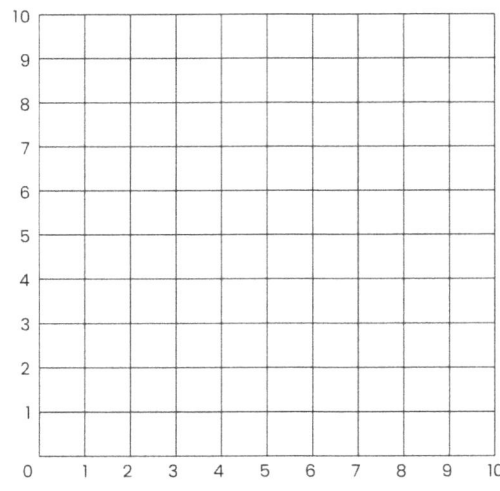

38 Silvia spends $49.80 on a new pair of pants. After paying for the pants, she has $13.97 left over. How much money did Silvia have originally?

39 Tina solves this equation.

$$6x = 12\frac{3}{7}$$

$$6x = \frac{85}{7}$$

$$\frac{85}{7} \times \frac{1}{6} = x$$

$$\frac{85}{42} = x$$

Do you agree with Tina's solution? Explain your reasoning.

40 Bronson buys a box of cookies for $49.99. The box has 4 different containers inside. Each container holds 15 cookies. Write and solve an equation to determine the cost n per chocolate to the nearest cent.

_____

41 Steffi and his 2 sisters share a computer. Each day, their parents allow them to spend no more than a total of 105 minutes on the computer. If Steffi and his sisters share the computer time equally, write an inequality to represent n, the number of minutes each sister will have on the computer.

_____

42 What expression can be used to find the area of this figure in square centimeters?

6cm

17cm

19cm

36cm

19cm

23cm

_____

43 The temperature in Raleigh is 19 degrees cooler than the temperature in Tampa. The temperature in Tampa is 49 degrees warmer than the temperature in Fargo. The temperature in Fargo is -16 degrees Fahrenheit. What is the temperature in Raleigh, in degrees Fahrenheit?

_____

44 Which mathematical expression represents this word statement? 9 times a number n.

(A) 9n

(B) n-9

(C) $\frac{n}{9}$

(D) n+9

45 Which expression has a value greater than 50 and less than 60?

Expression A	$(12 \frac{1}{2} - 10)(7\frac{1}{2})$
Expression B	2^3+3^2-5
Expression C	$14 \frac{1}{2} + 10(3)$
Expression D	$4 \frac{1}{2}(8+3)+7$

(A) Expression A

(B) Expression B

(C) Expression C

(D) Expression D

Next Chapter: Answers

ANSWERS AND EXPLANATIONS

TABLE OF CONTENTS

TABLE OF CONTENTS

1.RATIOS AND RATES

1.1 WRITE A RATIO

1. Answer: D
Explanation: Ratio of boys to girls =3:5
Total parts =8
Value of each part = $\frac{32}{8}$ =4
Number of girls = 4×5=20.

2. Answer: B
Explanation: The ratio is 24 to 16, or 3 to 2

3. Answer: 19:54
Explanation: BC=1.9
AD = 1.4 + 1.9 + 2.1 = 5.4
BC:AD = 19:54.

4. Answer: D
Explanation: Joel eats 10 cookies, and Emily eats 5 cookies. The ratio is 10:5 or 2:1.

5. Answer: 9:5
Explanation: Amount of sugar =$\frac{3}{5}$kg
Amount of milk =$\frac{1}{3}$kg
Sugar: Milk= $\frac{3}{5}:\frac{1}{3}$ =9:5

6. Answer: A
Explanation: Seven people are not allergic to eggs, and 4 people are allergic to eggs. The ratio is 7 to 4.

7. Answer: C
Explanation: 1 XXL pizza caters to 4 people
Ratio = 1:4
Number of people = 4x
So, 4x = 36; x = 9.

8. Answer: B
Explanation: Total capacity = 100 gallons
Amount of water = 25 gallons
Empty space = 100 - 25 = 75 gallons
Empty space: Capacity = 75:100.

9. Answer: A
Explanation: The number of girls is smaller than the number of boys. Thus, the number of girls in the ratio must be less than the number of boys.

10. Answer: B
Explanation: Ratio of sunfish to perch = 4:2
Number of sunfish = 4x
Number of perch = 2x
Number of fish = 180
4x+2x = 180 => 6x=180 => x = 30
Number of sunfish = 4x = 4×30 = 120.

11. Answer: 1:3
Explanation: Number of games won = $\frac{2}{3}$
Number of games lost = $1-\frac{2}{3}=\frac{1}{3}$
Ratio of games lost to games won = 1:3.

12. Answer: C
Explanation: If here are 14 correct answers and 6 incorrect answer, there are 20 questions on the test.

13. Answer: D
Explanation: Fraction of girls = $\frac{5}{6}$
Fraction of boys = 25
Ratio of boys to girls =25:30.

14. Answer: C
Explanation: 2 lengths = 3 widths
Length to width = 3:2, Length = $3x$, Width = $2x$,
Perimeter = $(2(\text{Length + width}) = 10x = 60$
$x = 6$; Length = $3 \times x = 3 \times 6 = 18$.

15. Answer: D
Explanation: Number of correct answers = x
Number of all answers =40
Number of incorrect answers = 40-x
Ratio of incorrect answers to all answers = 9:40 , So, 40-x = 9 , Hence, x = 31.

16. Answer: B
Explanation: The ratio of the scores of Cavaliers to Warriors is 88 to 222, which, in lowest terms, is 44 to 111.

17. Answer: A
Explanation: 1st number = 4
2nd number = 8, 3rd number = 2
Sum of the first two numbers = 12
Sum of the last two numbers = 10
Ratio = 12 : 10 = 6:5.

18. Answer: C
Explanation: Number of correct answers = x
Number of all answers = 45
Number of incorrect answers = 45-x
Ratio of incorrect answers to correct answers:
11 : 34, So, 45-x = 11, Hence, x = 34 .

19. Answer: 7:3
Explanation:
The perimeter of the rectangle = 20 cm
The width of the rectangle = 3 cm
The length of the rectangle = 7 cm
The ratio of the length to the width = 7:3.

20. Answer: 2:5
Explanation: Number of children who have 3
or more pets = 8+2 = 10
Number of children who have two or fewer
pets = 15 + 8 + 2 = 25
Ratio = 10:25 = 2:5

1.2 UNIT RATES AND PRICES

1. Answer: C
Explanation: Using division, students may
divide 15 by 5. The unit rate of this situation is
3 to 1. There are 3 pens in 1 box.

2. Answer: D
Explanation: Using division, students may
divide 45 by 9. The unit rate of this situation is
5 to 1. Each cupcake takes 5 minutes to cook.

3. Answer: B
Explanation: The unit rate should be $ 6
per watermelon. This can be calculated by
dividing 984 by 164.

4. Answer: A
Explanation: The unit rate should be 40
liters per minute. This can be calculated by
dividing 600 by 15.

5. Answer: 9 miles
Explanation: Prince walks in 2 hours = 6
miles. Prince walks per hour = 6 ÷ 2 = 3 miles.
If he walked 27 miles, dividing 27 by 3 results
in the number of hours he walked.

6. Answer: 8
Explanation: Divide the number of students
by the number of rows, $\frac{8656}{1082}$=8. There are 8
students per row.

7. Answer: C
Explanation: Unit price = $\frac{280}{7}$ =40.

8. Answer: A
Explanation: Unit rate = $\frac{38}{3}$ =12.67.

9. Answer: D
Explanation: Unit rate =$\frac{2400}{25}$=96.

10. Answer: C
Explanation: Distance = 5500 m = 5.5 km
Time = 50 min =$\frac{50}{60}$ = $\frac{5}{6}$ hours

Unit rate = $\frac{5.5}{\frac{5}{6}}$=5.5× $\frac{6}{5}$ = 1.1 × 6 = 6.6.

11. Answer: 7 miles per hour
Explanation: $4\frac{5}{4}$=$\frac{21}{4}$ miles in $\frac{3}{4}$ hour

$\frac{21}{4}$×$\frac{4}{3}$ = $\frac{21}{3}$=7 miles per hour.

12. Answer: 0.17 per pumpkin
Explanation: Twenty pumpkins costs = $3.40
$3.40 ÷ 20 = 0.17 per pumpkin.

13. Answer: A
Explanation: $20.80 for 4 hours
$20.80 ÷ 4 = $5.20 per hour.

14. Answer: 1,800 m per hour
Explanation:
Doug walks from point A to B = 1,200 m. Doug walks from point B to C = 2,400 m.
1200 + 2400 = 3600 m in 2 hours
3600 ÷ 2 = 1,800 m per hour.

15. Answer: B
Explanation: Grayson's time = 30 minutes
6 miles in 30 minutes
6 ÷ 30 = 0.2 mile per minute.

16. Answer: D
Explanation:
Butterflies fly 35 miles in 30 minutes
Multiply by 2
70 miles in 60 minutes; 1 hour = 60 minutes
The butterfly travels at a speed of 70 miles per hour.

17. Answer: 240 mile in 1 hour
Explanation: Kevin reach 140 mile in 35 minutes; Divide by 7; 20 mile in 5 minutes
Multiply by 12; 240 mile in 60 minutes
Larry reaches 240 mile in 1 hour.

18. Answer: B
Explanation: Manuel gains $48 selling 8 sofa
$48 ÷ 8 = 6; Manuel gains = $6 per sofa
Tristan gains $ 91 selling 13 sofa
$91 ÷ 13 = 7; Tristan gains = $7 per sofa
Together = $6 + $7 = $13 per sofa.

19. Answer: B
Explanation: 1st size = $15 for 500 ml
1 L=1000 ml; $15×2 = $30 per Liter
2nd size =$18 for 900 ml; $2 for 100 ml
$20 for 1 Liter. **2nd size is the better buy**

20. Answer: C
Explanation:
The juice shop charges $6; 50 for 9 glasses.
$6.50 ÷ 9 = $0.72 per glass
The shop charges $1; 15 for 4 packs of sugar
$1.13 ÷ 4 = $0.29 per pack.
Unit price $0.72 + $0.29 = $1 per juice.

1.3 EQUIVALENT RATIOS

1. Answer: B
Explanation: $\frac{7\times3}{9\times3}= \frac{21}{27}$
So $\frac{21}{27} \neq \frac{21}{28}$

2. Answer: A
Explanation: $\frac{103+5}{91-7} = \frac{108}{84} = \frac{9}{7}$
$\frac{18}{14} = \frac{9}{7}$ So $\frac{9}{7} = \frac{9}{7}$

3. Answer: A
Explanation: $14 :\frac{7}{5}=14\times \frac{5}{7}=10$
$18 :1\frac{4}{5}=18 :\frac{9}{5}=18\times\frac{5}{9}=10$

4. Answer: B
Explanation: Number of apples Mia cuts in 12 minutes =324 apples
Mia's unit rate = $\frac{324}{12}$ =27 apples per minute.
Number of apples Jamie cuts in 8 minutes =184 apples
Jamie's unit rate = $\frac{184}{8}$ =23 apples per minute.
No, they are not equivalent.

5. Answer: A
Explanation: Number of dishes Charles's family cook in 11 hours =220
Charles family unit rate = $\frac{220}{11}$=20 dishes per hour.
Number of dishes Dylan's family cook in $19\frac{1}{2} = \frac{39}{2}$ hours =390
Dylan's family unit rate
=$390 :\frac{39}{2} =390\times\frac{2}{39}$ =20 dishes per hour
Yes, they are equivalent.

6. Answer: A
Explanation: Sides of the first rectangle =5 :7
Sides of the second rectangle =10 :14=5 :7
Yes, they are equivalent.

7. Answer: C
Explanation: 465 carrots in 15 boxes = $\frac{465}{15}$=31
279 carrots in 9 boxes = $\frac{279}{9}$ =31

8. Answer: D
Explanation: Number of shaded squares =24
Number of all squares = 32
Ratio = 24:32 = 12:16 = 3:4.

9. Answer: B
Explanation:
Number of pages in Math book =280
Number of pages in English book =210
Number of pages in Science book =350
Math : English : Science =280 :210 :350=28 :21 :35=4 :3 :5

10. Answer: B
Explanation: AC =12
DC =6. AC : DC =12 :6=2 :1 . AB =5. DB =13
AB : DB =5 :13. No, they are not equivalent.

11. Answer: $\frac{9}{2}$
Explanation: The highest common factor for the numerator and denominator is 36. Hence, dividing them with 36, we get $\frac{9}{2}$.

12. Answer: r = −12
Explanation: $\frac{r}{18} = \frac{r+6}{9}$
$\frac{r}{18} \times 9 = r + 6$;
$\frac{r}{2} = r + 6$
$r = 2(r + 6)$; $r = 2r + 12$; $-12 = 2r - r$; $r = -12$.

13. Answer: C
Explanation: Number of hours to finish 17 problems =2
Write this as a ratio $= \frac{2}{17}$
Number of hours to finish 51 problems
$= \frac{2}{17} = \frac{?}{51}$. $\frac{2 \times 3}{17 \times 3} = \frac{6}{51}$

14. Answer: D
Explanation: Angela sold 8 boxes of dried blueberries =$ 36.54
Write this as a ratio $= \frac{36.54}{8}$
Angela sold 16 boxes of dried blueberries
$= \frac{36.54}{8} = \frac{?}{16}$. $\frac{36.54 \times 2}{8 \times 2} = \frac{73.08}{16}$

15. Answer: A
Explanation: The highest common factor for both numbers in the ratio is 17. Hence, dividing with 17, we get 35.

16. Answer: B
Explanation: Nile bought six sofas for =$551
Multiply by 6.
11 sofas for $1,010.13

17. Answer: C
Explanation: Ratio 4:7
There are 80 black pens in a bag.
Multiply by 20
80 black to 140 blue = 80 + 140 = 220 pens.

18. Answer: 2:27
Explanation: The highest common factor for both the number in ratio is 19. Hence, dividing them with 19, we get 27.

19. Answer: B
Explanation: $\frac{x+8}{50} = \frac{3}{5}$
$x+8 = \frac{3}{5} \times 50$
$x+8 = 3 \times 10$
$x+8 = 30$
$x = 30 - 8$
$x = 22$

20. Answer: p = −6
Explanation: $\frac{p}{12} = \frac{p+3}{6}$
$\frac{p}{12} \times 6 = p + 3$

$\frac{p}{2} = p + 3$
$p = 2(p + 3)$
$p = 2p + 6$
$-6 = 2p - p$
$p = -6$

1.4 SOLVING PROPORTIONS

1. Answer: A
Explanation: The grade 6 class has 33 girls and 45 boys.
Ratio of girls to boys =33 :45
Ratio as a fraction in simplest form $= \frac{33}{45} = \frac{11}{15}$
(divide the numerator and denominator by 3)

2. Answer: B
Explanation: $\frac{13}{3} = \frac{4}{q}$
$q = 3 \times \frac{4}{13}$
$q = \frac{12}{13}$

3. Answer: A
Explanation: $\frac{4}{12} = \frac{1}{3a-6}$
$43a-6=1\times12$
$12a-24=12.$ $12a=12+24.$ $12a=36.$ $a=\frac{36}{12}$
$a=3$

4. Answer: A
Explanation: $\frac{15}{18} = \frac{5}{6}$
$\frac{25}{30} = \frac{5}{6}$
Yes, the given ratios are proportional.

5. Answer: C
Explanation: Jackson ran 2 miles in 15.2 minutes.
Let y be the distance run in 30.4 minutes.
$\frac{2}{15.2} = \frac{Y}{30.4}$
$\frac{2}{15.2}\times30.4=y;$ $y=2\times2;$ $y=4$ miles.

6. Answer: D
Explanation: A motor bike travels 240 miles in 4 hours
Distance traveled in 1 hour $= \frac{240}{4}=60$ miles
Hence, distance traveled in 9 hours =
$9\times60 = 540$ miles.

7. Answer: a=33, x=42
Explanation: When you multiply 6 by 3, you get 18. So, multiply 11 by 3 to get a.
Hence, $a=11(3)=33$
When you multiply 11 by 7, you get 77. So, multiply 6 by 7 to get x.
Hence, $x=6(7)=42$

8. Answer: B
Explanation:
Let r be the denominator of the fraction
$\frac{3r-6}{r} = \frac{3}{2}$
$2(3r-6)=3r.$ $6r-12=3r.$ $6r-3r=12$
$3r=12.$ $r=\frac{12}{3}=4$
$r=4$
Required fraction$= \frac{3r-6}{r} = \frac{3(4)-6}{4} = \frac{12-6}{4} = \frac{6}{4} = \frac{3}{2}$

9. Answer: 90 miles per hour
Explanation: $\frac{630}{7}=90$
$\frac{270}{3} =90.$ $\frac{810}{9}=90.$ $\frac{450}{5}=90$

10. Answer: 20, 100, 140, and 220
Explanation: Number of months a year = 12
Total number of coins collected = 240
Number of coins collected a month $=\frac{240}{12}=20$

Month	1	5	7	11
Coins	20	100	140	220

11. Answer: 0.14
Explanation: Old constant of proportionality:
$= = = = =7$
$\frac{28}{4}$ $\frac{42}{6}$ $\frac{63}{9}$ $\frac{91}{13}$ $\frac{119}{17}$
Switch the rows:

B	4	6	9	13	17
A	28	42	63	91	119

New constant of proportionality:
$= = = = =0.14$
$\frac{4}{28}$ $\frac{6}{42}$ $\frac{9}{63}$ $\frac{13}{91}$ $\frac{17}{119}$

12. Answer: C
Explanation: $=$
$\frac{25}{35}$ $\frac{5}{7}$

13. Answer: A
Explanation: 1 inch = 15 miles
8.2 inches = 8.2 × 15 = 123 miles
The actual distance is 123 miles.

14. Answer: D
Explanation: Scale : 8 cm = 320 m
We know that, 1 m = 100 cm
8 cm = 320 × 100 cm. So, the scale is : 8 cm = 32,000 cm. Simplifying, 1 cm = 4,000 cm
The scale factor is 1:4000

15. Answer: B
Explanation: Scale : 3 cm = 30 m
We know that, 1 m = 100 cm
So, the scale is : 3 cm = 30 × 100 cm
3 cm = 3000 cm. The scale factor is 1:1000

16. Answer: A
Explanation: Scale factor: 5:16
(Multiply both sides by 5) = 25:80
Actual size = 80 = 0.8 m

17. Answer: C
Explanation: Scale factor of the house length = 1:5. Actual size of the house length 150 m= 15,000 cm
Scale size of the house length
$= \frac{15000}{5} \times 1 = 3000$ cm
Therefore, scale size of the house length = 3000 cm

18. Answer: D
Explanation: Scale factor = 1:12,000
Scale perimeter = 72 cm
Scale length of the square school $= \frac{72}{4} = 18$ cm
Actual length of the park =
18 × 12,000 = 216,000 cm = 2160 m = 2.16 km
Actual area of the park = 2.16 × 2.16 = 4.67 sq. km

19. Answer: B
Explanation: Distance between home and the beach is 7 units. From the scale,
2 units=4 km; 1 unit = 2 km. So, 7 units = 14 km
The distance from Sarah's home to the beach is = 14 km

20. Answer: 3 units = 5 m
Explanation: Diagram A:
Scale: 3 units = 6 m
1 unit = 2 m
Length of the field = 5 units = 5 × 2 = 10 m
Length of the field = 3 units = 3 × 2 = 6 m
Diagram B:
Length of the field = 6 units = 12 m
1 unit = 126 = 2 m
For the scale, 3 units = 2 × 3 = 6 m
Scale: 3 units = 6 m

1.5 CHAPTER REVIEW

1. Answer: B
Explanation: Number of grapes Avery eats in 4 minutes =172 grapes
Avery's unit rate $= \frac{172}{4} = 43$ grapes per minute.
Number of grapes Dixie eats in 7 minutes =217 grapes
Dixie's unit rate $= \frac{217}{7} = 31$ grapes per minute.
No, they are not equivalent.

2. Answer: B
Explanation: Number of shaded squares =12
Number of all squares =30
Ratio =12 :30=4 :10=2 :5.

3. Answer: $\frac{19}{3}$
Explanation: The highest common factor for the numerator and denominator is 23. Hence, dividing them with 23, we get $\frac{19}{3}$

4. Answer: B
Explanation: $\frac{29}{11} = \frac{2}{b}$
$b = 11 \times \frac{2}{29}$
$b = \frac{22}{29}$

5. Answer: C
Explanation: The ratio is 28 to 20, or 7 to 5

6. Answer: A
Explanation: Scale : 11 cm = 550 m
We know that, 1 m = 100 cm;
11 cm=550×100 cm
So, the scale is : 11 cm=55,000 cm
Simplifying, 1 cm=5,000 cm
The scale factor is 1 :5000

7. Answer: D
Explanation: The missing value can be found using the proportion: $\frac{13}{104} = \frac{?}{136}$
$\frac{?}{136} = \frac{13}{104}$
$? = \frac{13}{104} \times 136$
$? = 17$

8. Answer: B
Explanation: Dividing 492 by 41 is 12. The unit rate is 12 to 1.

9. Answer: A
Explanation: To determine whether two ratios are equivalent, write them as fractions and compare the fractions. If the fractions are equivalent, the ratios are equivalent. Both ratios can be written as $\frac{8}{1}$.

10. Answer: 3 days
Explanation: 10 deliveries in =6 days
5 deliveries in =3 days

ANSWERS AND EXPLANATIONS

11. Answer: C
Explanation: Carrots =3x
Beetroots =5x
Add 3 carrots and 5 beetroots
Carrots =3x+3=3(x+1)
Beetroots =5x+5=5(x+1)
Carrots to Beetroots = $\frac{3(x+1)}{5(x+1)} = \frac{3}{5}$

12. Answer: A
Explanation: $\frac{6}{21} = \frac{2\times3}{7\times3} = \frac{2}{7}$

13. Answer: B
Explanation: 140 miles in 7 hours
20 miles per hour
10 miles in $\frac{1}{2}$ hour
40 miles in 2 hour.

14. Answer: D
Explanation: $\frac{7}{9} : \frac{14}{3}$
$\frac{7}{9} \times \frac{3}{14} = \frac{1}{6}$

15. Answer: C
Explanation: $\frac{56}{a+2} = \frac{8}{3}$
56×3=8(a+2)
168=8a+16
168-16=8a
152=8a
a= $\frac{152}{8}$
a=19

16. Answer: D
Explanation: 36 :96=3:8
$\frac{w}{48} = \frac{3}{8}$
W= $\frac{3\times48}{8}$ =18
$\frac{27}{z} = \frac{3}{8}$
3Z=27×8
Z= $\frac{27\times8}{3}$ =72
Z-W=72-18=54

17. Answer: B
Explanation: Boys =7x; Girls =3x
7x=56. x=$\frac{56}{7}$
x = 8
3x = 3 × 8 = 24

18. Answer: A
Explanation: 3 in to 1 ft
x in to 45 ft
$\frac{3}{x} = \frac{1}{45}$
x=45×3=135 ft

19. Answer: 48 days
Explanation: 10 people – 12 days – 7 books
5 people – 24 days – 7 books
5 people – 48 days – 14 books

20. Answer: 14 erasers
Explanation: Pen =3x
Pencil =5x
Eraser =3x-37
Total =3x+5x+3x-33=11x-37
11x-37=150
11x=150+37
11x=187
x= $\frac{187}{11}$
x=17
Pen =3×17=51
Pencil =5×17=85
Eraser=3×17-37=51-37=14

2. FRACTIONS

2.1 LCM AND GCD

1. Answer: C
Explanation: $36 = 3 \times 3 \times 2 \times 2 = 3^2 \times 2^2$
$54 = 3 \times 3 \times 3 \times 2 = 3^3 \times 2$
GCF =(36, 54) = $3^2 \times 2 = 9 \times 2 = 18$.

2. Answer: A
Explanation: $63 = 3^2 \times 7$
$81 = 3^4$
$108 = 3^3 \times 2^2$
LCM = $3^4 \times 2^2 \times 7 = 2,268$.

3. Answer: B
Explanation: Animals stickers = $64 = 2^6$
Birds stickers = $96 = 2^5\times3$
GCF$(64, 96) = 2^5 = 32$

4. Answer: D
Explanation: Red balls = $152 = 2^3 \times 19$
White balls = $104 = 2^3 \times 13$
GCF$(152, 104) = 2^3 = 8$

5. Answer: A
Explanation: Apple = $30 = 2 \times 3 \times 5$
Banana = $70 = 2 \times 5 \times 7$
Raspberries = $90 = 2 \times 3^2 \times 5$
GCF $(30, 70, 90) = 2 \times 5 = 10$ bowls.

6. Answer: C
Explanation: Math class = 2nd day
Science class = 5th day
LCM $(2, 5) = 10$; July 11.

7. Answer: B
Explanation: $42 = 2 \times 3 \times 7$
$49 = 7^2$. LCM $(42, 49) = 2 \times 3 \times 7^2 = 294$

8. Answer: C
Explanation: $a \times b$ = GCF $(a, b) \times$ LCM (a, b)
$78,450 = 2615 \times$ GCF(a,b); GCF$(a,b) = \frac{78450}{2615} = 30$.

9. Answer: 5 packs of energy drink and 4 packs of water.
Explanation: Energy drink $= 8 = 2^3$
Water $= 10 = 2 \times 5$. LCM$(8,10) = 2^3 \times 5 = 40$
$40 \div 8 = 5$ packs of energy drink
$40 \div 10 = 4$ packs of water

10. Answer: D
Explanation: Black hair clip = $20 = 2^2 \times 5$
Yellow hair clip = $36 = 2^2 \times 3^2$
Pink hair clip = $60 = 2^2 \times 3 \times 5$
GCF $(20, 36, 60) = 2^2 = 4$.

11. Answer: 5 groups. In each group, there will be 15 apples, 10 oranges, 8 bananas, and 7 strawberries.
Explanation: Apples = $75 = 3 \times 5^2$
Oranges = $50 = 2 \times 5^2$; Bananas = $40 = 2^3 \times 5$
Strawberries = $35 = 5 \times 7$
GCF$(75, 50, 40, 35) = 5$ groups
$75 \div 5 = 15$ Apples in each group
$50 \div 5 = 10$ Oranges in each group
$40 \div 5 = 8$ Bananas in each group
$35 \div 5 = 7$ Strawberries in each group

12. Answer: n=14, 4 Mushrooms, 5 Onions, and 6 Radish.
Explanation: Mushrooms $= 56 = 2^3 \times 7$
Onions $= 70 = 2 \times 5 \times 7$. Radish $= n$.
GCF $(56, 70, n) = 14 = 2 \times 7$. $n = 14$
$56 \div 14 = 4$ Mushrooms
$70 \div 14 = 5$ Onions
$84 \div 14 = 6$ Radish

13. Answer: C
Explanation: $1568 = 2^5 \times 7^2$
$1248 = 2^5 \times 3 \times 13$
GCF$(1568, 1248) = 2^5 = 32$
$1568, 1248 = 32 \times 49 + 32 \times 39 = 32(49 + 39)$

14. Answer: B
Explanation: $1320 = 2^3 \times 3 \times 5 \times 11$
$825 = 3 \times 5^2 \times 11$
GCF$(1320, 825) = 3 \times 5 \times 11 = 165$
$1320 - 825 = 165 \times 8 + 165 \times 5 = 165(8-5)$

15. Answer: 1944, 5
Explanation: $x \times y =$ GCF $(x, y) \times$ LCM(x, y)
$x \times y = 18 \times 540 = 9720 = 2^3 \times 3^5 \times 5$
Possible answer:
1st number $= 2^3 \times 3^5 = 1944$
2nd number $= 5$

16. Answer: A
Explanation: LCM$(8, 16, 32) = 32$
But 32 is not a perfect square. The next number is $32 + 32 = 64$ that is a perfect square, so, Tom needs $64 \times 64 = 4096$ toy cars

17. Answer: C
Explanation: $a \times b =$ GCF $(a, b) \times$ LCM(a, b)
$56448 = 32 \times$ LCM(a,b)
LCM$(a,b) = \frac{56448}{32} = 1764$

18. Answer: B
Explanation: $a \times b =$ GCF $(a, b) \times$ LCM (a, b)
$51420 = 3428 \times$ GCF (a,b)
GCF $(a,b) = \frac{51420}{3428} = 15$.

19. Answer: C

Explanation: Number = n

$n = 20x_1 + 19 => n + 1 = 20\,(x_1+1)$

$n = 22x_2 + 21 => n + 1 = 22\,(x_2+1)$

$n = 24x_3 + 23 => n + 1 = 24\,(x_3+1)$

$n = 26x_4 + 25 => n + 1 = 26\,(x_4+1)$

Then n+1 is divisible by 20, 22, 24, 26

$20 = 2^2 \times 5$

$22 = 2 \times 11$

$24 = 2^3 \times 3$

$26 = 2 \times 13$

Thus, the smallest number n is

$n+1 = 2^3 \times 3 \times 5 \times 11 \times 13 = 17160 => n = 17160 - 1 = 17159$

20. Answer: 2:44 p.m

Explanation: $32 = 2^5$

$28 = 2^2 \times 7$

LCM(30, 28) $= 2^5 \times 7 = 224$ minutes $= 3$ hours 44 minutes At 2 :44 p.m

2.2 DIVIDE FRACTIONS

1. Answer: C

Explanation: This problem is equivalent to $\frac{5}{9} \times \frac{18}{15}$, which is equal to $\frac{2}{3}$

2. Answer: A

Explanation: Divide Harry's portion of the pie by 9. $\frac{7}{12} \div 9 = \frac{7}{12} \times \frac{1}{9} = \frac{7}{108}$.

3. Answer: D

Explanation: Jack receives half of the pears, so he gets 13 pears. He splits this with her two brothers : $13 \div 3 = \frac{13}{3}$ pears.

4. Answer: B

Explanation: $\frac{7}{10} \div \frac{1}{10} = \frac{7}{10} \times \frac{10}{1} = 7$

5. Answer: A

Explanation: Janet uses $1\frac{5}{4}$ cups of cheese for each pizza.

$6\frac{3}{4} \div 1\frac{5}{4} = \frac{27}{4} \div \frac{9}{4} = \frac{27}{4} \times \frac{4}{9} = 3$

6. Answer: C

Explanation: Tom has apple $= 4\frac{4}{5}$

Orange $= 1\frac{3}{5}$

$4\frac{4}{5} \div 1\frac{3}{5} = \frac{24}{5} \div \frac{8}{5} = \frac{24}{5} \times \frac{5}{8} = 3$ times

7. Answer: D

Explanation: $4\frac{1}{2} \div \frac{3}{4} = \frac{9}{2} \div \frac{3}{4} = \frac{9}{2} \times \frac{4}{3} = 6$

8. Answer: B

Explanation: Apple juice $= 14\frac{2}{2} \div \frac{5}{4} = \frac{30}{2} \times \frac{4}{5} = 12$

Orange juice $= 15\frac{4}{3} \div \frac{7}{3} = \frac{49}{3} \times \frac{3}{7} = 7$

9. Answer: A

Explanation: Hector has onion $= 7\frac{3}{5}$

Garlic $= 3\frac{4}{5}$

$7\frac{3}{5} \div 3\frac{4}{5} = \frac{38}{5} \div \frac{19}{5} = \frac{38}{5} \times \frac{5}{19} = 2$ times

10. Answer: B

Explanation: The product of two fraction $= 44\frac{1}{3}$

One of the fraction $= \frac{19}{30}$

$44\frac{1}{3} \div \frac{19}{30} = \frac{133}{3} \times \frac{30}{19} = 70$

11. Answer: 12 m

Explanation:

$85\frac{4}{4} \div 7\frac{1}{6} = \frac{344}{4} \div \frac{43}{6} = \frac{344}{4} \times \frac{6}{43} = 12$ m

12. Answer: D

Explanation: Adam has $= \$ 130176$

Price of one television $= \$ 90\frac{2}{5}$

$\$ 130176 \div \$ 90\frac{2}{5} = 130176 \div \frac{452}{5} = 130176 \times \frac{5}{452} = 1,440$

13. Answer: $\frac{4}{13}$

Explanation:

$\frac{8}{13} \div 2 = \frac{8}{13} \div \frac{2}{1} = \frac{8}{13} \times \frac{1}{2} = \frac{2 \times 2 \times 2}{13 \times 2} = \frac{4}{13}$

14. Answer: C

Explanation: $3\frac{3}{5} \div 3 = \frac{18}{5} \div \frac{3}{1} = \frac{18}{5} \times \frac{3}{1} = \frac{6}{5}$

15. Answer: B

Explanation: Max collected $\frac{2}{9}$ of a pound of potatoes. He has to divide them equally among 8 baskets.

$\frac{2}{9} \div 8 = \frac{2}{9} \div \frac{8}{1} = \frac{2}{9} \times \frac{1}{8} = \frac{1}{36}$ of a pound.

16. Answer: A

Explanation: $\frac{2}{5} \div 5 = \frac{2}{5} \div \frac{5}{1} = \frac{2}{5} \times \frac{1}{5} = \frac{2}{25}$

17. Answer: 2 chocolates
Explanation: $\frac{1}{7} \div 6 = \frac{1}{7} \div \frac{6}{1} = \frac{1}{7} \times \frac{6}{1} = \frac{1}{42}$
$84 \times \frac{1}{42} = 2$ chocolates

18. Answer: C
Explanation: $7\frac{3}{9} \div 9 = \frac{45}{6} \div \frac{9}{1} = \frac{45}{6} \times \frac{1}{9} = \frac{1}{42}$

19. Answer: D
Explanation: Shaded part $= \frac{3}{4}$
Divided into 4 vertical columns $= \frac{3}{4} \div 4$

20. Answer: $\frac{1}{32}$
Explanation: $\frac{1}{8} \div 4 = \frac{1}{8} \div \frac{4}{1} = \frac{1}{8} \times \frac{1}{4} = \frac{1}{32}$

2.3 EXPRESSIONS WITH FRACTIONS

1. Answer: D
Explanation:

$$\frac{1 + \dfrac{1}{1 + \frac{1}{5}}}{1 + \dfrac{1}{1 - \frac{1}{5}}} = \frac{1 + \dfrac{1}{\frac{6}{5}}}{1 + \dfrac{1}{\frac{4}{5}}} = \frac{1 + \frac{5}{6}}{1 + \frac{5}{4}}$$

$$= \frac{\frac{11}{6}}{\frac{9}{4}} = \frac{11}{6} \times \frac{4}{9} = \frac{22}{27}$$

2. Answer: A
Explanation:

$$\frac{7x}{y} = \frac{7 \times 1\frac{1}{7}}{\frac{7}{8}} = \frac{7 \times \frac{8}{7}}{\frac{7}{8}} = 8 \times \frac{8}{7} = \frac{64}{7}$$

$$\frac{x}{7y} = \frac{1\frac{1}{7}}{7 \times \frac{7}{8}} = \frac{\frac{8}{7}}{\frac{49}{8}} = \frac{8}{7} \times \frac{8}{49} = \frac{64}{343}$$

$$\frac{7x}{y} - \frac{x}{7y} = \frac{64}{7} - \frac{64}{343} = \frac{3136 - 64}{343} = \frac{3072}{343} = 8\frac{328}{343}$$

3. Answer: C
Explanation: Prince's share $= \frac{3}{8} \times \$240$
Peter's share $= \left(\frac{3}{8} \times \$240\right) \div 2$
Philip's share $= \$240 - \left(\frac{3}{8} \times \$240 + \left(\left(\frac{3}{8} \times \$240\right) \div 2\right)\right) = \$240 - (\$90 + \$45) = \$105$

4. Answer: B
Explanation: $\frac{3}{4}y - \frac{13}{16} - \frac{5}{8}$ $\frac{3}{4}y = \frac{3}{16}$

$$y = \frac{3}{16} \div \frac{3}{4} = \frac{3}{16} \times \frac{3}{4} = \frac{1}{4}$$

5. Answer: A
Explanation: Left: $3\frac{2}{4} - \frac{6}{7} = \frac{14}{4} - \frac{6}{7} = \frac{74}{28} = \frac{34}{14}$ m

Two pieces: $= \frac{5}{28} \times 2 = \frac{10}{28} = \frac{5}{14}$ m

Yes, there is enough ribbon

6. Answer: Total length $= 15\frac{1}{2}$, Difference $= \frac{3}{2}$
Explanation:

Total length $= 1\frac{1}{2} \times 2 + 2 \times 2 + 2\frac{1}{2} + 3 \times 2 = 3 + 4 + \frac{5}{2} + 6 = \frac{31}{2}$

$= 15\frac{1}{2}$,   Difference $3 - 1\frac{1}{2} = 3 - \frac{3}{2} = \frac{3}{2}$

7. Answer: <
Explanation:
$$\left(\frac{5}{6} + \frac{10}{11} \div \frac{5}{11}\right) \times \frac{1}{15} = \left(\frac{5}{6} + \frac{10}{11} \times \frac{11}{5}\right) \times \frac{1}{15} = \left(\frac{5}{6} + 2\right) \times \frac{1}{15} =$$
$$\frac{17}{6} \times \frac{1}{15} = \frac{17}{90}$$
$$\left(\frac{5}{6} + \frac{10}{11}\right) \div \frac{5}{11} \times \frac{1}{15} = \frac{115}{66} \times \frac{11}{5} \times \frac{1}{15} = \frac{23}{90}$$
$$\frac{17}{90} < \frac{23}{90}$$

8. Answer: C
Explanation: $\left(\frac{5}{6} - \frac{1}{12}\right) \times \frac{7}{9} = \frac{9}{12} \times \frac{7}{9} = \frac{7}{12}$

9. Answer: D
Explanation: $\left(\frac{9}{2} + \frac{5}{18}\right) \div \frac{14}{27} = \frac{1}{2} \times \frac{27}{14} = \frac{27}{28}$

10. Answer: Ben should order $= 12$ muffins
Explanation: Number of friends $= 18$
Each gets $= \frac{1}{12}$
Total $= 18 \times \frac{1}{12} = \frac{3}{2}$ muffins
Ben should order $= 12$ muffins

11. Answer: B
Explanation: Working $= \frac{2}{8} \times 24$ hours
Resting $= \frac{1}{4} \times 24$ hours
Altogether $= \frac{2}{8} \times 24 + \frac{1}{4} \times 24 = 6 + 6 = 12$ hours

273

12. Answer: C

Explanation: Cocoa powder = $3\frac{1}{2}$

Sugar = $\frac{1}{4}$

Cocoa butter = $1\frac{3}{4}$

Altogether = $3\frac{1}{2}+\frac{1}{4}+1\frac{3}{4}$ Cups

Number of chocolates = 10

Per one chocolate = $(3\frac{1}{2}+\frac{1}{4}+1\frac{3}{4})\div 10$

= $(\frac{7}{2}+\frac{1}{4}+\frac{7}{4})\div 10=\frac{22}{7}\times\frac{1}{10}=\frac{11}{20}$ cups

13. Answer: A

Explanation: Number of pears = 11

Martin leaves = $\frac{1}{6}\times 11$ pears

The rest = $11-\frac{1}{6}\times 11$ pears

Number of friends = 5

Each friend gets = $(11-\frac{1}{6}\times 11)\div 7=(11-\frac{11}{6})\times\frac{1}{7}=$

$\frac{55}{6}\times\frac{1}{7}=\frac{55}{42}=1\frac{13}{42}$ pears

14. Answer: C

Explanation: Demi had = $4\frac{1}{2}$ kg

Demi kept for herself = $1\frac{3}{4}$ kg

Remaining amount of flour $4\frac{1}{2}-1\frac{3}{4}$ kg

Brother's share = $4\frac{1}{2}-1\frac{3}{4}\div 2=\frac{11}{4}\times\frac{1}{2}=\frac{11}{8}=1\frac{3}{8}$ kg

15. Answer: B

Explanation: Distance walk by Roy = $5\frac{1}{5}$ miles

Distance walk by Ari = $5\frac{1}{5}+2\frac{1}{10}$ miles

Total distance ran in three days =

$5\frac{1}{5}+(5\frac{1}{5}+2\frac{1}{10})\times 3=\frac{26}{5}+(\frac{26}{5}+\frac{73}{10})\times 3=$

$(\frac{26}{5}+\frac{125}{10})\times 3=\frac{177}{10}\times 3=53\frac{1}{10}$

16. Answer: B

Explanation: Number of balls = 50

Red balls = $\frac{1}{5}\times 50$

Remaining number of balls = $50-\frac{1}{5}\times 50$

Number of blue balls =

$(50-\frac{1}{5}\times 50)\div 2=(50-10)\div 2=40\div 2=20$

17. Answer: $\frac{9}{14}$ **of a project**

Explanation:

Portion finished on Wednesday = $\frac{1}{7}$

Portion finished on Thursday = $\frac{1}{7}+\frac{1}{14}$

Portion left to finish = $1-(\frac{1}{7}+(\frac{1}{7}+\frac{1}{14}))=$

$1-\frac{5}{14}=\frac{9}{14}$ of a project

18. Answer: Kelly gave 4 times more saving

Explanation: Lara's part = $\frac{1}{8}$

Maya's part = $\frac{3}{8}$

Kelly's part = $1-(\frac{1}{8}+\frac{3}{8})$

Kelly gave = $\dfrac{1-\frac{1}{8}+\frac{3}{8}}{\frac{1}{8}}=\dfrac{1-\frac{1}{2}}{\frac{1}{8}}=\frac{1}{2}\times\frac{8}{1}=4$ times more saving.

19. Answer: C

Explanation: Each day = $\frac{5}{9}$ miles

During eight days = $\frac{5}{9}\times 8$ miles

9th day = $1\frac{1}{9}$ miles

Total = $\frac{5}{9}\times 8+1\frac{1}{9}=\frac{40}{9}+\frac{10}{9}=\frac{50}{9}=5\frac{5}{9}$ miles

20. Answer: $\frac{1}{3}$

Explanation: Number of friends = 5

Portion each ate = $\frac{2}{15}$

Portion left = $1-\frac{2}{15}\times 5=1-\frac{2}{3}=\frac{1}{3}$

2.4 CHAPTER REVIEW

1. Answer: B

Explanation: $256=2^8$

$728=2^3\times 7\times 13$

$GCF(256, 728)=2^3=8$

2. Answer: C

Explanation: $198=2\times 3^2\times 11$

$352=2^5\times 11$

$LCM(198, 352)=2^5\times 3^2\times 11=3,168$

3. Answer: 3,456, and 5
Explanation: $a \times b = GCF\ (a, b) \times LCM(a, b)$
$a \times b = 24 \times 720 = 17280 = 2^7 \times 3^3 \times 5$
Possible answer:
1st number $= 2^7 \times 3^3 = 3,456$
2nd number $= 5$

4. Answer: A
Explanation: $a \times b = GCF\ (a, b) \times LCM(a, b)$
$68356 = 46 \times LCM(a,b)$
$LCM(a,b) = \frac{68356}{46} = 1486$

5. Answer: C
Explanation: $15\frac{3}{4} \div 9 = \frac{63}{4} \div \frac{9}{1} = \frac{63}{4} \times \frac{1}{9} = \frac{7}{4}$

6. Answer: D
Explanation: $5\frac{2}{6} \div 8 = \frac{32}{6} \div \frac{8}{1} = \frac{32}{6} \times \frac{1}{8} = \frac{2}{3}$

7. Answer: B
Explanation: $5\frac{1}{2} \div 11 = \frac{11}{2} \div \frac{11}{1} = \frac{11}{2} \times \frac{1}{11} = \frac{1}{2}$

8. Answer: A
Explanation: Amount of time spent with the parrot $= \frac{6}{11} \times 3$
Amount of time feeding the parrot $= \frac{2}{11} \times 2$
Total amount of time spent with the parrot =
$(\frac{6}{11} \times 3) + (\frac{2}{11} \times 2)$ hours

9. Answer: C
Explanation: $\frac{1}{3}m = \frac{11}{18} - \frac{7}{12}$
$\frac{1}{3}m = \frac{1}{36}$
$m = \frac{1}{36} \div \frac{1}{3} = \frac{1}{36} \times \frac{3}{1} = \frac{1}{12}$

10. Answer: Total length $= 27\frac{1}{2}$, Difference $= \frac{5}{2}$
Explanation: Total length =
$1\frac{1}{2} + 2 \times 3 + 2\frac{1}{2} + 3 \times 2 + 3\frac{1}{2} + 4 \times 2$
$= \frac{3}{2} + 6 + \frac{5}{2} + 6 + \frac{7}{2} + 8 = \frac{15}{2} + 20 = \frac{55}{2} = 27\frac{1}{2}$
Difference $= 4 - 1\frac{1}{2} = 4 - \frac{3}{2} = \frac{5}{2}$

11. Answer: A
Explanation: $84 = 2^2 \times 3 \times 7$
$112 = 2^4 \times 7$
$LCM\ (84, 112) = 2^4 \times 3 \times 7 = 336$

12. Answer: B
Explanation: Randy has = \$94,604
Price of one smartphone $= \$87\frac{5}{4}$
$\$94604 \div \$87\frac{5}{4} = 94604 \div \frac{353}{4} = 94604 \times \frac{4}{353}$
$= 1,072$

13. Answer: D
Explanation: $2 \div \frac{1}{6} = 2 \times \frac{6}{1} = 12$

14. Answer: B
Explanation: Distance to shop $= 3\frac{1}{2}$ miles
Distance to work $= 1\frac{2}{4}$ miles
Distance from work to home $= 1\frac{7}{4}$ miles
Number of days $= 8$
Total distance covered =
$(3\frac{1}{2} + 1\frac{2}{4} + 1\frac{7}{4} \times 8) = (\frac{7}{2} + \frac{6}{4} + \frac{11}{4}) \times 8 = \frac{31}{4} \times 8 = 62$ miles

15. Answer: C
Explanation: Portion of cheesecake eaten during the celebration $= \frac{19}{31}$
Portion of cheesecake eaten next day =
$\frac{1}{3} \times (1 - \frac{19}{31}) = \frac{1}{3} \times \frac{12}{31} = \frac{4}{31}$
Total portions consumed $= \frac{19}{31} + \frac{4}{31} = \frac{23}{31}$
Portion of cheesecake left $= 1 - \frac{23}{31} = \frac{8}{31}$

16. Answer: A
Explanation: Aaron practiced violin for = $2\frac{1}{2}$ hours
This month he should practice $= 20\frac{5}{2}$ hours
$20\frac{5}{2} \div 2\frac{1}{2} = \frac{45}{2} \div \frac{5}{2} = \frac{25}{2} \times \frac{2}{5} = 5$ times

17. Answer: 61
Explanation: Number of mangoes $=64=2^6$
Number of cherries $=84=2^2 \times 3 \times 7$
Number of oranges $=104=2^3 \times 13$
Number of plants in each row GCF
$(64, 84, 104)=2^2=4$
Number of mango rows $=64 \div 4=14$
Number of cherry rows $=84 \div 4=21$
Number of orange rows $=104 \div 4=26$
Total number of rows $=14+21+26=61$

18. Answer: $17\frac{1}{3}$kg
Explanation: Total weight of watermelon =
$(2\frac{4}{4} \times 3)+(2\frac{1}{2} \times 2)+1\frac{7}{3}$
$=(\frac{12}{4} \times 3)+(\frac{5}{2} \times 2)+\frac{10}{3}=9+5+\frac{10}{3}$
$= \frac{27+15+10}{3}=\frac{52}{3}=17\frac{1}{3}$ kg

19. Answer: B
Explanation:
$21\frac{2}{3} \div 13=\frac{65}{3} \div \frac{13}{1} =\frac{65}{3} \times \frac{1}{13} = \frac{5}{3}$.

20. Answer: C
Explanation: $\frac{5}{8} \div 8=\frac{5}{8} \div \frac{8}{1}= \frac{5}{8} \times \frac{1}{8} = \frac{5}{64}$.

3. FACTORS AND MULTIPLES

3.1 IDENTIFY FACTORS

1. Answer: A
Explanation:
$1 \times 33=33$
$3 \times 11=33$
List of factors is 1 , 3 , 11, 33.

2. Answer: B
Explanation: $2+3+4+5+6=20$
Password: 123456, because $1+20=21$ is divisible by both 3 and 7.

3. Answer: C
Explanation: $1 \times 15=15$
$3 \times 5=15$
List of factors is 1 , 3 , 5, 15.

4. Answer: D
Explanation: Michale's number : 30*
It must end with 0 or 5, but it is an odd number, so it ends with 5. Hence, Michale's number is 315. 315 is divisible by 5 and by 7, and is not divisible by 2. So, 315 is the correct answer.

5. Answer: B
Explanation: $2 \times 18 = 36$
$3 \times 12 = 36$
$4 \times 9 = 36$
$6 \times 6 = 36$
List of factors is 2, 3 , 4, 6, 9, 12, 18.

6. Answer: C
Explanation: When she puts the pens in groups of 6; $55 = 9 \times 6 = 54+1$, then 1 extra pen is left. When she puts the pens in groups of 5, $55 = 11 \times 5 = 55$, no extra pen is left, so option C is correct.

7. Answer: A
Explanation: $2 \times 9=18$
$3 \times 6=18$
List of prime factors 2 , 3.

8. Answer: D
Explanation: $4 = 2 \times 2$
$24 = 3 \times 2 \times 2 \times 2$
$28 = 7 \times 2 \times 2$
$42 = 7 \times 3 \times 2$
the smallest number is $168 = 7 \times 3 \times 2 \times 2 \times 2$. So option D is correct.

9. Answer: A
Explanation: $2 \times 30 = 60$
$3 \times 20 = 60$
$4 \times 15 = 60$
$5 \times 12 = 60$
$6 \times 10 = 60$
List of prime factors 2 , 3, 5.

10. Answer: B
Explanation: $107 \times 18 + 107 \times 42 = 107 \times 18 + 42 = 107 \times 60$; 107 is a prime number
Factors of 60: 1, 2, 3, 4, 5, 6, 10, 12, 15, 20, 30, 60
So, 9 is not a factor of 60.
The correct option is B.

11. Answer: C
Explanation: $3 \times 15 = 45$
$5 \times 9 = 45$
List of prime factors 3, 5

12. Answer: C
Explanation: The number must end with 0, the sum of two remaining digits is 8.
$8 = 8 + 0 = 1 + 7 = 2 + 6 = 3 + 5 = 4 + 4$
The possible numbers are: 800, 530, 170, 260, 710, 350, 620, 440
So, the smallest 3-digit number is 170.

13. Answer: D
Explanation: Number 33 : $3 \times 11 = 33$, The prime factors are 3, 11. Number 44: $4 \times 11 = 44$, The prime factors are 4, 11. The greatest common prime factor of 33 and 44 is 11.

14. Answer: 15 years, 39 years, and 65 years
Explanation: 195 has factors 1, 3, 5, 13, 15, 39, 65, 195. The older brother is 15 years, the father is 39 years old and grandfather is 65 years old.

15. Answer: B
Explanation: Number 28 : $2 \times 14 = 28$
$4 \times 7 = 28$. The prime factors are 2, 7
Number 63 : $3 \times 21 = 63$. $7 \times 9 = 63$
The prime factors are 3, 7. The greatest common prime factor of 28 and 63 is 7.

16. Answer: B
Explanation: $5 \times 15 = 75$; $3 \times 25 = 75$
List of prime factors 3, 5.

17. Answer: C
Explanation: $5 \times 8 = 40$ chocolates;
$40 \div 10 = 4$ new boxes. Yes, students are able to redistribute the chocolates into 4 boxes.

18. Answer: A
Explanation: $9 \times 12 = 108$ pencils bought
$18 \times 6 = 108$ pencils needed. Yes, the teacher was able to divide pencils so that each student receives 6 pencils.

19. Answer: C
Explanation: Number 18 : $2 \times 3 \times 3 = 18$
The prime factors are 2, 3
Number 36 : $2 \times 2 \times 3 \times 3 = 36$
The prime factors are 2, 3; The greatest common prime factor of 18 and 36 is 3.

20. Answer: D
Explanation: In the given options, 42 is divisible only by 7 and not divisible by 4, 5, 9. $42 \div 7 = 6$. There should be 7 members on the team and each member should swim 6 laps.

3.2 IDENTIFY MULTIPLES

1. Answer: 7, 14, 21, 28, 35
Explanations: Multiples of 7: 7, 14, 21, 28, 35.

2. Answer: C
Explanations: $3 \times 5 = 15$ days. 3rd March + 12 days = 15th March, So option C is correct.

3. Answer: 12, 24, 36, 48, 60
Explanations: Multiples of 12: 12, 24, 36, 48, 60.

4. Answer: 96 stickers
Explanations:

Weeks	Number of stickers
1	24
2	48
3	72
4	96

Number of stickers, Sheena will have at the end of 4 weeks = 96 stickers.

5. Answer: 18, 36, 54, 72, 90.
Explanations: Multiples of 18: 18, 36, 54, 72, 90.

6. Answer: 4
Explanations: Prime number between 4 and 6 is 5. Number of car toys: 8 × 5 = 40
Number of car toys in each 10 rows: 40÷10=4.

7. Answer: 24, 32, 40, 56, 72
Explanations: Multiples of 8: 24, 32, 40, 56, 72

8. Answer: C
Explanations: 42−12=30 is not a multiple of 4.

9. Answer: 10, 15, 20, 35, 45
Explanations: Multiples of 5: 10, 15, 20, 35, 45

10. Answer: B
Explanations: The smallest 3-digit number: 100. Multiple of 3, 5 and 7: 105
105 is not a multiple of 4 and 6.

11. Answer: 14 and 28
Explanations: Multiples of 2: 2, 4, 6, 8, 10,12,14,16,18,20,22,24,26,28,30,32,34,36, ...
Multiples of 7: 7, 14, 21, 28, 35, 42, 49, ...
Two common multiples of 2 and 7: 14 and 28

12. Answer: B
Explanations: 24 = 9 + 8 + 7
Possible number: 987, 879, 798, 978, 897, 789
To be a multiple 4, the number must be an even number. The even numbers are 798 and 978, but the numbers are not a multiple of 4.

13. Answer: 15 and 30
Explanations: Multiples of 3: 3, 6, 9, 12, 15, 18, 21, 24, 27, 30, 33, 36, 39, ...
Multiples of 5: 5, 10, 15, 20, 25, 30, 35, ...
Two common multiples of 3 and 5: 15 and 30

14. Answer: 15, 51, 45, 54, 75, 57
Explanations:
Possible numbers: 15, 51, 45, 54, 75, 57

15. Answer: 7, 34, 51, 68, 85.
Explanations: Multiples of 17: 17, 34, 51, 68, 85

16. Answer: 44, 45; 80, 81
Explanations: Multiples of 4: 4, 8, 12, 16, 20, 24, 28, 32, 36, 40, 44, 48, 52, 56, 60, 64, 68, 72, 76, 80, …
Multiples of 9: 9, 18, 27, 36, 45, 54, 63, 72, 81, …
Consecutive pairs of multiples 4 and 9:   44, 45; 80, 81

17. Answer: 36 and 72
Explanations: Multiples of 4: 4, 8, 12, 16, 20 ,24, 28, 32, 36, 40, 44, 48, 52, 56, 60, 64, 68, 72, …
Multiples of 9:   9, 18, 27, 36, 45, 54, 63, 72, 81, 90, ……
Two common multiples of 4 and 9: 36 and 72

18. Answer: 105 photos
Explanations: Number of photos: 35 × 3 = 105
David put 105 photos into the album.

19. Answer: 9, 18, 36, 45, 63, 81
Explanations: Multiples of 9: 9, 18, 36, 45, 63, 81

20. Answer: 180 cards
Explanations: Minimum number: 12 × 15=180 cards. Peter is playing with 180 cards.

3.3 PRIME FACTORIZATION

1. Answer: 11, 12, 13
Explanation: $1,716 = 2 × 2 × 3 × 11 × 13$
Factors: 1, 2, 3, 4, 6, 11, 12, 13, 22, 26, 33, 39, 44, 52, 66, 78, ….
11, 12, 13 are three consecutive numbers with a product of 1,716.

2. Answer: 4 × 9=36
Explanation: Two smallest non-unit perfect squares: 4 and 9 have the product of 36.

3. Answer: C
Explanation: $12×250×70=(2×2×3)×(5×5×5×2)×(2×5×7) = 2^4 × 3 × 5^4 × 7$

4. Answer: A
Explanation: $30×28×144×60=(2×3×5)×(2×2×7)×(12×12)×(2×2×3×5)= 2^5×3^2×5^2×7×12^2$

5. Answer: 30
Explanation: $2 \times 3 \times 5 \times 11 = 330$
$330 \div 10 = 33$
$$\frac{24+28+21+42+46+50+19+32+38+x}{10} = 33$$
$300 + x = 330$
$x = 330 - 300 = 30$

6. Answer: $2^4 \times 17$
Explanation: Prime factorization of $2^4 + 4^4 =$
$2^4 + 2^8 = 2^4(1 + 2^4) = 2^4(1 + 16) = 2^4 \times 17$

7. Answer: 12 months, $42
Explanation: $616 - $112 = 504
$504 = 2^2 \times 3 \times 42$
12 months, She paid $42 each month.

8. Answer: 37 hours at a rate or 18 mph
Explanation: $666 = 2 \times 3^2 \times 37$
Lisa could spend
2 hours at a rate 333 mph (impossible)
3 hours at a rate 222 mph (impossible)
37 hours at a rate or 18 mph (possible)

9. Answer: 10 potatoes in each row.
Explanation: $320 = 2^6 \times 5$
The greatest number of rows = 32
The minimum number of potatoes in each row = 10

10. Answer: C
Explanation: $111 = 3 \times 37$ (accept)
$112 = 24 \times 7$ (reject)
113 is a prime number (reject)
$114 = 2 \times 3 \times 19$ (reject)

11. Answer: 7 baskets with 17 mangoes in each.
Explanation: $119 = 7 \times 17$
7 baskets with 17 mangoes in each.

12. Answer: A
Explanation: $21,560 = 2^3 \times 5^1 \times 7^2 \times 11 = 8 \times 5 \times 49 \times 11$

13. Answer: B
Explanation: $18 = 3 \times 3 \times 2$
$18 = 3^2 \times 2$

14. Answer: $80 = 2 \times 5 \times 8$
Explanation: $80 = 2 \times 5 \times 8$
The Different possible dimensions of the box are:
1 cm × 1 cm × 80 cm
1 cm × 2 cm × 40 cm
1 cm × 8 cm ×10 cm
2 cm × 5 cm × 8 cm
2 cm × 4 cm × 10 cm
2 cm × 2 cm × 20 cm.

15. Answer: D
Explanation: $1,044 = 2^2 \times 3^2 \times 29$
Prime factor less than 30 is 29
Length = 36 m, Width = 29 m.

16. Answer: $186 = 2 \times 3 \times 31$
Explanation: $186 = 2 \times 3 \times 31$
Possible answers:
186 pages per day on 1 day
93 pages per day on 2 day
62 pages per day on 3 day
31 pages per day on 6 day.

17. Answer: $36 = 2^2 \times 3^2$
Explanation: $36 = 2^2 \times 3^2$
Possible box dimensions: 1m × 36m
2m × 18m
3m × 12m
4m × 9m

18. Answer: A
Explanation: $24 = 2 \times 2 \times 2 \times 3$
$24 = 2^3 \times 3$

19. Answer: C
Explanation: $1,564 = 2^2 \times 17 \times 23$
Prime factor greater than 20 is a=23
Blessy has $1,564 \div 23 = 68$ followers.

20. Answer: D
Explanation: $6,664 = 2^3 \times 7^2 \times 17$
The greatest possible prime number of waiters is 17, each gets $392.

ANSWERS AND EXPLANATIONS

1. Answer: A
Explanation: 1 × 44 = 44;
4 × 11 = 44
List of factors is 1, 4, 11, 44.

2. Answer: 17, 34, 51, 68, 85
Explanation: Multiples of 17: 17, 34, 51, 68, 85

3. Answer: B
Explanation: 101 is a prime number (reject)
102 = 2 ×3×17 (reject)
106 = 2 ×53 (accept)
113 is a prime number (reject)

4. Answer: C
Explanation: 3 + 4 + 5 + 6 + 8 = 26
Password: 734568, because 7+26 = 33 is
divisible by both 3 and 11.

5. Answer: 27, 36, 45, 63, 72
Explanation: Multiples of 9: 27, 36, 45, 63, 72.

6. Answer: x = 30
Explanation: $(2×52×7)=350$
$350÷10=35$
$$\frac{22+26+19+38+44+48+17+30+36+x}{10}=35$$
$320 + x = 350$
$x = 350 - 320 = 30.$

7. Answer: B
Explanation: Mike's number : 24*
It must end with 0 or 5, but it is an odd
number, so it ends with 5. Mike's number is
245.
245 is divisible by 5 and by 7, and is not
divisible by 2. So, 245 is the correct answer.

8. Answer: D
Explanation: 1 × 24 = 24
2 × 12 =24
3 × 8 = 24
4 × 6 = 24, List of prime factors 2 , 3

9. Answer: A
Explanation: $35 ×28×169×90=(7×5)×(2×2×7)×$
$(13×13)×(2×3×3×5)= 2^3×3^2×5^2×7^2×13^2$

10. Answer: C
Explanation: Smallest 3-digit number: 100
Multiple of 3, 4 and 6 : 108
108 is not multiple of 5 and 7

11. Answer: B
Explanation: $15×375×105=(5×3)×(5×5×5×3)×$
$(3×5×7)=3^3×5^5×7$

12. Answer: 36 and 72
Explanation: Multiples of 4: 4, 8, 12, 16, 20, 24,
28, 32, 36, 40, 44, 48, 52, 56, 60, 64, 68, 72, ...
Multiples of 9: 9, 18, 27, 36, 45, 54, 63, 72, 81, 90,
....
Two common multiples of 4 and 9: 36 and 72.

13. Answer: 19 years, 38 years, and 95 years
Explanation: 190 has factors 1, 2, 5, 10, 19, 38,
95, and 190. The older sister is 19 years, the
mother is 38 years old and the grandmother
is 95 years old.

14. Answer: A
Explanations: 23 = 9 + 8 + 6
Possible number: 986, 869, 698, 968, 896, 689
To be a multiple of 4, the number must be
an even number. The even numbers are 986,
698, 968 and 896. 968, 896 are the only two
numbers that are multiple of 4.

15. Answer: D
Explanation: Number 22 : 2× 11=22, The
prime factors are 2, 11. Number 55 : 5× 11= 55,
The prime factors are 5, 11. So, the greatest
common prime factor of 22 and 55 is 11.

16. Answer: 270=2×3×45
Explanation: 270=2×3×45
Possible answers:
270 pages per day on 1 day
135 pages per day on 2 day
90 pages per day on 3 day
45 pages per day on 6 day

17. Answer: B
Explanation: The smallest 3-digit number is 100. 100+123 = 223 is not divisible by 9. The smallest sum divisible by 9 is 225, then x+123=225, x=225-123=102, so x= 102.

18. Answer: C
Explanation: No of greeting cards: 108
Greeting cards in each pack: 12
Number of packs: 108÷12=9 or 108 = 12×9
Steffi bought 9 packs of greeting cards.

19. Answer: A
Explanation: 105 =3×5×7

20. Answer: D
Explanation: In the given options, 49 is divisible only by 7 and not divisible by 4, 5, 9. 49÷7 = 7. There should be 7 members in the team and each member should swim 7 laps.

4. EXPONENTS

4.1 MULTIPLICATION EXPRESSIONS

1.Answer: 5×5×5
125
Explanation: Expanded form 5×5×5
Standard form 125.

2. Answer: 3^5
3×3×3×3×3
Explanation: Exponential form 3^5
Expanded form 3×3×3×3×3.

3. Answer: 9×9×9
729
Explanation: Expanded form 9×9×9
Standard form 729.

4. Answer: 7^3
7×7×7
Explanation: Exponential form 73
Expanded form 7×7×7.

5. Answer: 6^4
Explanation: 6×6×6×6.

6. Answer: A
Explanation: 8×8×8×8×8×8×8×8 = 8^8.

7. Answer: 39
Explanation: 4^3-5^2 = 64-25 = 39.

8. Answer: 271
Explanation: 10^3-9^3 = 1000-729 = 271.

9. Answer: 27
Explanation: $6^3÷2^3$ = 216÷8 = 27.

10. Answer: 5910
Explanation:
$6×(9^3 + 4^4)$ = 6×(729 + 256) = 6×985 = 5910.

11. Answer: 18
Explanation: $8^2-6^2-3^2-4^0$ = 64-36-9-1 = 18.

12. Answer: B
Explanation: 4a = 120→a = 30
Area = a^2 = 30^2 = 900 cm^2.

13. Answer: C
Explanation: Volume of a cube = a^3 = 343
Edge of the cube = a = $^3\sqrt{343}$ = 7 cm.

14. Answer: C
Explanation:
$3^5×3$ = 3×3×3×3×3×3 = 3^6 = 729 miles.

15. Answer: B
Explanation: 9×3×27=729=3^6 slices.

16. Answer: B
Explanation: 46656÷(6×36)=216=6^3 small packages.

17. Answer: A
Explanation: Width = 5^3 cm
Length = $5^3×5$ = 5^4 cm
Area = $5^3×5^4$ = 78,125 cm^2.

18. Answer: A
Explanation: 81×9×3=2187=3^7 apples.

19. Answer: C
Explanation: 2×256-4×64+3×32-5×16+6×1
=512-256+96-80+6=278.

20. Answer: C
Explanation:
Chris's age = x years
Tom's age = y years
$x+y^2 = 208$
$x^2+y = 158$
If x = 12 then $12^2 = 144$, this means x < 12
If x = 13 then $13^2 = 169$, false
If x = 12, then $12^2 = 144$, y = 158 - 144 = 14
Check: 12 + 196 = 208.

4.2 EVALUATE EXPONENTS

1. Answer: 625
Explanation: $(-5)4=(-5)×(-5)×(-5)×(-5)$
=25×25=625

2. Answer: 1
Explanation: $75^0=1$

3. Answer: B
Explanation: $(-8)^3+(3)^6$
$(-8)×(-8)×(-8)+3×3×3×3×3×3$
=(-512)+729
=217

4. Answer: D
Explanation:
$(\frac{1}{4})^3 = \frac{1}{4}×\frac{1}{4}×\frac{1}{4}=\frac{1}{64}$

5. Answer: A
Explanation: $(-\frac{5}{7})^3$
$=-\frac{5}{7}× -\frac{5}{7} × -\frac{5}{7} =-\frac{125}{343}$

6. Answer: C
Explanation: $3^4×4-4^3×3$
3×3×3×3×4-4×4×4×3
=324-192
=132

7. Answer: D
Explanation: $(-4)^4×(-\frac{1}{4})^3$
$=(-4)×(-4)×(-4)×(-4)×(-\frac{1}{4})×(-\frac{1}{4})×(-\frac{1}{4})$
$=256×(-\frac{1}{64})$
$=(-4)$

8. Answer: B
Explanation: $7^{11} × 7^5$;
$7^{11+5} = 7^{16}.$

9. Answer: C
Explanation: $\frac{3^6}{3^2}$
$=3^{6-2} = 3^4$

10. Answer: A
Explanation:
$\frac{10^7}{3×10^5} = \frac{10×10×10×10×10×10×10}{3×10×10×10×10×10}$
$=\frac{10×10}{3}= \frac{100}{3} = 33\frac{1}{3}$

11. Answer: B
Explanation: $x^2=225$
$x=15^2$
x=15 m
Perimeter =4×15=60 m

12. Answer: D
Explanation: $3^5×3^7=3^{12}$

13. Answer: A
Explanation: 4×4×16=256

14. Answer: C
Explanation: $6^2×6^3=6^5=7776$

15. Answer: A
Explanation: Jim: $216
Aaron: $2166 = $1296
1296 = 6 × 6 × 6 × 6 = 6^4

16. Answer: C
Explanation: $4^5÷4=4^4$
$4^4x4^3=4^7$

17. Answer: B
Explanation: $x^2 × x^2=625$
$x^2=25, x^2=5^2, x=5$ in, $A=x^2=25$ in^2

18. Answer: D
Explanation: $64 \times 8 = 8^2 \times 8$
$= 8^{2+1} = 8^3$

19. Answer: C
Explanation: $15 \times 20 = 300 \text{ m}^2$
$300 \text{ m}^2 \times 0.8^2 = 240 \text{ m}^2$

20. Answer: D
Explanation: $5^{5-x} = 625 = 5^4$

$5-x = 4$

$x = 1$

$\left(\frac{1}{5}\right)^{1-x} = \left(\frac{1}{5}\right)^{1-1}$

$\left(\frac{1}{5}\right)^0 = 1$.

4.3 MISSING EXPONENT

1. Answer: B
Explanation: $4^x = 256$
$4 \times 4 \times 4 \times 4 = 256$. Thus, $x = 4$.

2. Answer: C
Explanation: $9^x = 3^6$
$9 \times 9 \times 9 = 3 \times 3 \times 3 \times 3 \times 3 \times 3$
$x = 3$.

3. Answer: A
Explanation: $81^x = 9^2$
$9 \times 9 = 9 \times 9$
$x = 2$.

4. Answer: C
Explanation: $13^2 = 13 \times 13 = 169$
$x = 13$.

5. Answer: C
Explanation: Missing exponent
$5^4 = 5 \times 5 \times 5 \times 5 = 625$
Thus $x = 4$
Missing base
$25^2 = 625$
Thus $x = 25$.

6. Answer: B
Explanation: Missing exponent
$9^4 = 9 \times 9 \times 9 \times 9 = 6561$
Thus $x = 4$
Missing base
$3^8 = 3 \times 3 \times 3 \times 3 \times 3 \times 3 \times 3 \times 3 = 6561$
Thus $x = 3$.

7. Answer: C
Explanation: $17 \times 289 = 17 \times 17^2 = 17^x$
$x = 3$

8. Answer: C
Explanation: Missing exponent
$\left(\frac{1}{18}\right)^2 = \frac{1}{18} \times \frac{1}{18} = \frac{1}{324}$
Thus $x = 2$

Missing base
$\left(\frac{1}{18}\right)^2 = \frac{1}{18} \times \frac{1}{18} = \frac{1}{324}$
Thus $x = \frac{1}{18}$.

9. Answer: B
Explanation: $2 \times 256 \times 4 = 2^x$
$2 \times 2^7 \times 2^2 = 2^x$
$2^{10} = 2^x$
$x = 10$.

10. Answer: A
Explanation: $x^2 = 81$
Width: $x = 9$ m
Length: $3x = 36$ m.

11. Answer: C
Explanation: 1 km = 1,000 m = 1,000 × 100 cm
= 100,000 cm = 100,000 × 10mm
= 1,000,000 mm = 10^6 mm
$x = 6$.

12. Answer: B
Explanation: $42x^2 = 16800$
$x^2 = 400$
$x = 20$
$x^4 = 1,60,000$.

283

13. Answer: A
Explanation: $10,240 = 4x^2 \times 5x$
$20x^3 = 10240$
$x^3 = 512$
$x = 8$
Length: $4x^2 = 4 \times 8^2 = 256$ feet
Width: $5x = 5 \times 8 = 40$ feet

14. Answer: D
Explanation: $5 \times (x^2 \times x^2) = 12,500$
$5x^4 = 12,500$
$x^4 = 2500$
$x^2 = 50$

15. Answer: B
Explanation: $1764 = x^2$
$x = 42$

16. Answer: A
Explanation: $a_1 = 3$
$a_2 = 3 \times 3 = 9$
$a^3 = 9 \times 3 = 27$
$a_4 = 27 \times 3 = 81$
$a_5 = 81 \times 3 = 243$
$a_6 = 243 \times 3 = 729$
$a_7 = 729 \times 3 = 2187$
$a_8 = 2187 \times 3 = 6561$
$a_9 = 6561 \times 3 = 19,683$
$a_{10} = 19683 \times 3 = 59049.$

17. Answer: A
Explanation:
$9 \times 9 = 81$ pieces must be
1st: 1 piece
2nd: 2 pieces
In total: 3 pieces
3rd: 4 pieces
In total: 7 pieces
4th: 8 pieces
In total: 15 pieces
5th: 16 pieces
In total: 31 pieces
6th: 32 pieces
In total: 63 pieces
7th: 64 pieces
8th child will finish.

18. Answer: D
Explanation: $20^4 = 400^2$
$k = 4$
$k^2 = 16$

19. Answer: B
Explanation: Surface area: $6a^2 = 1536^2$
$a^2 = 256$
$a = 16$
Volume: $a^3 = 16^3 = 4096$ cm^3

20. Answer: D
Explanation: $c^3d^2 = 25000$
$c^3d^2 = 1000 \times 25 = 10^3 \times 5^2$
$c = 10$ and $d = 5$

4.4 POWERS OF TENS

1. Answer: C
Explanation: $10000000 = 10^7$

2. Answer: D
Explanation: $\frac{1}{1000} = 10^{-3}$

3. Answer: D
Explanation: $50 = 5 \times 10^1$

4. Answer: C
Explanation: $0.00085 = 8.5 \times 10^{-4}$

5. Answer: B
Explanation: $3.33 \times 10^3 = 3330$

6. Answer: D
Explanation: $7.22321 \times 10^5 = 722321$

7. Answer: C
Explanation: $5.8 \times 10^2 + 0.006 \times 10^3$
$= 580 + 6 = 586.$

8. Answer: A
Explanation:
$88.05 \times 10^5 + 6.54 \times 10^{-1} + 5 \times 10^0$
$= 8805000 + 0.654 + 5$
$= 88,05,005.654$

9. Answer: B
Explanation:
$5200 \div 10^5 + 4.25 = 0.052 + 4.25 = 4.302$

10. Answer: B
Explanation: $(5.2 \times 10^{11}) \times 10^{-8} = 5.2 \times 10^3$

11. Answer: D
Explanation: $(7 \times 10^3) \times (2.4 \times 10^{-6}) = 16.8 \times 10^{-3}$

12. Answer: C
Explanation: $\$50 \div 1000 = \$0.05$

13. Answer: A
Explanation: $(4.8 \times 10^6) \times (4.8 \times 10^6) = 23.04 \times 10^{12}$

14. Answer: A
Explanation: $50 \times 10^{-9} = 5 \times 10^{-8}$

15. Answer: C
Explanation: $(8 \times 10^{15}) \times (6 \times 10^{-11}) = 48 \times 10^4$

16. Answer: A
Explanation: $55800 = 5.58 \times 10^4$

17. Answer: C
Explanation: $8 \times 10^5 = 800000$ gold coins

18. Answer: C
Explanation:
$(10 \times 10^{25}) \div (5 \times 10^5) = (10 \div 5) \times (10^{25} \div 10^5) = 2 \times 10^5$
Should be
$(10 \times 10^{25}) \div (5 \times 10^5) = (10 \div 5) \times (10^{25} \div 10^5) = 2 \times 10^{20}$

19. Answer: B
Explanation:
$\frac{100^{15}}{100^7} \div 10^{-3} = \left(\frac{1}{10}\right)^x$
$\frac{100^{15}}{100^7} \div \frac{1}{1000} = 10^8 \times 1000 = 10^{11}$
$\left(\frac{1}{10}\right)^x = 10^{-x}$
$-x = 11$
$x = -11.$

20. Answer: C
Explanation: $2.2 \times 10^6 = 2200000$ square miles

1. Answer: $5 \times 5 \times 5$
125
Explanation: Expanded form $5 \times 5 \times 5$
Standard form 125

2. Answer: 30
Explanation: $9^2 - 5^2 - 2^4 - 10^1 = 81 - 25 - 16 - 10 = 30.$

3. Answer: C
Explanation: $16 \times 4 \times 64 = 4096 = 4^6$ slices.

4. Answer: A
Explanation: Width $= 6^3$ cm
Length $= 6^3 \times 6 = 6^4$ cm
Area $= 6^3 \times 6^4 = 2,79,936$ cm^2

5. Answer: A
Explanation: Volume of a cube $= a^3 = 729$
Edge of the cube $= a = \sqrt[3]{729} = 9$ cm.

6. Answer: −473
Explanation: $(-9)^3 + (2)^8$
$(-9) \times (-9) \times (-9) + 2 \times 2 \times 2 \times 2 \times 2 \times 2 \times 2 \times 2$
$-729 + 256 = -473.$

7. Answer: B
Explanation: $7^{25} \times 7^{-10}$
$7^{25-10} = 7^{15}$

8. Answer: A
Explanation: $5^4 \div 5 = 5^3$
$5^3 \times 5^2 = 5^5$

9. Answer: D
Explanation: $6^{6-x} = 1296 = 6^4$
$6 - x = 4$
$x = 2$
$\left(\frac{1}{6}\right)^{1-x} = \left(\frac{1}{6}\right)^{1-2}$
$\left(\frac{1}{6}\right)^{-1} = 6$

10. Answer: D
Explanation: $4^6 \times 4^5 = 4^{11}$

11. Answer: D
Explanation: $16^x=4^4$
$16\times16=4\times4\times4\times4$
$x=2$

12. Answer: B
Explanation: Missing exponent
$6^4=6\times6\times6\times6=1296$
Thus $x=4$
Missing base
$36^2=1296$
Thus $x=36$

13. Answer: B
Explanation: $18\times5832=18\times18^3=18^x$
$x=4$

14. Answer: A
Explanation: $x^2=121$
Width:$x=11$ m
Length:$3x=33$ m

15. Answer: A
Explanation: Surface area: $6a^2=1944^2$
$a^2=324$
$a=18$
Volume: $a^3=18^3=5832$ cm^3

16. Answer: B
Explanation: $c^3d^2=11664$
$c^3d^2=729\times16=9^3\times4^2$
$c=9$ and $d=4$

17. Answer: D
Explanation: $0.000095=9.5\times10^{-5}$

18. Answer: A
Explanation: $(8.2\times10^{15})\times10^{-7}=8.2\times10^8$

19. Answer: C
Explanation: $\$80\div1000=\$0.08$

20. Answer: B
Explanation: $4.2\times10^5=420000$ square miles

5. EXPRESSIONS, EQUATIONS, AND INEQUALITIES

5.1 VARIABLE EXPRESSIONS

1. Answer: A
Explanation: Sum of x and 5 :$x+5$

2. Answer: A
Explanation:
One-third of the sum x and 6 :$\frac{1}{3}(x+6)$

3. Answer: B

Expressions	Terms	Co-efficient	Constants
$6x^2 + 8$	$6X^2,8$	6	8

Explanation:
Expression: $6x^2+8$
Terms: $6x^2,8$
Coefficients: 6
Constants:2

4. Answer: D
Explanation: The quotient of x+8 and
9:$(x+8)\div9$
Expression: $\frac{(x+8)}{9}$

5. Answer: C
Explanation: Half of x:$\frac{1}{2}x$
Four decreased by half of x: $4-\frac{1}{2}x$
Expression: $4-\frac{1}{2}x$

6. Answer: D
Explanation: $2x^2-4x+8$, when x = 3
$2(3)^2-4(3)+8 = 18-12+8 = 14$

7. Answer: A
Explanation: $t^2-7u+5ut$, when t=60 and u=40
$(60)^2-7(40)+5(60)(40)=$
$3600 - 280 + 12000 = 15320.$

8. Answer: B
Explanation: Lisa gave 8 books from h,
So, the expression is $h-8$

9. Answer: A
Explanation: 2nd week: x balloons
1st week: x+11 balloons
3rd week: 3x balloons
Total: (x+11)+ x + 3x balloons

10. Answer: D
Explanation: $x^3y - y^3x$, when x=5, y=4
$(5)^3(4)-(4)^3(5)=500-320=180$

11. Answer: C
Explanation: Amount of money John earned working h hours = 8.50h

12. Answer: A
Explanation: Your contribution: $(y+5)
Eight friends' contribution: $8y
Total: $((y+5)+8y)
When y=20, $((y+5)+8y) = $((20+5)+8(20))
= $(25+160) = $185.

13. Answer: D
Explanation: No. of strawberries in a box: 12
Cost of a box with 12 strawberries: $k
Cost of each strawberry in the box: $($\frac{k}{12}$)

14. Answer: A
Explanation: Perimeter: 2(6+(d-4)) cm
When d=12 cm, the perimeter is
2(6+(d-4))=2(6+(12-4))=12+16=28 cm

15. Answer: A
Explanation: Number of pages read: 83
Number of pages read in y hours: xy
Number of pages read after y hours: 83+xy

16. Answer: B
Explanation: Total amount paid for h hours:
$(45+10h) When h=5, $45+10(5) = $95

17. Answer: B
Explanation: Middle side: x cm
Longest side: x+5.5 cm
Shortest side: (x+5.5)-8 cm
Perimeter: ((x+5.5)-8+x+(x+5.5)) cm

18. Answer: C
Explanation: Cost of dinner: $x
Cost of lunch: $0.6x
Cost of I lunches: $(I×0.6x)

19. Answer: C
Explanation: Sum of twice the number a and 4 is b : b=2a+4. Difference of twice the number b and 6: = 2(2a+4)-6 = 4a+2

20. Answer: A
Explanation: The algebraic expression which contains only two terms is called binomial. It is a two-term polynomial. Also, it is called a sum or difference between two or more monomials. It is the simplest form of a polynomial.

5.2 EQUIVALENT EXPRESSIONS

1. Answer: B
Explanation: $x(x-4)+5=x \times x-4 \times x+5 =x^2-4x+5$

2. Answer: B
Explanation:
$m(5-m)+m^3 \times 4m = (m \times 5-m \times m)+4m^4$
$= 4m^4-m^2+5m$

3. Answer: B
Explanation:
$b^3-4b^3+7b^2-2-5b^2+8 = -3b^3+2b^2+5.$

4. Answer: A
Explanation:
$-b-5b^2+8b+9b^2-11+8=4b^2+7b-3$

5. Answer: A
Explanation: Kiraz: 82x+5
Linda: 88y+7. Total: 82x+5+88y+7=82x+88y+12

6. Answer: C
Explanation:
Area of the rectangle: $x(x - 4)= x^2 - 4x.$

7. Answer: A
Explanation: Width: h in
Length: h+8 in
Height: $(h+8)+6=h+14$ in
Volume: $= h(h+8)(h+14) = h^2+8h(h+14)=$
$h^3+14h^2+8h^2+112h$ in^3
When h=15, then the volume is
$15^3+14(15)^2+8(15)^2+112(15) =$
$3375+3150+1800+1680 = 10005$ in^3

8. Answer:6a+4b+14 points
Explanation:
Aaron: $3(a+2)+2b = 3a+2b+6$ points
Robert: $3a+2(b+4) = 3a+2b+8$ points
Total number of points of two basketball
players: $3a+2b+6+3a+2b+8=6a+4b+14$ points

9. Answer: D
Explanation: $\$a\times(a+8)=\$(a^2+8a)$

10. Answer: A
Explanation: $4c-5+15-2c=2c+10=2(c+5)$
Pizza slices Becky ordered from "Pizza House":
$2(c+5)$

11. Answer:14(n+10)
Explanation: $200-2(30-6n)+2n=200-$
$60+12n+2n = 14n+140 = 14(n+10)$
Pencils and erasers Mike buy altogether :
$14(n+10)$

12. Answer: A
Explanation: Daises : 2d
Roses : d-2
Lilies : $2d+d-2=3d-2$
Total number of plants : $2d+d-2+3d-2=6d-4$

13. Answer:290
Explanation: First: 2x mangos, 4y nectarines,
and 3z pomegranates, Then: 2x+3z
nectarines; Total: 2x mangos, 4y+2x+3z
nectarines, and 3z pomegranates
Total number of fruits:
$2x+4y+2x+3z+3z=4x+4y+6z$
When x=15, y=20, z=25
$4(15)+4(20)+6(25)=60+80+150=290$

14. Answer: $(21.375h-135)$
Explanation: $\$(1-0.25)(60+9.5h)=\$(7.125h-45)$
In 3 weeks: $\$3(7.125h-45)=\$(21.375h-135)$

15. Answer: A
Explanation: 3y+11-5 and 6+3y
When y=2; $3(2)+6$ and $6+3(2)$, 12 and 12, They
are equivalent, and Kennedy is correct.

16. Answer: B
Explanation: Shark: m mph
Human:$\frac{1}{4}$m mph
Difference per hour: $m-\frac{1}{4}m=\frac{3}{4}$ m miles
In a hours: $\frac{3}{4}$ma miles

17. Answer: B
Explanation: Jace's age: x years
Lincoln's age: x-4 years
In a years: Jace's age:x+a years
Lincoln's age: x+a-4 years
Total age: $x+a+x+a-4=2x+2a-4$ years
If x=18 and a=4,
then $2x+2a-4=2(18)+2(4)-4=40$ years

18. Answer: D
Explanation: Width: x cm
Length: x+10 cm
Perimeter: $2(x+(x+10)) = 2(2x+10) = 4x+20$
$2(2x+20)$ cannot represent the perimeter of
the rectangle

19.Answer: D
Explanation: Width: x cm
Length: x-12 cm
Perimeter: $2(x+(x-8)) = 2(2x-8) = 4x-16$ cm
$2(2x-4)$ cannot represent the perimeter of
the rectangle

20. Answer: A
Explanation:
Jim: (10d+5n) pennies
Tom: $3\times(10d+5n) = 30d+15n$ pennies
The amount of money they both have
altogether: $(10d+5n)+30d+15n = 40d+20n$
pennies

5.3 SOLVING EQUATIONS

1. Answer: A
Explanation: 15x−5=10
Add 5 on both sides of the equation
15x−5+5=10+5
15x=15. Divide both sides by 15. x=1

2. Answer: A
Explanation: x−2=4
Add 2 on both sides of the equation
x−2+2=4+2. x=6

3. Answer: A
Explanation:
$\frac{1}{3}$−x=9x
Group the variable terms and constant terms together.
10x=$\frac{1}{3}$.Divide both sides by 10. x=$\frac{1}{30}$

4. Answer: C
Explanation: 4(x+2)−3(x+3)=12
Use the distributive property and multiply out the brackets. 4x+8−3x−9=12
x−1=12. x=13

5. Answer: B
Explanation: 6(x+5)−4(x+5)=20
Use the distributive property and multiply out the brackets. 6x+30−4x−20=20
2x+10=20. 2x=10. Divide both sides by 2. x=5

6. Answer: D
Explanation: 9(1−3x)+7(2+5x)=3(x+8)+30
Use the distributive property and multiply out the brackets. 9−27x+14+35x=3x+24+30
23+8x=3x+54 ; 5x=31 ; x=6.2.

7. Answer: C
Explanation: 5(3+x)−8(2x+6)=5(x+5)−10
15+5x−16x−48=5x+25−10
−11x−33=5x+15 ; −16x=48 ; x=−4816 ; x=−3.

8. Answer: B
Explanation: $\frac{x+6}{4}$ − $\frac{x+2}{3}$ = $\frac{1}{12}$
Multiply both sides by 12.
3(x+6)−4(x+2)=1 ; 3x+18−4x−8=1
−x+10=1 ; x=9.

9. Answer: A
Explanation: 6−4x+x = 2−2x−x−8
6−3x = −3x−6; 6 = −6
So, the equation has no solutions.

10. Answer: C
Explanation: 25+4x−2x = 5+x+x+20
25+2x=25+2x
0 = 0. The equation has Infinite Solution.

11. Answer: B
Explanation: Tom ate: x cookies
Tony ate: 9 cookies
Together: x+9 cookies; x+9=16
x=16−9=7; Tom ate 7 cookies.

12. Answer: B
Explanation:
$\frac{4x-2}{3}$ = $\frac{5x-20}{3}$
Multiply both sides by 3
4x−2=5x−20.
x=18 So, the equation has One Solution.

13. Answer: A
Explanation: Number of doughnuts: x doughnuts. Total price: $4.50x
$4.50x=40.50
x= $\frac{40.50}{4.50}$
x=9; Steve bought 9 doughnuts..

14. Answer: B
Explanation: Number of cups: x cups
Cups cost: $5x
Spent:$(5x+25)
(5x+25)=200−45
5x=130
x=26; Lisa bought 26 cups.

289

15. Answer: C
Explanation: Number of friends: x
Gave: $\frac{1}{3}x$
Left:4
Total:$\frac{1}{3}x+4$
$\frac{1}{3}x+4=10$, $\frac{1}{3}x=6$
$x=18$; Lincoln gave apples to 18 friends.

16. Answer: C
Explanation: Shirt: $\$x$; Pant: $\$3x$
Total:$\$x+\$3x=\$4x$;
$4x=100$, $x=25$, $3x=3\times25=75$
The price of the shirt is $25.

17. Answer: B
Explanation: Number of weeks: x
Savings in x weeks: $20x.
Savings in total: $(20x+120)$
$20x+120=380$, $20x=260$, $x=13$
Olivia saved money for 13 weeks.

18. Answer: A
Explanation: Harden: x years
Harden in 6 years: $x+6$ years
$x+6=35$, $x=35-6=29$,
Harden is 29 years old.

19. Answer: B
Explanation: 1st number: x
2nd number: $x+1$
Sum: $x+x+1=2x+1$
$2x+1=321$, $2x=320$, $x=160$, $x+1=161$
The smallest of these numbers is 160.

20. Answer: A
Explanation: Cost of the Candy: $\$x$
Cost of the Hotdog: $\$3x$
Total Cost:$\$x+\$3x=\$4x$
$4x=76$,
$x=\frac{76}{4}=19$,
$3x=3\times19=57$
The price of the hotdog is $57.

5.4 SOLVING INEQUALITIES

1.Answer: C
Explanation: ' x is at most 12 ' means that the most x allowed to be is 12; So, the value of x can be 12, or any number less than 12.
' x is at most 12 ' means $x\le12$.

2. Answer: B
Explanation: ' a is less than 12.5' means that the value of a is less than 12.5. ' a is less than 12.5 ' means $a<12.5$.

3. Answer: A
Explanation: sum of x and 5: $x+5$ 'The sum of x and 5 is fewer than −4 means the value of $x+5$ is less than −4. $x+5 < -4$.

4. Answer: B
Explanation: Ten times a number z is more than or equal to 1000. $10z\ge1000$.

5. Answer: A
Explanation: $x-2>4$
When $x=7$, $7-2=5>4$, 5 is greater than 4
$x=7$ is a solution to the inequality $x-2>4$.

6. Answer: B
Explanation: A game is designed for ages 5 and up. $x \ge 5$.

7. Answer: B
Explanation: Let x be the other expenses. Total expense is $20+x$. The sum of the $20-ticket and the other expenses must be no more than $50 means $20+x$ is equal to 50 or less than 50. $20+x\le50$.

8. Answer: A
Explanation: Let x be the expenses of buying books. Already spent $14+x$. Total expense is 40
$14+x\ge40$.

9. Answer: B
Explanation: Let x be the number of miles James rides. Total cost for the ride is 5.20+0.80x. James has no more than $15 to spend on a ride. $5.20 + 0.80x \le 15$.

10. Answer: A
Explanation: It takes a teacher more than 30 minutes but less than 3 hours to prepare for the lesson. One Lesson:$30 \le x \le 180$.
Five Lessons:$150 \le x \le 900$.

11. Answer: B
Explanation: $x-5>-2$, Add 5 on both sides $x-5+5>-2+5$, $x>3$.

12. Answer: A
Explanation: $-\frac{2-x}{4} \ge 4$, $\frac{2-x}{4} \ge -4$
Multiply 4 on both sides $\frac{2-x}{4} \times 4 \ge -4 \times 4$
$2-x \ge -16$, Subtract 2 on both sides
$2-x-2 \ge -16-2$, $-x \ge -18$, $x \ge 18$.

13. Answer: A
Explanation: $2.5x-5 \le 7.5$
Add 5 on both sides
$2.5x - 5 + 5 \le 7.5 + 5$; $2.5x \le 12.5$
Divide both sides by $\frac{2.5x}{2.5} \le \frac{12.5}{2.5}$
$x \le 5$.

14. Answer: C
Explanation: $4x-13 \le 19$
Add 13 on both sides, $4x-13+13 \le 19+13$
$4x \le 32$, Divide both sides by 4
$\frac{4x}{4} \le \frac{32}{4}$
$4x \le 4324$
$x \le 8$.

15. Answer: D
Explanation: To buy new bag, Becky has to save more than $45; $x > 45$.

16. Answer: A
Explanation: First exam score 85
Total exams:2
Let the score in second exam be x
Average score is 90, So, $\frac{85+x}{2} > 90$
$85 + x > 180$
$x > 95$.

17. Answer: C
Explanation: $7x \le 42$
$x \le \frac{42}{7}$
$x \le 6$ So, Chris can buy 0,1,2,3,4,5 or 6 dresses.

18. Answer: Refer to Explanation
Explanation: Lilies=5x
Jasmines=x
Total=x+5x=6x
$6x \le 360$
$x \le 60$
$5x \le 300$.

19. Answer: D
Explanation: $5x + 1000 \le 6000$
$5x \le 6000 - 1000$
$5x \le 5000$
$x \le 1000$.

20. Answer: B
Explanation: $15-x>27-7x$
$6x > 12$
$x > \frac{12}{6}$
$x > 2$.

5.5 CHAPTER REVIEW

1. Answer: A
Explanation: Sum of x and 6 : $x+6$

2. Answer: B
Explanation: $3x^2-6x+10$, when x=5
$3(5)^2-6(5)+10 = 75-30+10 = 55$

3. Answer: C
Explanation: The amount of money Antony earned working b hours = 11.50b

291

4. Answer: C
Explanation: Perimeter: $2(8+(d-16))$ cm
When d=32 cm, the perimeter is
$2(8+(d-16))=2(8+(32-16))=16+32=48$ cm

5. Answer: A
Explanation: Number of pages read: 53
Number of pages read in y hours: xy
Number of pages read after y hours: 53+xy

6. Answer: B
Explanation: $x(x-7)+14=x\times x-7\times x+14=x^2-7x+14$

7. Answer: D
Explanation: Area of the rectangle:
$x(x+5)=x^2+5x$

8. Answer: 6a+4b+19 points
Explanation: Jim: $3(a+3)+2b=3a+2b+9$ points
Tom: $3a+2(b+5)=3a+2b+10$ points
Total number of points of two basketball
players: $3a+2b+9+3a+2b+10=6a+4b+19$
points

9. Answer: 12n+40
Explanation: $120-2(40-4n)=120-80+8n+4n$
$=12n+40$. Pens and Glue stick Lincoln buy
altogether: 12n+40

10. Answer: $(29.9h+208)
Explanation: $\$(1-0.35)(80+11.5h)=$
$\$(7.475h+52)$
In 4 weeks: $\$(47.475h+52)=\$(29.9h+208)$

11. Answer: B
Explanation: 40x+5=85
Subtract 5 on both sides of the equation
40x+5-5=85-5, 40x=80
Divide both sides by 40, x=2

12. Answer: A
Explanation: $5(1+2x)+6(1+4x)=4(x+6)+20$
Use the distributive property and multiply out
the brackets.
$5+10x+6+24x=4x+24+20$
$11+34x=4x+44$, 30x=33, x=1.1

13. Answer: B
Explanation: $5-11x+x=2-4x-x-7$
$5-10x=-5x-5$, x=2
The equation has One solution.

14. Answer: C
Explanation: Number of weeks: x
Savings in x weeks: $15x
Savings in total: $(15x+80)$
15x+80=305, 15x=225, x=15
Jenny saved money for 15 weeks

15. Answer: D
Explanation: Number of wraps: x wraps
Total price: $6x, $6x=66, $x=\frac{66}{6}$
x=11 ; Jack bought 11 wraps.

16. Answer: B
Explanation: 1st number: x
2nd number:x+1, Sum:x+x+1=2x+1
2x+1=521, 2x=520, x=260 , x+1=261
The smallest of these numbers is 260.

17. Answer: C
Explanation: 'x is at most 25' means that the
most x allowed to be is 25; So, the value of x
can be 25, or any number less than 25.
'x is at most 25' means $x \leq 25$.

18. Answer: B
Explanation: A book is available for ages 9
and up. $x \geq 9$.

19. Answer: B
Explanation: Let x be the other expenses.
Total expense is 30+x. The sum of the
$30-ticket and the other expenses must be
no more than $60 means 30+x is equal to 60
or less than 60; $30 + x \leq 60$.

20. Answer: D
Explanation: $6x-12 \leq 18$
Add 12 on both sides $6x-12+12 \leq 18+12$
$6x \leq 30$, Divide both sides by 6
$\frac{6x}{6} \leq \frac{30}{6}$,
$x \leq 5$.

6. AREA, VOLUME, AND NETS

6.1 AREA OF TRIANGLES

1. Answer: A
Explanation: Area of the triangle $=\frac{1}{2}\times b\times h$
Base $=15$, Height $=12$
Area $=\frac{1}{2}\times15\times12=90$ cm^2

2. Answer: A
Explanation: Area of the triangle $=\frac{1}{2}\times b\times h$
Base $=b$, Height $=16$
Area $=\frac{1}{2}\times b\times16=40=>8b=40=>b=\frac{40}{8}$
Base (b) $=5$ cm

3. Answer: C
Explanation: Area of the triangle $=\frac{1}{2}\times b\times h$
Base $=9.5$ m, Height $=20$ m
Area $=\frac{1}{2}\times20\times9.5=95$ m^2

4. Answer: A
Explanation: Area of the triangle $=\frac{1}{2}\times b\times h$
Base $=27$ cm
Height $=11.2$ cm
Area $=\frac{1}{2}\times11.2\times27=151.2$ cm^2

5. Answer: D
Explanation: Area of the triangle $=\frac{1}{2}\times b\times h$
Area $=\frac{1}{2}\times7\times8=28$ mm^2

6. Answer: A
Explanation: Area of the triangle $=\frac{1}{2}\times b\times h$
Area $=\frac{1}{2}\times45\times14=315$ m^2

7. Answer: B
Explanation: Area of the triangle $=\frac{1}{2}\times b\times h$
Area $=\frac{1}{2}\times(5.3+12.7)\times10.5=>\frac{1}{2}\times18\times10.5=94.5$ cm^2

8. Answer: C
Explanation: Area of the triangle $=\frac{1}{2}\times b\times h$
Base of the cloth $=4.8$ m
Height of the cloth $=2.2$ m
Area $=\frac{1}{2}\times4.8\times2.2=5.28$ m^2

9. Answer: D
Explanation: Area of the triangle $=\frac{1}{2}\times b\times h$
Base of the piece of cardboard $=24$ cm
Height of the piece of cardboard $=22$ cm
Area $=\frac{1}{2}\times22\times24=264$ cm^2

10. Answer: A
Explanation: Area of the triangle $=\frac{1}{2}\times b\times h$
Base of the floor $=26$ feet
Height of the floor $=28$ feet
Area $=\frac{1}{2}\times26\times28=364$ ft^2

11. Answer: B
Explanation: Area of the triangle $=\frac{1}{2}\times b\times h$
Base $=2x$ cm
Height $=3x$ cm
Area $=\frac{1}{2}\times2x\times3x=3x^2$ cm^2
$3x^2=75=>x^2=25=>x=5$
Base $=2\times5=10$ cm

12. Answer: 101.25 cm^2
Explanation: Area of the triangle $=\frac{1}{2}\times b\times h$
Base $=15$ cm, Height $=0.9\times15=13.5$ cm
Area $=\frac{1}{2}\times15\times13.5=101.25$ cm^2

13. Answer: 18 cm
Explanation: Area of the triangle $=\frac{1}{2}\times b\times h$
Height $=17$ cm, Base $=17+y$,
Area $=\frac{1}{2}\times17\times(17+y)$
$\frac{17}{2}\times(17+y)=153$
$17+y=153\times\frac{2}{17}$
$17+y=18$, $y=18-17$, $y=1$, Base $=17+1=18$ cm

14. Answer: B
Explanation: Side $=x$ mm
$3x=96=>x=32$
Area $=\frac{1}{2}\times32\times21=336$ mm^2

15. Answer: D
Explanation: Area of the triangle $=\frac{1}{2}\times b\times h$
$\frac{1}{2}\times428\times h=84744$
$214h=84744$
$h=\frac{84744}{214}$
$h=396$ cm

16. Answer: C

Explanation: $Area_{XYZ}=4\ Area_{XYW}=>Area_{XYZ}=$ $\frac{1}{2}\times24=6\ cm^2$

17. Answer: 98 cm²

Explanation: $Area_{square}=14\times14=196\ cm^2$ $Area_{part}=\frac{1}{2}\times196=98\ cm^2$

18. Answer: A

Explanation: Area of the triangle $=\frac{1}{2}\times b\times h$

Base $=30$ cm

Height $=h$

Area $=\frac{1}{2}\times30\times h=330=>15h=330=>h=\frac{330}{15}$

Height $=22$ cm

19. Answer: D

Explanation: Area of the triangle $=\frac{1}{2}\times b\times h$

Base of the cake $=50$ cm

Height of the cake $=40$ cm

Area $=\frac{1}{2}\times50\times40=1000\ cm^2$

20. Answer: 130 cm²
Explanation:
$Area_{recrangle}=13\times(10+10)=260\ cm^2$
$Area_{shaded}=\frac{1}{2}\times260=130\ cm^2$

6.2 AREA OF QUADRILATERALS AND POLYGONS

1. Answer: D
Explanation: $7\times2+4\times2+9\times4=14+8+36=58$ square units

2. Answer: A
Explanation: $8\times7+7\times3+\frac{1}{2}\times2=78$ square units

3. Answer: C
Explanation: Height $=8$ m
Area $=96\ m^2$
Base $=\frac{A}{h}=\frac{96}{8}=12$ m

4. Answer: B
Explanation:
$6\times6+12\times7=36+84=120$ square units

5. Answer: A
Explanation: Width $=12$ m
Area $=204\ m^2$
Length $=\frac{A}{w}=\frac{204}{12}=17$ m

6. Answer: D
Explanation: Width $=16$ cm
Length $=22$ cm
Area $=16\times22=352\ cm^2$

7. Answer: B
Explanation: Width $=11.5$ cm
Length $=19.5$ cm
Area $=11.5\times19.5=224.25\ cm^2$

8. Answer: C
Explanation: Area $=\left(\frac{15+9}{2}\right)\times7=\frac{24}{2}\times7=84\ cm^2$

9. Answer: B
Explanation: Area $=44\ cm^2$
Height $=4$ cm
Base $=\frac{A}{h}=\frac{44}{4}=11$ cm

10. Answer: D
Explanation: Area $=100\ cm^2$
Width $=10$ cm
$H=\frac{A}{w}=\frac{100}{10}=10$ cm

11. Answer: B
Explanation: Area $=b\times h$
Area $=12\times15=180\ m^2$

12. Answer: A
Explanation:
$10\times6+12\times6=60+72=132$ square units

13. Answer: 25 cm2
Explanation: Area of square $=a^2$
Area $=5^2=25\ cm^2$

14. Answer: A
Explanation: $3x-6=14-x$
$3x+x=14+6$, $4x=20$, $x=5$
Length $=3\times5-6=15-6=9$ units
Width $=3\times5-3=15-3=12$ units
Area $=9\times12=108$ units^2

15. Answer: 27 cm²
Explanation: $4.5\times6=27$ cm^2

16. Answer: 96 cm²
Explanation: Area of trapezoid $=\frac{1}{2}(a+b)\times h$
Area $=\frac{1}{2}(17+7)\times8=96$ cm^2

17. Answer: B
Explanation: Base $=9$ m
Area $=189$ m^2
Height $=\frac{A}{b}=\frac{189}{9}=21$ m

18. Answer: C
Explanation: Height $=20.5$ m
Base $=22.5$ m
Area $=20.5\times22.5=461.25$ m^2

19. Answer: 77 cm²
Explanation: Area of rectangle $=w\times l$
Length $=11$ cm
Width $=7$ cm
Area $=11\times7=77$ cm^2

20. Answer: 121 mm²
Explanation: Area of square $=a^2$
Area $=11^2=121$ mm^2

6.3 THE VOLUME OF RECTANGULAR PRISMS

1. Answer: Number of cubes $=24$
Volume of prism $=3$ cm³
Explanation:
Volume of a prism $=2\times3\times\frac{1}{2}=3$ cm^3
Side of the cube $=\frac{1}{2}$ cm
Volume of the cube $=\frac{1}{2}\times\frac{1}{2}\times\frac{1}{2}=18$ cm^3
Number of cubes $=3\div\frac{1}{8}=3\times\frac{8}{1}=24$

2. Answer: Number of cubes $=8$
Volume of prism $=64$ cm³
Explanation:
Volume of a prism $=4\times8\times2=64$ cm^3
Side of the cube $=2$ cm
Volume of the cube $=2\times2\times2=8$ cm^3
Number of cubes $=64\div8=8$

3. Answer: Width of the prism $=1.8$ m
Volume of prism $=17.28$ m³
Explanation: Side of the cube $=0.6$ m
Volume of the cube $=0.6\times0.6\times0.6=0.216$ m^3
Number of cubes $=80$
Volume of the prism $=0.216\times80=17.28$ m3
Width of the prism $=\frac{17.28}{6\times1.6}=1.8$ m

4. Answer: Length of the prism $=32$ mm
Volume of prism $=8000$ mm³
Explanation: Side of the cube $=4$ mm
Volume of the cube $=4\times4\times4=64$ mm^3
Number of cubes $=125$
Volume of the prism $=64\times125=8000$ mm^3
Length of the prism $=\frac{8000}{10\times25}=32$ mm

5. Answer: B
Explanation:
Volume of rectangular prism $=l\times w\times h$
Volume $=15\times3\times3=135$ ft^3

6. Answer: C
Explanation:
Volume of rectangular prism $=l\times w\times h$
Volume $=10\times5\times6=300$ m^3

7. Answer: A
Explanation:
Volume of rectangular prism $=l\times w\times h$
Volume $=30\times10\times5=1500$ cm^3

8. Answer: D
Explanation: Height $=\frac{13.6}{27.2}=\frac{1}{2}$ cm^2

9. Answer: B
Explanation: Height $=\frac{6}{33}=\frac{2}{11}$ mm^2

10. Answer: B
Explanation: Base $=\frac{40}{5}=8$ m^2

11. Answer: A

Explanation: Base =
$$\frac{18\frac{2}{6}}{11\frac{2}{3}} = \frac{\frac{110}{6}}{\frac{35}{5}} = \frac{110}{6} \times \frac{5}{35} = 1\frac{4}{7} \text{ mm}^2$$

12. Answer: D
Explanation:
Volume of rectangular prism = l×w×h
Volume = 6×15×20 = 1800 mm³

13. Answer: 306 m³ > 80 m³
Explanation: 1st prism = $8 \times 4\frac{1}{2} \times 8\frac{1}{2}$ = 306 m³
2nd prism = 5×4×4 = 80 m³

14. Answer: B
Explanation:
Volume of one cube = $\frac{7}{448} = \frac{1}{64}$ cm³
Side of the cube = $\frac{1}{4}$ cm

15. Answer: C
Explanation:
Volume of one cube = $\frac{135}{5}$ = 27 cm³
Side of the cube = 3 cm

16. Answer: Length of the prism = 20 mm
Volume of prism = 160 mm³
Explanation: Side of the cube = 2 mm
Volume of the cube = 2×2×2 = 8 mm³
Number of cubes = 20
Volume of the prism = 20×8 = 160 mm³
Length of the prism = $\frac{160}{4\times2}$ ×2 = 20 mm

17. Answer: D
Explanation: Prism B = x m³
Prism A = 2x m³
x+2x = 43.2
3x = 43.2
x = 14.4 m³

18. Answer: B
Explanation: Prism B = x cm³
Prism A = 2x cm³
x+2x = 27, 3x = 27 , x = 9 cm³
Prism A = 2×9 = 18 cm²

19. Answer: C
Explanation:
Volume of one cube = $\frac{5}{625} = \frac{1}{125}$ m³
Side of the cube = $\frac{1}{5}$ m

20. Answer: B
Explanation:
Volume of one cube = $\frac{2410}{7}$ = 343 mm³
Side of the cube = 7 mm

6.4 REPRESENT 3-D FIGURES

1. Answer: 5, 9, 6
Explanation: Number of faces = 5
Number of edges = 9
Number of vertices = 6

2. Answer: 5, 8, 5
Explanation: Number of faces = 5
Number of edges = 8
Number of vertices = 5

3. Answer: B
Explanation:
Option B net diagram is
a triangular pyramid net.

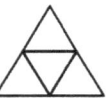

4. Answer: A
Explanation:
Option A net diagram is
a cuboid's net.

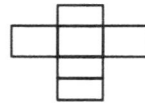

5. Answer: C
Explanation:
Option C net diagram is
not a cylinder net.

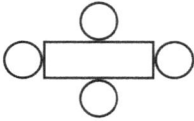

6. Answer: B
Explanation: Cone

7. Answer: D
Explanation: Hexagonal prism

8. Answer: B
Explanation: No

9. Answer: Triangular pyramid
Explanation:

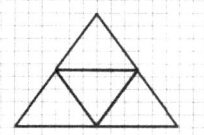

10. Answer: A
Explanation: Sphere

11. Answer: C
Explanation: The side 3 will touch the side 8

12. Answer: D
Explanation: The side 12 will touch the side 11

13. Answer: A
Explanation: The side 1 will touch the side 10

14. Answer: 10
Explanation: The side 11 will touch the side 10

15. Answer: 4
Explanation: The side 8 will touch the side 4

16. Answer: 7
Explanation: The side 2 will touch the side 7

17. Answer: Trapezoidal prism's net
Explanation:

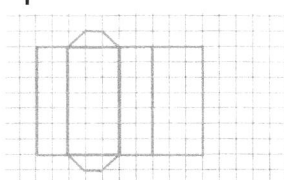

18. Answer: 7, 12, 7
Explanation: Number of faces =7
Number of edges =12, Number of vertices =7

19. Answer: Not correct
Explanation: The correct
net of a square pyramid is

20. Answer: B
Explanation: No, the given net cannot make a cube's net.

6.5 SURFACE AREA

1. Answer: B
Explanation: The Length of each side is 20 inches.

2. Answer:

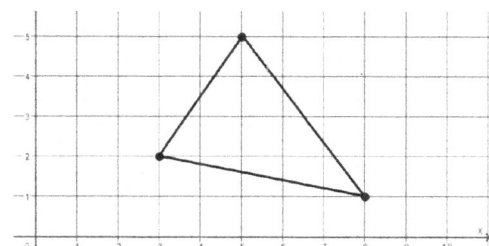

Explanation: To graph the point (3, 2), you must move 3 to the right and 2 up. To graph the point (5,5), you must move 5 to the right and 5 up. To graph the point (8,1), you must move 8 to the right and 1 up. All from the origin. Then connect the points to form a triangle.

3. Answer: John is incorrect
Explanation: The surface area of the cube is 9×9×6 or 486 sq ft.

4. Answer:

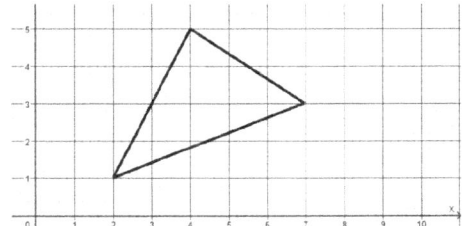

Explanation: To graph the point (7, 3), you must move 7 to the right and 3 up. To graph the point (4,5), you must move 4 to the right and 5 up. To graph the point (2,1), you must move 2 to the right and 1 up. All from the origin. Then connect the points to form a triangle.

ANSWERS AND EXPLANATIONS

5. Answer: Mary is correct
Explanation: The surface area of the cube is
6×6×6 or 216 sq ft.

6. Answer: A
Explanation: 65×5=150 unit²

7. Answer: C
Explanation: $8×5+2(\frac{1}{2}×8)=48$ unit²

8. Answer: B
Explanation:
Surface area =6(10×10)=600 unit²

9. Answer: D
Explanation: Surface area
=215×5+15×3+5×3=270 units²

10. Answer: Yes
Explanation: Surface area of the prism
=2(6×12+6×16+12×16) Yes, the expression
could be used to calculate the surface area
of the prism.

11. Answer: No
Explanation: Base area of the pyramid
=(2×2)in²
Area of each triangular face = $\frac{1}{2}$×(2×4)
Area of four triangular faces =$4×\frac{1}{2}$
(2×4)=2×(2×4)
Total surface area of the pyramid =
((2×2)+2(2×4)) in²
Given expression: ((2×2)+4(2×4)) in²
The given expression could not be used to
calculate the surface area of the pyramid.

12. Answer: Yes
Explanation:
Base area of the pyramid =(7×7)in²
Area of each triangular face = $\frac{1}{2}$×(7×11)
Area of four triangular faces =$4×\frac{1}{2}$ (7×11)
=2×(7×11)
Total surface area of the pyramid =
((7×7)+2(7×11) in²
Given expression: ((7×7)+2(7×11)) in²
Yes, the given expression could be used to
calculate the surface area of the pyramid.

13. Answer: B
Explanation: Cuboid: length =13 cm; width =11
cm, and height =9 cm
Surface area of the box
=2(13×11+13×9+11×9)=718 cm²

14. Answer: A
Explanation: Surface area of the pyramid
= area of the square base + 4 (area of the
triangular faces)
=$10×10+4(\frac{1}{2}×6×10)=100+120=220$ cm²

15. Answer: B
Explanation: If base area =100 cm², then the
base side is 10 cm long
Slant height =x cm
Surface area: $100+4(\frac{1}{2}×10×x)=140$
20x=140−100
20x=40
x=2 cm

16. Answer: C
Explanation: Side length =y cm
Surface area of cube =$6(y×y)=6y^2=384$
$y^2=64$ [divide both sides by 6]
y=8 cm [take square root on both sides]

17. Answer: D
Explanation: 400=2(14x+8x+14×8)
400=2(22x+112)
22x+112=200
22x=200−112
22x=88
x=4 cm

18. Answer: $ 5222.4
Explanation:
Box 1=2(15×13+15×7+13×7)=782 cm²
Box 2=2(19×18+19×5+18×5)=1,054 cm²
Difference on one box =1,054−782=272 cm²
Difference on 16 boxes =272×16=4,352 cm²
Savings = 4352 × $1.2 = $5222.4.

19. Answer: B
Explanation: Surface are
2(20 × 5 + 5 × 10 + 20 × 10)= 700 unit² .

20. Answer: B
Explanation: Side length = x cm
Surface area of cube = $6(x \times x) = 6x^2 = 216$
$x^2 = 36$ [divide both sides by 6]
$x = 6$ cm [take square root on both sides].

6.6 CHAPTER REVIEW

1. Answer: C
Explanation: Area of the triangle $= \frac{1}{2} \times b \times h$
Base $= 25$, Height $= 22$
Area $= \frac{1}{2} \times 25 \times 22 = 275$ cm^2

2. Answer: A
Explanation: Area of the triangle $= \frac{1}{2} \times b \times h$
Base $= 5x$ cm, Height $= 6x$ cm
Area $= \frac{1}{2} \times 5x \times 6x = 15x^2$ cm^2
$15x^2 = 240 => x^2 = 16 => x = 4$
Base $= 5 \times 4 = 20$ cm

3. Answer: B
Explanation: Area of the triangle $= \frac{1}{2} \times b \times h$
Base $= 5.2$ cm, Height $= 10.5$ cm
Area $= \frac{1}{2} \times 5.2 \times 10.5 = 27.3$ cm^2

4. Answer: D
Explanation: Height $= 11$ m
Area $= 242$ m^2
Base $= \frac{A}{h} = \frac{242}{11} = 22$ m

5. Answer: B
Explanation: Area $= b \times h$
Area $= 7 \times 14 = 98$ m^2

6. Answer: C
Explanation: $\frac{1}{2} \times 9 \times 18 = 81$ cm^2

7. Answer: A
Explanation:
$5 \times 3 + 13 \times 4 + 5 \times 5 = 15 + 52 + 25 = 92$ unit^2

8. Answer: 7,500,000 m³
Explanation: Volume of rectangular prism
$= l \times w \times h$
Volume $= 200 \times 150 \times 250 = 7,500,000$ m^3

9. Answer: A
Explanation: $32 \times 20 \times x = 4480$
$x = \frac{4480}{32 \times 20} = 7$
$7 \times \frac{1}{2} = 3\frac{1}{2}$ cm

10. Answer: C
Explanation:
Volume of rectangular prism $= l \times w \times h$
Volume of the rectangular prism:
$13 \times 6 \times \frac{7}{3} = 182$ cm^3

11. Answer: Width of the prism = 6 cm
Volume of the prism = 60 cm³
Explanation: Side of the cube = 1 cm
Volume of the cube = $1 \times 1 \times 1 = 1$ cm^3
Number of cubes = 60
Volume of the prism = $1 \times 60 = 60$ cm^3
Width of the prism $= \frac{60}{2 \times 5} = 6$ cm

12. Answer: 3,645
Explanation:
Volume of rectangular prism $= l \times w \times h$
Volume = $18 \times 15 \times 13.5 = 3,645$

13. Answer: B
Explanation: Height $= \frac{21}{63} = \frac{1}{3}$ mm^2

14. Answer: D
Explanation:
Volume of one cube $= \frac{14}{1750} = \frac{1}{125}$ cm^3
Side of the cube $= \frac{1}{5}$ cm

15. Answer: C
Explanation: Area of one face = 92 cm^2
Surface area = $6(92) = 552$ cm^2

16. Answer: A
Explanation: Area: $289 = x^2$, $x = 17$ in.

17. Answer:

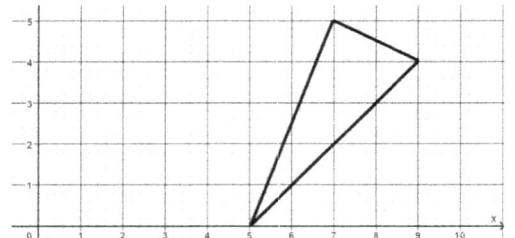

Explanation: To graph the point (9, 4), you must move 9 to the right and 4 up. To graph the point (5,5), you must move 7 to the right and 5 up. To graph the point (5,0), you must move 5 to the right and 0 to the right. All from the origin. Then connect the points to form a triangle.

18. Answer: B
Explanation: $428 = 2(19×4+4z+19z)$
$428 = 2(76+23z)$
$23z + 76 = 214$
$23z = 214 - 76$
$23z = 138$
$x = 6$ cm.

19. Answer: 6, 12, 8
Explanation: Number of faces =6
Number of edges =12
Number of vertices =8

20. Answer: C
Explanation: Pentagonal pyramid

7. COLLECTING AND INTERPRETING DATA

7.1 STATISTICAL VARIABILITY

1. Answer: B
Explanation: The median value is the middle value of the data set. When the data set has an even number of elements, the median is the average of the middle two numbers when the data set is arranged from smallest values to largest values.

2. Answer: D
Explanation: Graphs that are skewed to the right have fewer dots on the right side of the center.

3. Answer: 9.4
Explanation: The mean is a way of measuring the center of a data set. The mean is recognized as an average, or a balance point of all data points. The mean is calculated by adding the values in the data set and dividing by the number of data values in the set.

4. Answer: A
Explanation: The mean is a way of measuring the center of a data set. The mean is recognized as an average, or a balance point of all data points. The mean is calculated by adding the values in the data set and dividing by the number of data values in the set.

5. Answer: B
Explanation: The number 24 is minimum in the given data list.

6. Answer: C
Explanation: The number 489 is maximum in the given data list.

7. Answer: 87
Explanation: Range = Largest value − Smallest value
$89-2=87$

8. Answer: 10
Explanation: 5, 6, 11, 11, 14, 17, 19, 19, 21, 32, 43
$Q_1=11$
$Q_3=21$
$Q_3-Q_1=21-11=10$

9. Answer: B
Explanation: Ordered set of numbers: 1, 3, 9, 11, 12, 13, 16, 17, 21, 21, 23, 27, 35
$= \frac{1+3+9+11+12+13+16+17+21+21+23+27+35}{13} = \frac{209}{13} = 16\frac{1}{13}$

10. Answer: Mean B $=30\frac{6}{9}$
Explanation:

Mean A $= \frac{5+18+21+23+29+34+41+43+44}{9} = \frac{258}{9} = 28\frac{6}{9}$

Mean B $= \frac{7+20+23+25+31+36+43+45+46}{9} = \frac{276}{9} = 30\frac{6}{9}$

Mean C $= \frac{9+11+13+27+27+28+31+39+42}{9} = \frac{227}{9} = 25\frac{2}{9}$

Mean D $= \frac{8+11+12+15+22+25+29+37+39}{9} = \frac{198}{9} = 22$

11. Answer: III
Explanation: $Q_1=7$
$Q_3=35$
$Q_3-Q_1=35-7=28$

12. Answer: IV
Explanation:

MAD I $= \frac{11+12+16+23+26+32+34+45+61}{9} = 28.89$

MAD II $= \frac{9+15+19+20+21+26+27+31+45}{9} = 23.67$

MAD III $= \frac{7+9+14+17+17+21+24+32+35}{9} = 19.56$

MAD IV $= \frac{4+10+13+13+17+19+25+31+43}{9} = 19.44$

13. Answer: A
Explanation: Grade 5= 72 - 10 = 62
Grade 6 = 57 - 19 = 38

14. Answer: B
Explanation: Grade 1 = 69-9 = 60
Grade 2 = 52-6 = 46

15. Answer: A
Explanation: Cake = Q_3-Q_1 = 44-22 = 22
Pizza = Q_3-Q_1 = 42-21 = 21

16. Answer: B
Explanation:

Grade 3$= \frac{31+56+12+8+5+21+12+54+37+22+23}{11} = 25.55$

Grade 5$= \frac{24+28+43+32+16+8+2+12+1+16+30}{11} = 19.27$

17. Answer: 63
Explanation:
Range = Largest value – Smallest value
Range = 72 - 9 = 63

18. Answer: 421
Explanation: Range = Largest value – Smallest value Range =989-568=421

19. Answer: 78
Explanation: The mean is a way of measuring the center of a data set. The mean is recognized as an average, or a balance point of all data points. The mean is calculated by adding the values in the data set and dividing by the number of data values in the set.
Mean $= \frac{80+102+58+72}{4} = 78$

20. Answer: B
Explanation: MAD $= \frac{34+37+45+48+51}{5} = 43$

7.2 MEAN AND MEDIAN

1. Answer: B
Explanation: Ordered set of numbers =2, 5, 6, 7, 8, 11, 15, 18
Mean $= \frac{2+5+6+7+8+11+15+18}{8} = \frac{72}{8} = 9$

2. Answer: D
Explanation: When the numbers are arranged from least to greatest, the median is the number in the middle or center.

3. Answer: C
Explanation: Arrange the numbers from least to greatest. The number 15 must be in the middle to be the median.

4. Answer: A
Explanation: The "mean" is the average. Add all the numbers in the data set, and then divide by how many numbers there are. The mean is $\frac{40}{10} = 4$

5. Answer: B
Explanation: Arrange the numbers from smallest to largest. The median is the center number. The data set contains 11 numbers, so the median is in the 6th position.

6. Answer: D
Explanation: The mode is the number that appears most often. The number 4 appeared most often.

7. Answer: C
Explanation:
Ordered set of numbers: 11, 12, 12, 12, 14, 15, 17
Mode: 12 (appears 3 times)
Median: 12 (middle value)
Mean: $\frac{11+12+12+12+14+15+17}{7} = \frac{93}{7} = 13.3$
After 12 is removed : 11, 12, 12, 14, 15, 17 (ordered set of numbers)
Mode: 12 (appears 2 times)
Median: $\frac{12+14}{2} = \frac{26}{2} = 13$ (mean of middle two terms)
Mean: $\frac{11+12+12+14+15+17}{6} = 13.5$
Hence, only the mode remains the same after 12 is removed.

8. Answer: C
Explanation:
List of numbers = 11, 16, 13, 8, 10, 16, 17
Ordered set = 8, 10, 11, 13, 16, 16, 17
Mode = 16
Median = 13
Mean = $\frac{8+10+11+13+16+16+17}{7} = \frac{91}{7} = 13$
Ordered set of numbers after 16 and 10 are replaced by numbers 17 and 8 :
8, 8, 11, 13, 17, 17, 17
New mode = 17
New median = 13
New mean = $\frac{8+8+11+13+17+17+17}{7} = \frac{91}{7} = 13$
The mode after the values are changed.

9. Answer: A
Explanation: Let the last test score be y
Mean = $\frac{85+91+72+86+y}{5} = \frac{334+y}{5}$
$\frac{334+y}{5} \geq 82$
$334 + y \geq 410$; $y \geq 410 - 334$
$y \geq 76$; Minimum score = 76.

10. Answer: B
Explanation:
Ordered list = 11, 18, 19, 20, 30
Median = 19
New ordered list = 11, 18, 19, 19, 20, 30
New median = $\frac{19+19}{2} = \frac{38}{2} = 19$
The median doesn't change.

11. Answer: 63
Explanation: There are
$3+2+1+6+4+7+2+6+3+1+7 = 42$ students
Ordered list = 27, 32, 35, 50, 58, 63, 65, 71, 76, 78, 85
Median = 63

12. Answer: B
Explanation:
Orange's mean = $\frac{65+72+54+79}{4} = \frac{270}{4} = 67.5$
Mango's mean = $\frac{56+62+63+81}{4} = \frac{262}{4} = 65.5$
Apple's mean = $\frac{81+78+70+62}{4} = \frac{291}{4} = 72.8$
Blueberry's mean = $\frac{87+58+62+80}{4} = \frac{287}{4} = 71.8$
By comparing means, Mango sold least in four months.

13. Answer: B
Explanation:
Orange's mean = $\frac{55+67+51+83}{4} = \frac{256}{4} = 64$
Mango's mean = $\frac{63+52+69+78}{4} = \frac{262}{4} = 65.5$
Apple's mean = $\frac{71+60+75+68}{4} = \frac{274}{4} = 68.5$
Blueberry's mean = $\frac{85+66+74+88}{4} = \frac{313}{4} = 78.3$

14. Answer: 57
Explanation:
Ordered list = 28, 38, 57, 57, 60, 65
Median = $\frac{57+57}{2} = \frac{114}{2} = 57$

15. Answer: D
Explanation: Ordered list = 0, 0, 1, 1, 1, 1, 2, 2, 2, 2, 2, 3, 3, 3, 3, 4, 4
Mean = $\frac{0+0+1+1+1+1+2+2+2+2+2+3+3+3+3+4+4}{17} = \frac{34}{17} = 2$
Median = 2
Mode = 2

16. Answer: A
Explanation: Ordered list =5, 6, 7, 8, 9, 10, 10, 10, 11, 12, 15

Mean = $\frac{5+6+7+8+9+10+10+10+11+12+15}{11}$ = $\frac{103}{11}$=$9\frac{4}{11}$

Median =10
Mode =10

17. Answer: $5\frac{2}{11}$
Explanation: There are
3+2+1+6+4+7+2+6+3+1+7 = 42 students
Ordered list = 27, 32, 35, 50, 58, 63, 65, 71, 76, 78, 85

Mean $\frac{27+32+35+50+58+63+65+71+76+78+85}{11}$=$\frac{640}{11}$=$58\frac{2}{11}$

Median = 63
Difference = 63 – $58\frac{2}{11}$= $5\frac{2}{11}$

18. Answer: C
Explanation: List =x, 16, x+14
Mean = $\frac{x+16+x+14}{3}$ =16
2x+30=48
2x=48–30
2x=18
x=9

19. Answer: 170
Explanation: Numbers: x, x+1, x+2
x+x+1+x+2=510
3x+3=510
3x=510–3
3x=507
x=169
m=x=169, n=x+2=171
Mean of m and n = $\frac{169+171}{2}$ = $\frac{340}{2}$=170

20. Answer: 29
Explanation: Sum of 16 numbers =36×16=576
Sum of another 14 numbers =21×14=294
Sum of all 30 numbers =576+294=870
Mean of all 30 numbers =$\frac{870}{30}$=29

7.3 USE DOT PLOTS, BOX PLOTS, AND HISTOGRAMS TO REPRESENT DATA

1. Answer: B
Explanation: The data shown on the dot plot is represented by each dot. The number of dots placed at each value point expresses the frequency.

2. Answer: (1, 2, 2, 3, 4, 5, 5, 5, 6, 7, 7)
Explanation: There are 11 data points on the dot plot; 3 of the data points are repeated values.

3. Answer: C
Explanation: The minimum and maximum values of the box plot are 1 and 9, the median is 6.

4. Answer: A
Explanation: The frequency and numerical values align with each bar of the histogram.

5. Answer:

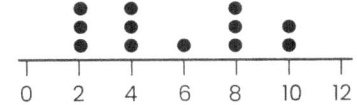

Explanation: Number 2 : 3 times
Number 4 : 3 times
Number 6 : 1 time
Number 8 : 2 times
Number 10 : 2 times

6. Answer:

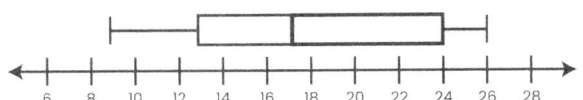

Explanation: The first quartile is thirteen, the median is seventeen, and the third quartile is Twenty-three. The smallest value is nine, and the largest value is twenty-six.

7. Answer:

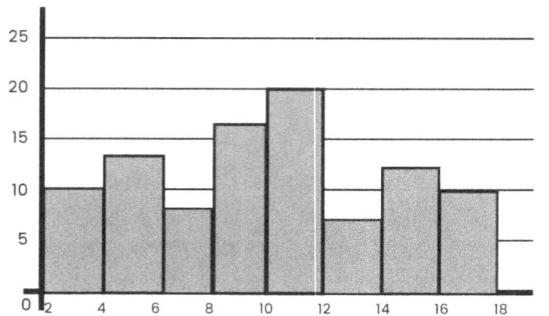

Explanation: The process of making a histogram using the given data is described below:

Step 1: Choose a suitable scale to represent weights on the horizontal axis.

Step 2: Choose a suitable scale to represent the frequencies on the vertical axis.

Step 3: Then draw the bars corresponding to each of the given weights using their frequencies.

8. Answer: B

Explanation: Number 4, 12, 24, 36=2 times==>total=8 times
Number 16, 32, 40, 48=1 time==>total=4 times
Number 8, 28, 44=3 times==>total=9 times
Number 20=5 times==>total=5 time
Therefore the answer is 26.

9. Answer: C

Explanation: To find the mode of this dataset, we can identify the values that occur most often. This data set has two modes: 25.

10. Answer: A

Explanation:

Mean $= \frac{6+7+5+6+6+7+8+9+8+10+8+7+10+9+9+7+6+8+9}{19} = \frac{145}{19} = 7\frac{12}{19}$

11. Answer: 49, 100

Explanation: The marks scored =68, 79, 83, 99, 100, 80, 95, 78, 58, 63, 49, 93, 86
Minimum =49
Maximum =100

12. Answer: 5

Explanation: To find the mode of this dataset, we can identify the values that occur most often: This dataset has modes: 5 Each of these values occurs five times in the dataset. Therefore, the answer is 5.

13. Answer: D

Explanation: The lower quartile, or first quartile (Q1), is the value under which 25% of data points are found when they are arranged in increasing order. Here $Q_1 = 60$

14. Answer: A

Explanation: To find the mode of this dataset, we can identify the values that occur most often:

15. Answer:

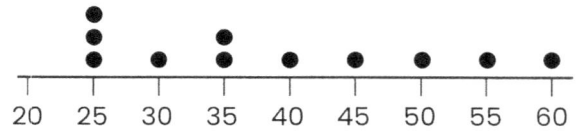

Explanation: 45, 52, 38, 49, 35 2 times, 25 3 times, 30, 40.

16. Answer: B

Explanation: In the given data diagram there are 91 answered the question

17. Answer:

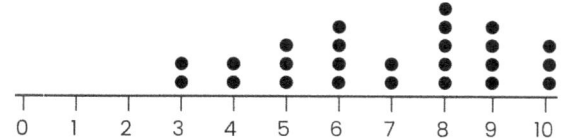

Explanation: The dot shows the number of responses.

18. Answer:

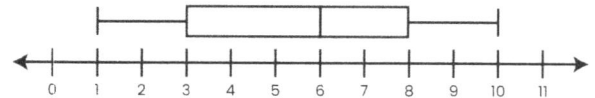

Explanation: The box dot shows the response of 15 customers.

19. Answer: C
Explanation: The dot plot shows the number of hours a student spent on gardening per week. The largest number of hour is 4.

20. Answer: A
Explanation: The number of motorbikes exceeding allowable speed =6+5+7=18

7.4 CHAPTER REVIEW

1. Answer: B
Explanation: The number 268 is maximum in the given data list.

2. Answer: D
Explanation: Ordered set of numbers =
12, 16, 16, 17, 19, 19, 20, 21, 23, 23
$= \frac{12+16+16+17+19+19+20+21+23+23}{10} = \frac{186}{10} = 18\frac{6}{10}$.

3. Answer: A
Explanation: Apple $=Q_3-Q_1=72-24=48$
Orange $=Q_3-Q_1=69-19=50$

4. Answer: 38
Explanation: Range = Largest value − Smallest value Range =45−7=38

5. Answer: C
Explanation: The mean is a way of measuring the center of a data set. The mean is recognized as an average, or a balance point of all data points. The mean is calculated by adding the values in the data set and dividing by the number of data values in the set.
Mean $= \frac{45+36+90+51+38+64}{6} = 54$

6. Answer: C
Explanation: List of numbers =16, 21, 18, 13, 15, 21, 22
Ordered set =13, 15, 16, 18, 21, 21, 22
Mode =21 , Median =18
Mean $= \frac{13+15+16+18+21+21+22}{7} = \frac{126}{7} = 18$
Ordered set of numbers after 21 and 15 are

replaced by numbers 22 and 13 :
13, 13, 16, 18, 22, 22, 22
New mode =22
New median =18
New mean $= \frac{13+13+16+18-22+22+22}{7} = \frac{126}{7} = 18$
So, the mode after the values are changed.

7. Answer: C
Explanation: Ordered list =1, 2, 2, 2, 2, 2, 3, 3, 3, 3, 4, 4, 4, 5, 5
Mean $= \frac{1+2+2+2+2+2+3+3+3+3+4+4+4+5+5}{15} = \frac{45}{15} = 3$
Median =3, Mode =2

8. Answer: A
Explanation: There are 8+6+7+9+9+3+1+8=51 students
Ordered list =25, 55, 65, 72, 78, 80, 95, 98
Mean= $\frac{25+55+65+72+78+80+95+98}{8} = \frac{568}{8} = 71$
Median =75, Difference =75−71=4

9. Answer: D
Explanation: List =z, 26, z+24
Mean $= \frac{z+26+z+24}{3} = 26$
2z+50=78
2z=78−50
2z=28
z=14

10. Answer: 160
Explanation: Numbers: x, x+1, x+2, x+3, x+4
x+x+1+x+2+x+3+x+4=800
5x+10=800
5x=800−10
5x=790
x=158
p=x=158, q=x+4=162
Mean of p and q $= \frac{158+162}{2} = \frac{320}{2} = 160$

11. Answer: B
Explanation: Range = Largest value − Smallest value Range =−3−(−13)=10

12. Answer: C
Explanation: The mode is the number that appears most often in the data set.

13. Answer: B
Explanation: Ordered list =31, 38, 39, 40, 50
Median =39
New ordered list =31, 38, 39, 39, 40, 50
New median $=\frac{39+39}{2}=\frac{78}{2}=39$
The median doesn't change.

14. Answer: D
Explanation: The mode is the number that appears most often in the data set.

15. Answer: A
Explanation: The first quartile is thirty, the median is forty-five, and the third quartile is seventy. The smallest value is ten, and the largest value is eighty.

16. Answer: B
Explanation: The first quartile is thirty-six.

17. Answer: 31
Explanation: The first quartile is nineteen, the median is thirty-nine, and the third quartile is fifty. The smallest value is eleven, and the largest value is sixty-two.
$Q_3-Q_1=50-19=31$

18. Answer:
(5, 10, 10, 15, 15, 15, 15, 20, 20, 20 25, 25)
Explanation: There are 12 data points on the dot plot; 4 of the data points are repeated values.

19. Answer:

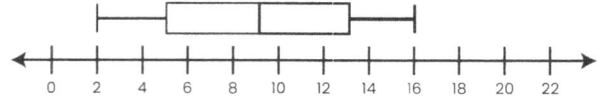

Explanation: The first quartile is five, the median is nine, and the third quartile is thirteen. The smallest value is two, and the largest value is sixteen.

20. Answer: C
Explanation: In the given data diagram there are 68 answered the question

---

COMPREHENSIVE ASSESSMENT – I

1. Answer: A
Explanation: The average speed is 72 mph, 72 x 5.5 = 396.

2. Answer: C
Explanation: There are 3 cookies in a serving. Lisa takes 18 cookies, so she takes 6 servings.

3. Answer: $1.75
Explanation: Find the price per pound by dividing the total price by the number of pounds. 5.25 ÷ 3 = 1.75. Each row in the table results in a price of $1.75 per pound of oranges.

4. Answer: D
Explanation: Two times 8.93 seconds is 17.86 seconds

5. Answer: 20
Explanation: There are 2 wheels on each motorcycle and 4 wheels on each car and the ratio of cars to motorcycles is 10:4, in which 10(4)x is the number of tires on the cars and 4(2)x is the number of tires on the motorcycles.

6. Answer: D
Explanation: To identify the least number of days, find the least common multiple of the two numbers. The least common multiple of 12 and 10 is 60.

7. Answer: 40 strawberries 24 apples
Explanation: The ratio of dogs to cats in the table is 4:8. Each column in the table contains the same ratio.

8. Answer: C
Explanation: The definition of the absolute value of a number is the distance the number is from 0 on the number line.

9. Answer: 24
Explanation: The rate is 6 stories every 15 minutes or $\frac{1}{4}$ hour. Multiplying the number of stories by 4 yields 24 stories per hour.

10. Answer: A
Explanation: If he needs to buy at least 5 gallons of paint. At least is represented by.

11. Answer: Jessy.
Explanation: Three songs in 4 days is a rate of 0.75 songs per day, and 5 songs in 6 days is a rates of 0.833 songs per day. Jessy learns songs at a faster rate.

12. Answer: B
Explanation: Eight times 10 is 80, so the height is 80 inches. Then, 80 divided by 16 is 5.

13. Answer: 1.5 miles per hour
Explanation: The total time hiking is 18.5 hours. The ratio would be 28 miles per 18.5 hours. Divide 28 by 18.5 to get the rate per hour.

14. Answer: D
Explanation: A balance of zero would mean that Mercy is not in debt to her credit card company and the credit card company does not owe her any money.

15. Answer: 28
Explanation: The ratio of red stripes to blue stripes is 4:1. Solve the equation $4x + x = 35$. There are 7 blue stripes and 28 red stripes on the shirt.

16. Answer: A
Explanation: The amount of flour used to make 52 muffins is (4.5×4) or 18 cups. The amount of flour used to make 4 cakes is (2.5×4) or 10 cups. The total amount of flour is $18 + 10$ cups or 28 cups.

17. Answer: B
Explanation: $7 \times 10 = 70$ roses; $70 \div 14 = 5$ new bouquets; Yes, students are able to redistribute the roses into 5 bouquets.

18. Answer: 16 sketches
Explanation: Students may create a ratio table to discover there are 32 crayons and 16 sketches, or solve the equation $4x + 8x = 48$ where x represents anunknown in the ratio 4x:8x.

19. Answer: C
Explanations: $4 \times 5 = 20$ days. 2th June + 20 days = 22th June, So option C is correct.

20. Answer: 12 months, $61.
Explanation: $836 - $104 = $732; 732 = 22 \times 3 \times 61$
12 months; She paid $61 each month.

21. Answer: B
Explanation: Simplify the expression as follows: $9+197+2-727$; $9+19(9)-7$; $9+171-7$
$180-7$; 173.

22. Answer: 485
Explanation: The figure can be decomposed into smaller rectangles.
$A = 6 \times 8 + 19 \times 23 = 485$ ft^2.

23. Answer: A
Explanation: $8 \times 15 = 120$ pencils bought $20 \times 6 = 120$ pencils needed ; Yes, the teacher was able to divide pencils so that each student receives 6 pencils.

24. Answer: 12
Explanation: Area = base • height, which Is 176 cm2. The height is 11 cm, so $176 \div 11 = 16$, $4+TY=16$, $TY=16-4=12$.

25. Answer: 8
Explanation: $5+ 8d + 59$
A coefficient is a number in front of the variable.

26. Answer: A
Explanation: Multiply the sides of the cube by 2 to converting the large cube's dimensions to match the units of the small cube. The large cube's volume is 11 × 11 × 11 small cubes or 1,331 small cubes.

27. Answer: B
Explanation: Combine like terms and factor out 7.

28. Answer: B
Explanation: The dimensions of the larger prism must be converted to the same units of the small cube, and then multiplied. Multiply each dimension by 2.
The correct expression for determining the number of cubes is 11 × 12 × 9.

29. Answer: C
Explanation: The point at (7, 6) creates a 4-sided polygon with equal sides. The missing vertex is up 3 units and right 3 units from the point (4, 3).

30. Answer: A
Explanation: 18 5 − t>5 ; 18 5 − 3>5 ; 36>5
If t=3 then the left side is 36 which is greater than 5

31. Answer: C
Explanation: The last 2 points of the hexagon are located at (6, 3) and (8, 4) in order for the hexagon to have an area of 12 square units.

32. Answer: 51 feet and 45 feet
Explanation: The length of the first board (closest to the top of the stairs in the picture) is 30+25−4=51 feet. The length of the second board is 65−35+15=45.

33. Answer: 109
Explanation: 25+12n = 25+12×7 = 25+84 = 109.

34. Answer: Yes, She needs approximately 165 square inches.
Explanation: Find the surface area of Jolene's box by calculating the area of each rectangle in the net. The area is approximately 165 square inches. The wrapping paper has an area of 168 square inches

35. Answer: 22
Explanation: Peter has $339.36 left after buying a phone. He earned $459.36 from his job (339.36+120). Find the number of hours worked by dividing this amount by $20.88.

36. Answer: 4(x+4)
Explanation: Combine like terms and factor out the common factor of 4
6x+7−2x+9 = 4x+16 = 4(x+4).

37. Answer: y=0.96x
Explanation: Divide the y-values by the x-values. Tim pays $0.96 for each song he downloads.

38. Answer: D
Explanation: The data shown on the dot plot is represented by each dot. The number of dots placed at each value point expresses the frequency

39. Answer: Neither
Explanation:
The expression to calculate the surface area is 2(14 × 6) + 2(6 × 6) + 2(14 × 4).

40. Answer: 15
Explanation: List the numbers in numerical order from smallest to largest. Then, find the center number.

41. Answer: B
Explanation: The smallest value shown in the box plot is 200 minutes, and the largest value is 900 minutes.

42. Answer: {20, 20.2, 20.2, 20.4, 20.4, 20.4, 20.5, 20.6, 20.7}
Explanation: There are 9 data points on the dot plot; 3 of the data points are repeated values.

43. Answer: B
Explanation: This is not a statistical question because it is not answered by collecting data that may vary.

44. Answer: A
Explanation: The "range" of a list of numbers is the difference between the largest and smallest values.

45. Answer: C
Explanation: Graphs that are skewed to the left have fewer dots on the left side of the center.

COMPREHENSIVE ASSESSMENT – II

1. Answer: C
Explanation: The mean is found by adding the 5 values given ($0.61, $0.70, $0.51, $0.80,and $0.63) together, and dividing the sum by 5 is 0.65. Since these values represent money, this value is $0.65.

2. Answer: D
Explanation: Each hash mark represents 10. The first point represents 64 − 14 or 50. Point B is located at 80.

3. Answer: A
Explanation: This is a statistical question because to answer this question, you collect data by asking students about their favorite subjects, and there is variety in the data. The favorite subject is not the same for every student.

4. Answer: B
Explanation: The "range" of a set of numbers is the difference between the largest and smallest values.

5. Answer: D
Explanation: To take half of something is to divide it by 2.

6. Answer: C
Explanation: The net represents a prism with an eight-sided figure as the base. (an octagonal prism)

7. Answer: B
Explanation: Combining the variables results in 8a − 2a = 6a, so when the numbers are combined, the simplified expression is 7. The derived expression is (6a-7).

8. Answer: C
Explanation: By adding the number of hours spent studying for each test and multiplying for each test and multiplying it by the number of days spent studying, (x), Shyam can determine the total number of hours he will study.

9. Answer: D
Explanation: $6(8x) = 48x$ and $6(9)=54$. $6(8x-9) = 48x-54$.

10. Answer: A
Explanation: The greatest common factor is the largest whole number factor between 2 numbers. Factored into prime numbers gives $68=2\times2\times17$ and $56=2\times2\times2\times7$. The common factors are 4.

11. Answer: C
Explanation: $e=54.6\div6.5=8.4$, Solve the equation by dividing both sides by 6.5. The solution is 8.4.

12. Answer: B
Explanation: $9x=9+27$; $x=36\div9=4$, Combine like terms on the right side and divide both sides by 9. The solution is 4.

13. Answer: D
Explanation: John's bottle has 15 ounces of juice. This is $1\frac{1}{2}$ servings of juice (15 oz/10 oz).

14. Answer: C
Explanation:
Steve owes Kim $10, which is 32−22.

15. Answer: A
Explanation: The area of the base is given, so use the formula V = Bh.

16. Answer: B
Explanation: Divide both sides by 9. The value of m must be less than 6.

17. Answer: C
Explanation: The area of a triangle can be determined by multiplying base length and height, and dividing by 2.

18. Answer: D
Explanation: The least common multiple of 6 and 9 is 18.

19. Answer: A
Explanation: The most logical way to represent his distance from his starting place is up 11 and down 6 or +11 and -6.

20. Answer: D
Explanation: The vertical distance is the change in the y-values between the points. The distance between 7 and 13 is 6.

21. Answer: A
Explanation: The marks are 1 unit apart. Thus, the missing values are -3 and -1.

22. Answer: B
Explanation: In mathematics, the dividend is the number being divided in a division problem.

23. Answer: A
Explanation: Arrange the numbers from smallest to largest. The median is the middle number of the rearranged set.

24. Answer: 8
Explanation: The range is the difference between the minimum and maximum values. The difference between 12 and 4 is 8.

25. Answer: 10
Explanation: The limiting number is the number of boys. Divide 40 by 4.

26. Answer: Stock B
Explanation:
The change in stock price of - 8.5 is the biggest decrease of the three stocks.

27. Answer: 132
Explanation: The solid, an octagonal pyramid, has 8 faces, each with an area of 26 sq.cm. The area of the base is 340 - (26×8) = 340 − 208 = 132.

28. Answer: Yes.
Explanation: His weight (z) is greater than his brother's weight (y), so by subtracting 6 ½ from his own weight, Tom can determine her brother's weight.

29. Missing values : 1½, 3 , $3\frac{3}{4}$. There are 12 inches in 1 foot.

Inches	Feet
12	$\frac{12}{12}$ or 1
18	$\frac{18}{12}$ or $\frac{3}{2}$ or $1\frac{1}{2}$
26	$\frac{26}{12}$ or $2\frac{2}{12}$ or $2\frac{1}{6}$
36	$\frac{36}{12}$ or 3
45	$\frac{45}{12}$ or $3\frac{9}{12}$ or $3\frac{3}{4}$

30. Answer: $ 1.21
Explanation: Find the unit cost, or the cost of each crate, by dividing $14.52 by 12.

31. Answer: 5
Explanation: Volume of a rectangular prism is length × width × height.
Divide ($102\frac{9}{20}$ by $6\frac{5}{6}$ × 3).

32. Answer: $8.4
Explanation: Divide the total bill by the number of people splitting it equally.
($58.8 ÷ 7 = 8.4$).

33. Answer: $377
Explanation: The balance is determined by subtracting the amount withdrawn and adding the amount deposited to the balance.
$(513.85 - 215.97) + 79.12 = 377$.

34. Answer: AD=17.5 cm
Explanation: Area of the triangle:
$\frac{1}{2}$×b×h = $\frac{1}{2}$×7×22 = 77.
Area of a parallelogram = base x height.
The area of the quadrilateral is 5 times x Area of the triangle=77×5=385 cm², the height is 22 cm.
So, AD = 385 ÷ 22 = 17.5 cm.

35. Answer: Catherina has $8\frac{1}{4}$ cups of apple juice. Each serving of orange juice is $\frac{5}{4}$ cups. Catherina has $6\frac{3}{5}$ servings of apple juice.
Explanation: The student should create a word problem to represent the given division situation.

36. Answer: 40
Explanation: Calculate the number of strawberry on each plant by dividing 1,120 by 28.

37. Answer: (5,1), (3, 6), and (7, 8).

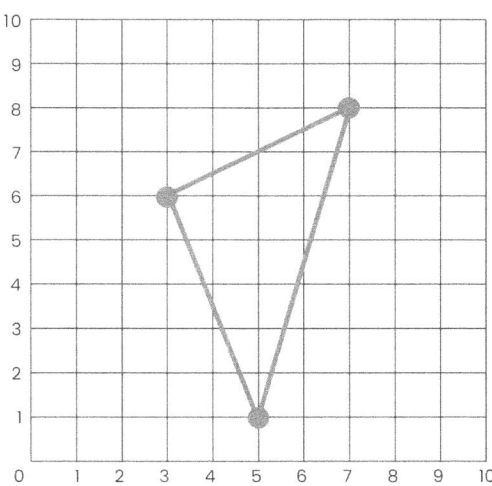

Explanation: To graph the point (5, 1), move 5 to the right and 1 up or down. To graph the point (3, 6), move 3 to the right and 6 up. To graph the point (7, 8), move 7 to the right and 8 up. All from the origin. Then connect the points to form a triangle.

38. Answer: $63.77
Explanation: To find the original amount of money Silvia has, add the amount of money she has left to cover the cost of the pants.
($49.80 + $13.97 = 63.77).

39. Answer: No.
Explanation: While solving the equation, Tina made a mistake in converting the mixed number into an improper fraction, then she divides the fraction by 7. So the solution found is incorrect.

40. Answer: n = ($\frac{49.99}{60}$) n = $0.83
Explanation: The cost per chocolate is $0.83. The divisor in the equation, 60, is found by multiplying the number of cookies inside each container by the number of containers inside the box (15 x 4).

41. Answer: n ≤ 35
Explanation: There are 3 sisters. If each person is allowed the same amount of Time on the computer, they will have less equal to 35 minutes of time each. (105÷3=35).

42. Answer:
(23×19) + (17×6) or (36×23) − (19×17)
Explanation: Decompose the figure into smaller rectangles. Find the area by adding the areas of the smaller rectangles together: (23×19) + (17×6) Find the area by subtracting the area of the rectangle formed by the entire figure minus the area of the unshaded portion of the entire figure.(36×23) − (19×17).

43. Answer: 14
Explanation: The temperature in Tampa is 33 degrees Fahrenheit, found by
−16 + 49 − 19 = 14. The temperature in Raleigh is 14 degrees Fahrenheit.

44. Answer: A
Explanation: The word "times" means multiply.

45. Answer: D
Explanation: The expression 4 ½(8+3)+7 has a value of 56.5.